FUNCTIONING OF REGIONAL PUBLIC LIBRARIES IN ANDHRA PRADESH

FUNCTIONING OF REGIONAL PUBLIC LIBRARIES IN ANDHRA PRADESH

A Study

L.V. CHANDRA SEKHARA RAO

PUBLICATIONS

KALPAZ PUBLICATIONS

DELHI-110052

Functioning of Regional Public Libraries in Andhra Pradesh:
A Study

Rs. 890

ISBN: 81-7835-682-1

Published in 2008 in India by
Kalpaz Publications
C-30, Satyawati Nagar,
Delhi-110052
E-mail: kalpaz@hotmail.com
Phone : 9212729499

Laser Type Setting by: Quick Media, Delhi
Printed at : Singhal Print Media, Delhi

Contents

List of Tables

List of Figures

Abbreviations

A.L.A.	:	American Library Association
A.P.	:	Andhra Pradesh
A.P.G.P.	:	Andhra Pradesh Grandhalaya Parishad
A.P.P.L.	:	Andhra Pradesh Publish Libraries (Act)
A.P.P.L.A.	:	Andhra Pradesh Public Libraries Association
A.V.	:	Audio Visual
B.A.	:	Bachelor of Arts
B.C.	:	Before Christ
B.Com.	:	Bachelor of Commerce
B.L.I. Sc.	:	Bachelor of Library and Information Science
B.Sc.	:	Bachelor of Science
CDs.	:	Compact Discs
C.L.I.Sc.	:	Certificate Course in Library and Information Science
CD-ROM	:	Compact Disc - Read only Memory
CLAMS	:	Cape Libraries Automated Materials Sharing
CoBISS	:	Cooperative online Bibliographic System
D.B.(Act)	:	Delivery of Books Act
D.C.L.	:	District Central Library
D.D.L.	:	Dewey Decimal Classification
D.E.O.	:	District Educational Officer
D.P.L	:	Department of Public Libraries
Dr.	:	Doctor
EALA	:	East African Library Association

EDA	:	Economic Development Activity
G.R.L	:	Government Regional Library
I.A.S.	:	Indian Administrative Service
I.F.L.A.	:	International Federation of Library Association
I.F.S.	:	Indian Forest Service
I.L.A.	:	Indian Library Association
I.P.S.	:	Indian Police Service
IASLIC	:	Indian Association of Special Librarians and Information Centres
INB	:	Indian National Bibliography
L.C.	:	Library Committee
LAN	:	Local Area Network
LISA	:	Library and Information Science Abstracts
LSCA	:	Library Services and Construction Act
M.A.	:	Master of Arts
M.Com.	:	Master of Commence
M.L.A.	:	Member of Legislative Assembly
M.L.I.Sc.	:	Master of Library and Information Science
M.Phil.	:	Master of Philosophy
M.R.O.	:	Mandal Revenue Officer
M.Sc.	:	Master of Science
MSCPLIC	:	Memphis and Shelby Country Public Library and Information Centre
NAEP	:	National Adult Education Programme
P.G.	:	Post Graduation
Ph.D.	:	Doctor of Philosophy
PWD(R&B)	:	Public Works Department (Roads & Buildings)
R.P.L.	:	Regional Public Library
R.R.R.L.F.	:	Raja Rammohun Roy Library Foundation

RDBMS	:	Relational Database Management Systems
S.C.	:	Scheduled Castes
S.C.L.	:	State Central Library
S.R.L.	:	State Regional Library
S.T.	:	Scheduled Tribes
SCECSAL	:	Standing Conference of Eastern, Central and South African Libraries
T.V.	:	Television
U.G.C.	:	University Grants Commission
U.K.	:	United Kingdom
U.P.	:	Uttar Pradesh
U.S.A.	:	United States of America
UNESCO	:	United National Educational, Scientific and Cultural Organization
V.C.D.	:	Video Cassette
V.C.R.	:	Video Cassette Recorder
WALA	:	West African Library Association
WAN	:	Wide Area Network
Z.G.S.	:	Zilla Grandhalaya Samastha(s)

Acknowledgements

I wish to express my deep sense of gratitude to **Dr. P. Bhaskara Rao**, my Research Director, for his sententiously valuable and immensely useful suggestions all through my research work. Without any hesitation to declare this as verity that he is towering and perennial source of inspiration, which motivated me to fulfill this gigantic task successfully with a quality perspective.

I immensely express my sense of gratitude to **Prof. K. Somasekhara Rao,** Department of Library and Information Science for his continuous encouragement, guidance and suggestions in completing my Ph.D. work.

I may be failing in my duty, if I do not thank **Prof. C. Sasikala,** Chairperson, Board of Studies (P.G.) for her pedagogical suggestions throughout this work.

I thank **Prof. R.S.R. Varalakshmi**, Head of the Department of Library and Information Science, for her academic and moral support in completion of this research work.

I would like to acknowledge with thanks the cooperation extended by **Smt. J. Vijaya Kumari,** and **Dr. N. David Livingstone,** Associate Professors, Department of Library and Information Science for their ethical support.

I cannot forget the help and cooperation rendered in every stage of this research work by **Dr. Chelli Nageswara Rao,** Librarian, Government Polytechnic, Visakhapatnam.

I am thankful to the Commissioner of Public Libraries, Andhra Pradesh, Hyderabad for providing permission to collect the data for all the Regional Public Libraries and also for sparing time in sharing his views on the research work in my interview with him.

I am highly indebted to the Librarians and other professionals of all the Regional Public Libraries for their cooperation extended in responding to the questionnaires and I am also thankful to the users who gave their valuable suggestions in response to my quarries.

My heartfelt thanks are due to teaching and non-teaching members, Government Polytechnic, Visakhapatnam, for their valuable support and suggestions.

My special thanks are extended to the Director, M.R. College, P.G. Courses, Vizianagaram for his kind co-operation in completing my Research Work.

My whole hearted thanks are due to the professional staff of Dr. V.S.K. Library, Sri L.Satyanarayana, Sri G. Ayyababu and Sri G.Nageswara Rao and my thanks are due to the semi-professionals of Dr. V.S.K. Library, Sri Viswanadha and S. Trinadha Rao, etc. for their cooperation and suggestions in various academic aspects of the study.

My absence at home due to research caused inconvenience abundantly to my parents Sri L. Appa Rao and Smt. L.Lakshmi Devi and my life partner Smt. L.V. Satyavathi and children L.J. Chandra Prasad, L. Meena Kumari Chinmaye. This is my special acknowledgement for their forbearance.

My thanks are also extended to Dr. M. Sudhakar Babu, Population Research Centre, Visakhapatnam, for his valuable suggestions during analysis and tabulation of my research work. I also my thank Mr. D. Appa Rao, for his patience in typing of this research work neatly.

I am responsible and pardonable for shortcomings and omissions.

L.V. Chandrasekhara Rao

1
Introduction

The reading of books for education, for information, for social status, for emotional relief, for spiritual satisfaction, and for pleasure became universal phenomenon. Gradually, the reading habit became one of the major factors of life. To augment this habit, the establishment and development of libraries for public became essential. "The library should be developed not with a view to achieve prestige by having large number of books but to make it as a useful institution to spread over education among the people"[1].

Library is an organized collection of books and other materials used for study, research, and recreation; also, the room or building that houses such a collection. The word is from the Latin *Liber* (book). Usually a library is thought of as simply a collection of books and periodicals. Most libraries, however, also contain nonprint materials - recordings, motion pictures, slides, filmstrips, art reproductions, and other still pictures, maps, music scores and microforms (microfilmed materials).

Types of Libraries

Libraries are of many types and these can be grouped on the basis of services offered to the different types of clientele such as public, academic, students, researchers, businessmen, scientists, workers, children, agriculturists, etc. To meet their varied needs the following kinds of libraries have came into existence.

1. Academic Librariries,

2. Special Libraries, and
3. Public Libraries

A brief narration about the public libraries in general, as well as history and development of Public Library System in the state of Andhra Pradesh in particular, is presented here, as it is pertinent to the present study.

Public Libraries

The main reason for the development of Public libraries could be the spread of general education, research and evolution of democratic ideas of the states responsibility towards common citizens.

A public library is a tax-supported institution serving a city, town, country, or other local area. Its basic function is to make books and other library materials available to all the citizens in the community it serves. Public libraries provide materials for general reference and research, for continuing education, and for recreation. Many public libraries are small and can offer only basic materials; however, large public libraries often provide materials for specialized reference and research, coordinate programs for continuing education and sponsor cultural and recreational events. Public library service is most highly developed in the United States, Canada, Great Britain, the Soviet Union and the Scandinavian countries.

There are more than 8,700 public libraries in the United States. Both municipal and country libraries often have branches and some offer bookmobile service. (A bookmobile is a specially equipped van that takes library materials to areas without easy access to a library building). Areas not served by public libraries often participate in programs organized by the state library or a regional library system, that provide materials through bookmobiles or the mail. Any person, regardless of place of residence, can use materials within any public library. Most public libraries, however, require non-residents to pay an annual fee for the privilege of borrowing materials.

A public library is one that serves the entire population of a community. Everyone in the community, regardless of nationality, race, colour, creed, age, sex, status, educational attainments, language or any such considerations has a claim to its services as a matter of right. It is generally established and maintained out of public funds under the mandate of legislation. Public library service is generally free of charge, but some libraries charge a nominal fee. They are usually referred to as subscription libraries. This contention finds support in the modern definition of a public library as approved by the UNESCO and IFLA, which is "Public Libraries are those libraries which serve the population of a community or region free of charge or for a nominal fee".

A public library functions as an intellectual powerhouse, aspiring to meet the intellectual, educational, recreational, informal and cultural requirements of the masses. A public library should act as a multi-purpose information - education - culture agency. A public library should make :

Education: To foster and provide means for self-development of the individual/group at whatever stage of education, closing the gap between the individual and recorded knowledge.

Information: To bring to the individual/group accurate information quickly and in depth, particularly on topics of current concern.

Culture: To be one of the principal centers of culture life and promote a keener participation, enjoyment and appreciation of all the arts.

Leisure: To play a part in encouraging the positive use of leisure and providing material for change and relaxation.

Public Library Development in India

Ancient and Medieval Period

In India since the ancient times, a library has been functioning as lighthouse for those who wanted to read and to extend the boundaries of various disciplines. The great Indian Universities like Nalanda, Taxasila (600 B.C.) and Vikramashila had massive collections of rare books in their libraries. Hueigen Sang the Chinese traveler is known to have visited the library at Nalanda in the 7th century. This great library was completely destroyed by Bakhtiar **Khilji** who invaded India during 1205 A.D. The advent of Muslim rule during the 13th century marked the dawn of another era of learning and scholarship. They established many academic institutions and it was found that a well-known library was established by Jalal-U-din Khilji at Delhi. Royal and pompous libraries were set-up by the Mughal Emperor Humayun at Agra fort with Lal Beg as Librarian[2],

The earliest libraries that survived are the Tanjavur Maharaja Sarfoji's Swaraswati Mahal Library which had a collection of about 43,000 manuscripts. It was started around 1535 A.D. by Telugu Nayakas who ruled Tanujore in the 16th Century. Khuda Baksh Library at Patna is another oldest library, which dates back to 1876 and is still flourishing. Khan Bahadur Baksh Khan at the time of his death, left a collection of 1,500 manuscripts, which become the nucleus of the library. His son Moulana Khuda Baksh Khan developed this library. Consequent to the Act of 1969, this library was known as Khuda Baksh Oriental Public Library.

British Period

The Britishers first set up public libraries in the presidency towns of Bombay, Calcutta and Madras. "The first library was established in Bombay by East India Company in 1715 A.D. In 1804, the Rayal Asiatic Society established its library in Calcutta". In Calcutta around 1818 the Calcutta Library was formed and was housed in the Town Hall.

In the year 1860, a small library was established by Jesse Mitchel, as a part of Madras Museum. Gradually it had grown in size during the period of Dr. Edgar Thurston and was shifted to the present building in 1890. Foundation for new building was laid by Lord Connemera on 22nd March 1890, and was opened to the public in 1896. After the library legislation in Madras province in the year 1948, this library became the State Central Library in 1950. Lord Curzen, the Viceray, was keen to save the Calcutta Public Library and made arrangements in 1899 to takeover the library by paying adequate compensation. The Calcutta public library and a number of Secretarial Libraries in Calcutta were merged in 1901. With the result the Imperial Library was started. The Imperial Library was opened to the public again in 1903. After the independence, its name has been changed to National Library of India, through an act 'Imperial Library (Change of name) Act 1948.

19th Century Libraries

Library movement geared up in Baroda on the invitation of Maharaja Sayaji Rao (Gaikwad III, the then ruler of the erstwhile Baroda state, who was the first Indian ruler to declare compulsory elementary education in his state in 1907). The famous American Librarian William Allenson Borden, student of Melwil Dewey came to Baroda and organized a free public library service. By the year 1910, Borden was able to establish a network of public libraries which included conventional libraries and mobile libraries.

Role of Government

The Committee appointed by the Government of Bombay under the Chairmanship of A.A.A. Fyzee[3] in Bombay in the year 1939 contributed to the development o f public libraries.

The committee in its report, submitted in 1940, recommended building up a strong network of public library system in the state with state Central Library, District Libraries, Taluk Libraries, Block Libraries etc., linked with each other in the form of a chain but there is no mention about the 'Regional Library System'.

Public Libraries Development in Five-Year Plans

The first milestone in the development of Public Libraries was declaring the Imperial Library (Calcutta) as the National Library of India in 1948. Another significant step was the establishment in 1951 of the Delhi Public Library, a UNESCO Pilot Project for Asia.

The Government of India created a history in the Public Library Movement by including the scheme of Improvement of Library Service in the First Five Year Plan of Educational Development. The development of the Public Libraries, under Five Year Pans, (upto Eighth Five Year Plan) was enumerated in the Annexure-I, for further details. Proposals were formulated to set up a National Central Library at Delhi and an idea was also mooted that each State should have a Central Library of its own with a network of circulating libraries in villages served through deposit stations and mobile vans. During this Plan 9 States (Assam, West Bengal, Madhya Pradesh, Punjab, P.E.P.S.U., Rajasthan, Saurashtra, Bhopal and Vindya Pradesh) have set up State Central Libraries and by the end of this Plan period (1951-56) these states (except Punjab) had either set up or were in the process of setting up District Libraries in 100 of their Districts.

National Book Depositories in India

On May 21, 1954[4], the Government of India enacted the Delivery of Books (Public Libraries) Act, 1954 making it obligatory for the publisher of every book to deliver at his own expense a copy of the book to the National Library, Calcutta; Connemara Public Library, Madras and Asiatic Society Library, Bombay. In 1982, Delhi Public Library also got the copyright privilege. In 1956, through an amendment, the Government wisely extended the Act to include newspapers as well. The Act has laid the foundation for the four National Book Depositories in India.

Under the Second Five Year Plan (1956-61) the Government spent about Rs. 12,943,000 on public libraries for setting up a country wide network (excluding Assam and U.P.) of libraries in her 320 districts. An additional provision of Rs.10 lacs was made to set up a Central Institute for Training of Librarians at Delhi affiliated to Delhi University. The first refresher course on "The Public Library and National Development" was inaugurated in March 1959. By and large, the achievement of this plan period was not encouraging.

In the Second Plan, an Institute of library science was established for training of librarians at Delhi and it is during this plan, some universities were encouraged for research in library science and training library personnel.

Advisory Committee for Libraries

The Ministry of Education, Government of India on the recommendations of a Seminar on the 'Role of Libraries in Social Education' set up an Advisory Committee for libraries under the Chairmanship of Sri K.P. Sinha. This committee submitted its report in 1958 with the following terms of reference.

Firstly, the report recommended that library service should be free to every citizen of India. Secondly, the library pattern in the country should consist of National Library, State Central Libraries, District Libraries, Block Libraries and Panchayat Libraries. Thirdly, it was deemed desirable to have an independent Directorate of Social Education and Libraries in every state. Fourthly, it strongly recommended the levy of library cess @ 6 paisa per rupee on property and house tax. Finally, it was recommended that the state and Central Governments should supplement the amount collected by levying the cess.

During the Third Five Year Plan (1961-66), the Central Government realized that "an adequate system of libraries is an essential part of any well-organized system of education.... Steps will be taken to set up or develop all the four national libraries at Delhi, Bombay, Calcutta and Madras. Provisions were also made for strengthening libraries at State headquarters and for increasing the number of libraries at the district and taluq levels.

The National Library of India

The history of the National Library falls into three distinct periods. The first is when a few public spirited people started public library service; the second is when, Lord Curzon started the Imperial Library, and the third is the Post-Independence period. The National Library, Kolkatta has its origins in the establishment in 1836 of a public library in Calcutta, for which, municipality of Calcutta agreed to maintain in 1890. In 1903 Lord Curzon effected amalgamation of the Calcutta Public Library and official Imperial Library to form the new Imperial Library. Since the amount for book purchase was inadequate, the Library was largely built from gifts, from individuals and Government departments in the early days. The First two gifts of importance were the Bihar and Tripura Collections. The Government of Bengal offered books received under the Press and Registration of Books Act, 1867. In 1949 the personal collections of Asutosh Mukhopadhyay were added to the library[5].

In 1948 it was renamed as the National Library and was moved to a beautiful site called Belvedere (once the residence of Vice-regal lodge). It was formerly opened to public on 1st February, 1953 by the Late Moulana Abdul Kalam Azad, the then Union Minister for Education. Holdings by March 1984 included 2 million volumes approximately and 3000 manuscripts. A notable development has been the publication of the National Bibliography. The first step was the enactment of the Delivery of Books Act of 1954 which required every publisher to send a copy of every book to the National Library in Calcutta and 3 copies to other public libraries in India. In 1956, the Act was amended to cover periodical publications in all the 14 official languages. The Indian National Bibliography began its publication in 1958. Preservation of books is of great importance in tropical climate. The work is shared by the laboratory, preservation of rare books and reprography divisions. Bibliographical assistance to the scholars is extended. A pilot children's library was run. A review committee was appointed in 1968 by the Government of India to review the working of the Library and to suggest measures for the efficient functioning and future development. The committee made a number of recommendations and they were accepted by the Government. The basic functions of the National Library according to the committee are :

1. Acquisition and conservation of all significant production of printed material.
2. Collection of printed materials concerned with India even if it is published outside the country.
3. Acquisition and conservation of foreign material required by the country.
4. Rendering of bibliographical and documentation services of current and retrospect materials.

5. Provision for photocopying and reprographic service.
6. Acting as the centre for international book exchange and international loan.

Modernisation Activities

The Computer Division was established in 1988 to augment the modernization activities in the Library. It started with a Mini Computer - HP 3000. MINISIS, a RDBMS software was installed for bibliographic control activities. In 2001 the Library switched over to Client - Server Environment with SUN E450 as the server. At present a Campus Wide Network is being developed with 98HP Pentium III PCs as nodes.

The digitization and archiving of rare and brittle books and other documents on compact disc was also undertaken. English and documents published before 1900 and Indian Publications of pre 1920s are selected for this. So far 6,600 selected books in Indian and English languages have already been scanned and stored on 548 CDs - covering a total of 25,00,000 pages. Some of the East India titles which already archived on CDs are viz., Report of the proceedings of the East India Company in regard to the production of cotton wool: 1788; Bengal selection of records : 1826; Prabasi—a journal in Bengali; Land settlement reports etc. As on September, 2002 the total number of books in National Library are 22,70,954; number of books in Indian languages are 5,58,516; number of Maps are 86,682; number of manuscripts are 3,227; number of books received under the D.B. Act are 9,19,724; number of current periodical titles are 17,530 and number of Newspapers (titles) are 902.

Raja Rammohun Roy Library

Raja Rammohun Roy Library Foundation came into being in May 1972 on the auspicious occasion of the bicentennial birth anniversary of Raja Rammohun Roy. Coincidentally, it was also the International Book Year and the Silver Jubilee Year of our Independence. The Foundation is an autonomous organization, established and sponsored by the Department of Culture, Government of India. It is registered under the West Benga Societies Registration Act, 1961. Its headquarters is located at DD-34, Sector-I, Salt Lake City, Calcutta. The Foundation started functioning from this new premises since September 1985[6].

Objectives

The main objective of the Foundation is to promote and support public library movement in the country by providing adequate library services and by developing reading habits all over the country. This objective is proposed to be achieved with the active co-operation of State Governments and Union Territories and of Voluntary Organizations operating in the field of library services, cultural activities, adult education and the like.

The Memorandum of Association has listed a number of other objectives too :

1. Enunciation of national library policy and working towards its adoption by the central and state governments and persuading them to enact library legislation where such legislation does not exist.
2. Helping build up a national library system by integrating the services of National Library, State Central Libraries, District Libraries, and other types of libraries, for instance through on inter-library lending system.
3. Providing financial assistance to libraries, to regional and national library associations and to other organizations engaged or interested in the promotion of library development.

4. Acting as a clearing house for ideas and information on library development;
5. Promoting research in problems of library development and
6. Taking all such measures as may be found necessary to promote library development and its utilization in the country.

Obviously, the Foundation can not work towards the fulfillment of these objectives all or once because of financial and other constraints. Besides, library and library services being a state subject, willing participation and cooperation of the states will also have to be enlisted patiently and stage by stage. Then, there is the paucity of the right type of books in some of the Indian languages relating to our country and technology suitable for the general reader. Another great limitation is the unavailability of trained personnel who should be prepared to work with missionary zeal and involvement in the ideal of service to the masses.

Library Legislation

One of the principal objectives of the foundation is to propagate the idea of enforcing library legislation in the country. The idea behind library legislation is to lay down an efficient administrative structure on legislative footing for effective utilization of available resources. The ultimate goal is to provide free or easy access to the source of knowledge for all sections of the community. With this objective the foundation appeals to the State and Union Territories which have not yet adopted a public library act to enact a library legislation on any model suitable for the state or the union territory keeping in view the New Education Policy (1986) and also other pressing social needs.

Achievements

Not withstanding various administrative and procedural constraints, the foundation has taken long strides in promoting library services in the country. The foundation during, the 7th Five Year Pan (1985-90) received Rs. 614.40 lakhs from the Government of India as Plan grant and Rs. 279.75 lakhs from different state governments and union territory administrations as state contribution, with an average annual plan grant @ Rs. 122.88 lakhs and average annual state contribution @ Rs. 55.95 lakhs. In turn, the foundation rendered assistance to the tune of Rs. 495.00 lakhs with an average annual assistance @ Rs. 99.00 lakhs.

With the expanded activity during the 8th Five Year Plan (1992-97) the total plan grant reaches Rs. 1175.70 lakhs from the Government of India with an average annual plan grant @ Rs. 235.14 lakhs and state contribution reaches Rs. 645.97 lakhs from different state governments with an average annual contribution @ Rs. 129.19 lakhs. Consequently the amount of assistance rendered to libraries during the 8th Five Year Plan also reached Rs. 1188.52 lakhs thus aggregating to an annual average of Rs. 247.70 lakhs. The RRRLF foundation has made significant contribution to the expansion and improvement of library services in the country as a whole.

Working Group on Development of Public Libraries

During the Third Plan, the Planning Commission (India) appointed the Working Group on Libraries in June, 1964[7]. The group formulated over-all policies, priorities and programmes of public library development costing Rs. 30.99 crores.

The Group strongly recommended that $1\frac{1}{2}$ per cent of education grants should be earmarked for public libraries. Unfortunately, its recommendations like those of Advisory Committee's were not honoured by the State Governments. Hence, it is futile to indulge in the evaluation of the result of these exercises.

The eradication of poverty and attaining self-reliance were the two watch-words of the Fifth Five Year Plan. With regard to education including libraries, this plan put emphasis on :

* Ensuring of educational opportunities as part of the overall pan ensuring social justice,
* Establishing closer links between the patterns of education on the one hand; the needs of development and the employment market on the other,
* Improvement of the quality of education imparted, and
* Involvement of the academic community, including students in the tasks of social and economic development.

No separate mention was made of libraries. Similar is the case with Sixth and Seventh Five Year Plans. Nevertheless, Rs.352 crores have been earmarked for education for the year 1986-87. One can take clue from the UGC (India), which allows 25 percent of her grants allocated to the Universities for the purchase of library books and journals.

The Delivery of Books and Newspapers (Public Libraries) Act, 1954

The Delivery of Books Act[8], which was passed in 1954 and later amended in 1956 to include newspapers also, acted as the first milestone towards the acquisition of Indian language publications in a systematic manner in Independent India. According to Section 3 of the Act, every publisher has to supply four copies of his publication to the National Library, Kolkata and the three other designated libraries viz: (1) The Cannemara Public Library (State Central Library), Chennai; (2) The Central Library (Town Hall), Mumbai; (3) The Delhi Public Library, Delhi. The copy deposited at the National Library is passed on to the Central Reference Library at Kolkata for the preparation and publication of the Indian National Bibliography (INB). This Act was not applicable to the newspapers in the beginning. In order to acquire newspapers to the public libraries for reference and record, Government of India amended the act as "Delivery of Books and Newspapers (Public Libraries) Act" in 1956 vide Amendment Act 99 of 1956. According to Section 3A as inserted by the Amendment Act, every publisher of a newspaper has to supply at his own expenses of each issue of newspaper to the libraries notified by the Central Government.

Objectives of the act

1. To institutionalize a system that helps the preservation of country's cultural and intellectual heritage embodied in documents.
2. To achieve total or comprehensive coverage through compulsory deposit of a copy of everything published in the country to the National Library and each of the three other depository libraries.
3. To ensure the total output of the country's contemporary intellectual and cultural work stored and preserved for posterity.
4. To conform to the objectives of the National Library and,
5. To provide a legal depository status to one or more designated in the country.

UNESCO and Public Libraries

UNESCO[9], through its assistance programmes, helps member states to establish and improve their library services. Particular attention is paid to the development of public library service to support adult education and literary programmes. UNESCO Public Library Manifesto (1994) gave a new image and a wider scope to the library services. UNESCO's faith in public libraries as institutions where people can obtain objective knowledge and enjoy the pleasure of reading and recreation.

UNESCO has played a vital role in the development of National Libraries through seminars and symposiums. One may recall UNESCO's symposiums on National Libraries in Europe (Vienna, Austria, September, 1958), Regional Seminar on the Development of National Libraries in Asia and Public Area (Manila, 1964).

UNESCO's recommendations to the Member States are :

- Requested to establish, a national library in each state;
- encouraged the formation of a library association;
- they should ratify the provision of the UNESCO's Convention, 1958, relating to the international exchange of official publications and government documents;
- and ratify the provisions of the International Copyright Convention; and
- a National Library Legislation is a *sine qua non* for the development of a net-work of the public library system.

Freedom, prosperity and the development of society and of individuals are attained through the ability of well-informed citizens, to exercise their democratic rights and to play an active role in society. Constructive participation and the development of democracy depend on satisfactory education as well as on unlimited access to knowledge, thought, culture and information.

The public library is the local gateway to knowledge, provides a basic condition for lifelong learning, independent decision-making and cultural development of the individual and social groups.

This manifesto proclaims UNESCO's belief in the public library as a living force for education, culture and information, and as an essential agent for the fostering of peace and spiritual welfare through the minds of men and women. UNESCO[10] therefore encourages national and local governments to support and actively engage in the development of public libraries.

Activities of Public Library

The public library is the local centre of information, making all kinds of knowledge and information readily available to its users. The services of the public library are provided on the basis of equality in access for all, regardless of age, sex, religion, nationally, language or social status. Specific services and materials must be provided for those users who cannot for whatever reason, use the regular services and materials, for example linguistic minorities, people with disabilities or people in hospital or prison.

High quality and relevance to local needs and conditions are fundamental. Material must reflect current trends and the evolution of society, as well as the memory of human endeavour and imagination. Collections and services should not be subject to any form of ideological, political or religious censorship, nor commercial pressures.

Functions

Being a social institution, the public library has to perform multi-faceted functions: For the overwhelming majority, the quickest and easiest access to the world's best thought is through the public library.

* The library must be current as well as retrospective. Its materials are provided,
* to facilitate informal self-education of all people in community;
* to enrich and further develop the subjects on which individuals are undertaking formal education;
* to meet the information needs of all;
* to support the educational, civic, and cultural activities of groups and organizations;
* to encourage wholesome recreation and constructive use of leisure time.

Provision of materials

The library is a dependable source for most of the people. In addition to books, the public library should provide pamphlets, documents, and other non-book materials, and special materials i.e., films, tapes, discs and other non-print sources. The provision of materials are so designed to encourage the over and to provide the current information to meat the user needs.

Information Services

The services performed by a modern library include :

1. The organization of material to make it easily accessible through shelf-arrangement, classification, and cataloguing;
2. Lending of material so that it may be used at the time and place most suited to the public;
3. Guidance to assist the user to find what he wishes, either in the materials immediately at hand or in whatever library may possess it;
4. The public library, thus, serve not only the earnest users, but also those who are seeking relaxation and recreation.

In essence, the public library provides materials and services to promote the diffusion of knowledge and information. The basic principle underlying the library service is that it exists for the training of the good citizen.

Educational Functions

(3) To J.H. Shera[11], the library is "handmaiden of universal education", with the aim of bringing enlightenment, improvement and happiness to one and all. In the words of Dr. S.R. Ranganathan, "libraries are social institutions charged with the duty of providing the means for the perpetual self-education to one and all", leading to material happiness, mental joy, spiritual delight and

the spread of mass literacy. Books remain the sole comprehensive and proven method of self-teaching; and public library being the repository of our cultural heritage provides opportunity and encouragement for children, men and women to educate themselves continuously.

Adult Education

The idea of adult education lay embedded in the realization that education is a life-long process, and that universal education is the life-blood of modern society. The Adult Education Committee of Great Britain[12] defined it that "all the deliberate efforts by which men and women attempt to satisfy their responsibilities as citizens and members of society. The American Association for Adult Education states that the aim of adult education is "to inspire grown-ups to be something more than they are now, and to do their work better than they do it now.

In India, the concept of adult education has been broadened. Maulana A.K. Azad, once the Union Education Minister of India, gave a new orientation, a new life, and later on a new name to this concept by enlarging its base and giving it the apt title of Social Education - an education for the complete man. "The real aim of Social Education", says Humayun Kabir, "is to create an educated mind among the adult literate," for helping them to evolve a philosophy of life and to develop interests which will enrich their leisure. Probably, it inspired Alvin Johnson to hair the public library as a People's University and assigned it a vital role in fighting illiteracy and helping people in their intellectual, cultural and material advancement. As an agency of adult education, the public library has used various instruments of mass-communication, with increasing use of audio-visual materials for disseminating knowledge.

The National Adult Education Programme launched by the Central Government through Ministry of Education and Social Welfare on 2nd Oct., 1978, could have worked much effectively through the efficient public library services. Their due recognition in NAEP would have given an opportunity to public libraries to educate people to learn to be useful citizens by developing their abilities, individual judgement and sense of moral and social responsibility.

Community Information Services

The term community information service is of recent origin and it refers to services offered by public libraries to disadvantaged groups. Community information services have been emerging as one of the important information service of the public library system in the contemporary society. It is an essential and integral part of the public libraries. The concept of public libraries is a fundamental and qualitative institutional development in the context of the modern democratic and industrial society. The public library professionals responded to these developments and evolved different variety of community information services to the user group. This is a significant effort by the library professionals to serve the society and to measure the adaptability and innovative ability of the library profession.

All these developments in the provision of public library services reached culmination in the provision of community information services. These services are first started in United States of America under the name of 'War on poverty programme'. The basic aims of these services are :

(*i*) To link the clientele with a problem to appropriate agency which can provide solution to the problem.

(*ii*) To provide feedback information to the agencies regarding people's problem.

The Library Association in 1980 defined the term 'Community Information Services' as "Services, which assist individuals and groups with daily problem solving and with participation in the democratic process. The services concentrate on the most popular problems that people have to face, problems to do with their homes, their jobs and their rights".

Extension Services

The main object to extension work is to attempt to turn the library into a social centre whose function is to encourage reading habit. It's main aim is to create awareness of the use of library among the non-users, so that they will be converted into actual users.

The public library personnel should promote the library consciousness among the people and the user group. The user is the dynamic component of any library system, the librarian should see, to make available the right document with exhaustive information to the right reader, at the right time and in the right form. The librarian should encourage the users to use the library so as to improve the image of librarianship among the people. To achieve this, the librarians should extend their service from not only helping the users, but also to help those who are not demanding service for various reasons. In other words they should aim at converting the non-users into users through the community and cultural programmes and various techniques of spreading the information about library sources and services. For this, the following techniques are used :

Display

Display of the important collections of the library is one of the important extension programmes of library. Display is designed to bring together the readers with the :

* Interdisciplinary nature of the subjects which are separated on the shelves by the scheme of classification;
* The latest additions of the library collection;
* The special services rendered by the library; and
* The special collection of the library, which is of more useful to the Local community.

A display will be more beneficial to the readers if it has a theme or a purpose. Something concrete which could be appreciated and remembered by the reader. The Topical Displays' are designed around a centenary or a felicitation of a well known man of letters, about a learned local man, the publication of a new book authorized by a local prominent writer, the events of national importance, like the Independence or the Republic Day celebrations, national festivals, library weeks or to discuss the current topics and so on. Subject displays are arranged to display the book having related and allied interests of the community. A display of books on sport can be enlivened by such shop-window dressing as the introduction of a foot-ball, a tennis racquet or a cricket score board; a window show of books on costume and dress making could be augmented by medals, dress models, dress materials etc.

Mobile displays are on the increase to promote the library consciousness especially in the rural community through a network of book distributing points. In all types of displays, colour captions and a skillful arrangement of the books and the display of book jackets of new titles or pictures help them to be more attractive. The displays can also be augmented by using photographs, cut-out pictures, charts and models. The lettering used for display work and posters should always be simple and eyecatching.

Exhibitions

Exhibitions are mostly arranged to publicize less-known materials, encourage reading, promote interest in a specific field or group of subject fields or celebrate events like 'Children's Book Week' to highlight their literature and the facilities provided for them in the library. Exhibitions on local history, art or subjects of common interests, a representative collection of local maps and plans, a pictorial survey of the district's architectural treasures or picture gallery of local personalities afford an opportunity to enrich the library permanently - either by encouraging gifts or loan of library materials. Each exhibition should have a specific objective to attract the users to participate in it.

Since the holding of an exhibition needs investment of a lot of money, energy and time, it should be well planned in advance. The librarians may take the help of booksellers or publishers and the Department of Information and Public Relations of the State Government, Department of Field Publicity of the Government of India or other organizations like travel agencies or foreign embassies to hold displays relating to various regions or various countries. It is also essential that the selection of material for the exhibition should be evaluated carefully, to draw the attention of the user group.

Formation of Reading Circles

Organizing Reading Circles in the library is another form of extension work. Subject specialists may be brought together by the librarians to constitute a reading circle. Such reading circles are usually effective agencies in thoroughly exploiting the library resources for the study of respective subjects by the experts. Mutual cooperation and coordination between the librarians and the experts is essential for the success of these reading circles. This sort of intervention between the people of various subject interests are grouped together and help in the collection development and thus rise the quality of document collection in the public libraries.

Festivals and Fairs

During the celebration of local festivals special programmes may be organized viz. conducting games, essay writing competitions, details etc. so that the readers may be attracted and ambled in the public library. And special days of the year may be dedicated to the participation in local fairs as it forms another potential form of the extension service of the public libraries. It helps to make the people aware of the library and its services so that they can make use of it whenever they are in need. It also helps the younger generation to know the cultural and traditional aspects of their localities, in other words their local history. This form of extension service is full of great potentialities in our country, as such celebrations will attract huge crowds of people especially the urban masses and the rural community.

Adult Education

Illiteracy is the main cause for poverty in India. Eradication of illiteracy in turn eradicates poverty from the country. World wide, it is estimated that approximately nine million people are illiterate. The library extension service programmes may be beneficial for illiterate adults in learning the basic reading and writing skill. In other worlds, the extension programmes may promote the functional literacy, which is essential for the national development[13].

The participants of the seminar on 'Functional Literacy in Latin America' observed that "literacy is traditional in so far as it is limited to the simple transmission of reading and writing skills and some elements of arithmetic", and is functional, when, as part of an over-all integrated educational process it helps people to see themselves in perspective, to acquire the qualifications needed to act on the reality of their condition through work and to play a conscious and creative part in public life. It is also functional in so far as it is integrated with regional and national development plan and is of assistance in their implementation. Consequently, functional literacy programme covers various integrated areas: fundamental education, technical and professional initiation and training for taking part in local and national life.

Distance Education

Education for all, especially for those who are deprived of education due to social and economic reasons, the 'Distance Education' has come into help them. Distance education eliminates the barriers of literacy and provides an opportunity to select choice of subjects and help the people in studying independently. In this system, as the student-teacher interaction is not possible regularly, it can be substituted by the librarian by providing necessary information and materials to the users. He can act as a liaison officer between the student and the distance educational institution. The librarians should collect the necessary information about their courses and should provide those required documents for reference. He could also give counseling for them in general skills like how to prepare themselves for examinations and also how to study independently to improve their knowledge etc. Thus the libraries can play very good role to extend their "student support services" to the students of distance learning.

User Education

The infrequent use of libraries has significant implications about quality of education. For example, a majority of the undergraduates can successfully complete their academic pursuits with a limited use of books, in turn, less use of library. The librarians should provide information about the cataloguing and educate the users how to get help from the library professionals and how to use the computer terminals if it is an automated library etc. to create interest among the users. The important benefit of public relations and library instruction efforts are aimed at attracting non-users into the library, thus the reading habits may be created among the users, in turn, to increase the use of library. The user-education programme should create positive learning experiences for people who use the library and to motivate non-users by providing special materials and programmes to nominate the non-users, towards the writing and reading habit. Both the public relations and the library instruction activities of a library require good planning to develop variety of users education programmes.

The libraries in addition to strengthening of its public relations through librarian and different media, it also conducts some of the extension services to improve its use by the existing users and to motivate interest among the non-users to use its collections.

IFLA and Public Library Standards

According to International Federation of Library Associations and Institutions (IFLA) standards, there should be one public library for every 3000 people with every 1 billion people. India needs according to this standard more than 3,30,000 public library units. One of the IFLA standards stipulates that the library unit should not be more than a mile away from the residential areas.

In view of this, IFLA suggested urgent attention on networking of libraries for resource sharing to avoid duplication; creation of compatible computerized databases; modernization and automation of libraries for easy accessibility; resource mobilization for development of libraries.

The thrust of library services in the Andhra Region before the dawn of Indian Independence was on community information services. The leaders of Andhra Library Movement[14] sponsored and organized a number of information servaices through the public libraries. These services partly met the information needs of the community; contributed to the awakening of the community, solved the problems of the community and individuals and helped the development and use of the resources and talents of the community.

As far as the community information services in the Andhra Pradesh Public library system is concerned, no mention is made in the Act or the development plans of Zilla Granthalaya Samsthas about the nature of services to the illiterates, neoliterates and non-users of the library who constitute more than eighty percent of population. The Granthalaya Parishad is yet to prepare developmental plans. If community information services are introduced in the public library system of Andhra Pradesh according to the given programme, public library services will be an effective and useful instrument in bringing about social change.

Public Library Movement in Andhra Pradesh

Andhra Pradesh has a cultural history for over five thousand years. During the 10th Century, Madhusudhana, a famous general of Chalukya King Raja Narayana, founded a college called Chati Kalasala and appointed six librarians called as Saraswati Bhandarikas besides other staff members. By 1800 the British established their political establishment over Andhra Region. The British initiated the dams across Krishna and Godavari rives providing irrigation and moderate industrialization was promoted. Thus the economic growth created demand for educational opportunities. The Western system of education was slowly spread into the districts and towns. At the same time, the social reform movement was picked up. Among the important social reformers in Andhra are Sri Kandukuri Veerasalingam Pantulu, Sri Gurajada Appa Rao, Sri Raghupati Venkata Ratnam Naidu, Sri Gidugu Venkata Rama Murthi Pantulu and others. All these developments created state for socio-cultural and political movement in Andhra region. Libraries came into being out of the initiative, planning and enthusiasm of individuals and groups, dedicated selfless workers.

During 1800 there is a 'Paravasthu' family library at Visakhapatnam, later developed into Arsha Grandhalaya and opened to public use. In 1820, the Saraswathy Mahal Library established by Raja Sarfoji at Thanjavuru, Wanaparthy's Raja Rameshwar Rayalu's library (1821-1865) was opened to the public. The first telugu book was printed in 1834, and it initiated starting of a wave of reading clubs and libraries. Even during this period at Rajahmundry a public library was opened by justice James Thomas in 1839. And the Theosophical Society started a library in 1850 at Guntur. Sri Mudigonda Sankararadhya promoted the 'Sanakarananda Library' in 1872, at Secunderabad. A School teacher, Sri Mantena Adinarayana Murthy established a

'Saraswathi Nilayam Library' in 1886. Abdul Quyum, a nationalist and partriot and Moulvi Syed Hussain Bilgrami (nawab Emadul Mulk) in the year 1886. Later this was acquired by the Nizam's Government and declared open to public, this was known as the Asafia Library finally converted into the State Central Library.

In the year 1911, the Rama Mohan Library at Vijayawada, the Saraswati Niketanam at Vetapalem in 1911 and Sarada Nilayam at Sattenapalli in 1920. The Andhra Desa Grandhabhandagara Sangham was established in 1914. A batch of library workers (Grandhalaya Sevakas) planned to tour a group of villages. This core group of library workers called 'Ramadandu' were divided into six sections, viz. (1) Advance Information Section, (2) The Bhajan Section, (3) Exhibition Section, (4) The Gramphone Section, (5) The lecturing section, and (6) The Magic Lantern section, held discussions with villagers, established a library, if there is no library.

Government of Andhra Pradesh appointed a committee under Chairmanship of Justice Sri Gopala Rao Ekbote to review the working of the Andhra Pradesh Public Libraries Act 1960 and to suggest amendments to improve the private libraries (aided libraries) in Andhra Pradesh and the Government has appointed another Committee under the Chairmanship of Sri Vavilala Gopala Krishnayya in July, 1978. The government have in principle accepted the majority of the recommendations of this committee. And even the accepted recommendations could not be implemented due to financial and political reasons[15].

Hyderabad Public Libraries Act (1955)

The Hyderabad Library Association stated in 1951 took-up the cause of library legislation. Shri K.M.Ujlambkar, who took lead in this regard, persuaded Shri Gopalrao Ekbote, the Minister for Education, Hyderabad State to take-up library legislation.

A Bill was drafted on the lines of the Madras Library Act and introduced the same in the Assembly in August 1954. The First All Hyderabad Library Conference was organised in December 1954 and Dr. S.R. Ranganathan was invited to preside over the conference. Dr. S.R. Ranganathan stressed the need for library legislation for a systematic growth of libraries. The Minister in his inaugural address assured to get the Bill passed in the next session of the Assembly and he got it done. The Hyderabad Public Libraries Act (1955) was a short lived one, because of the State Reorganization in 1956.

The salient features of this Act are :

1. The Minister of Education shall be State Library Authority.
2. State Library Council is advisory in nature.
3. The Director of Public Instruction will also act as the Director of Public Libraries.
4. Local Library Authority - One each for Hyderabad and Secunderabad, and for each district.
5. Library cess on property tax or house tax at the rate of 7 pies (oki) on every rupee.

Andhra Pradesh Public Libraries Act (1960)

Andhra Pradesh was formed in 1956 in accordance with the recommendation of the States Reorganization Commission. Before the formation of Andhra Pradesh, the Madras Public Libraries Act was in operation in the eleven districts of Andhra region. And the Hyderabad Public Libraries Act was in force in the nine districts in Telangana region. In order to have a composite Act, the Andhra Pradesh Public Library Act was enacted in I960[16]. This Act was amended successively in 1964, 1969, 1987, 1989 and 1990.

This Act is called the Andhra Pradesh Public Libraries Act, 1960. It was implemented from 1st April, 1960 in the

State of Andhra Pradesh which comprises Andhra and Telangana areas.

Salient features of the Andhra Pradesh Public Libraries Act are :

(*i*) Constitution of Andhra Pradesh Granthalaya Paishad, as an apex body with statutory powers and functions.

(*ii*) Constitution of a Directorate of Public Libraries to direct, supervise and control the public library system.

(*iii*) Constitution of City/Zilla Granthalaya Samsthas through the nomination of Chairman and members by the Government.

(*iv*) Librarians of City/District Central Libraries as ex-officio Secretaries of the City/Zilla Granthalaya Samsthas.

(*v*) Collection of eight paise as library cess; on house tax and property tax collected by Local Bodies.

(*vi*) Payment of staff salaries, working in the City/Zilla Granthalaya Samsthas.

Public Library System in Andhra Pradesh

The integrated Andhra Pradesh Public Library Act of 1960 helped in an orderly development of public libraries in the State. This Act created a network of public libraries, which started functioning and offering effective service in urban and rural areas of the state.[17]

The public library system of the state constitutes a central library at the 'apex' of the system, followed by the regional libraries, the district central libraries, the branch libraries, village libraries, deposit centers and mobile libraries. Besides the above, there are aided libraries, Panchayat libraries, and co-operative society libraries, which are also functioning in the net work of public libraries in the state receiving grants from Zilla Grandhalaya Samastha. Though the Act declared that the state central library is the 'apex' library in the system, but there is no mention about the functions of this library.

Now there are seven regional libraries in our state. Out of the seven regional libraries, one regional library at Hyderabad is also called the State Central Library. The other six-regional libraries are at Nizamabad, Warangal, Tirupathi, Rajahmundry, Guntur and Visakhapatnam. The 1960 Act was completely silent on the activities, the relationship between the state central library and the district central libraries. But the State Central Library and State Regional Libraries are working under the control and supervision of the Department of Public Libraries.

The district central libraries were established by the ZGS, and it is constituted under section (1) of APPL Act 1960. At present there are 23 Samasthas one for the city of Hyderabad known as city Grandhalaya Samastha and one each at 23 revenue districts of the state. The outline of the development plan for urban areas given in Rule 16 of APPL Rules 1961, held that, each municipal town should have a main library, if the municipal town exceeds the population of 50,000. In addition to this, there may be a branch library for every 25,000 - 50,000 population. This norm prompted the Zilla Grandhalaya Samstha to open libraries in all the municipalities in cities and towns.

The development plan of the Rural Library System, under Rule 16(4) at APRL Rules 1961, states that there shall be a district central library in each district head quarters, and a branch library for each panchayat, where the population is 5,000 and above, there must be one book deposit centre for each village or group of villages with a population between 1,000 and 5,000.

A.P. Public Library Structure

Based on the Act, the Andhra Public Library System is given below :

GOVERNMENT OF ANDHRA PRADESH

↓

Andhra Pradesh Grandhalava Paishad

↓

Department of Public Libraries

↓

Govt. Libraries	City Granthalaya Samstha/ Zilla Granthalaya Samsthas/Libraries	Aided Libraries
1. State Central Library.	City Central Library and District Central Libraries	Libraries Managed by
2. Regional Libraries.	↓ Branch Libraries	↓ 1. Voluntary Organisations
3. Mobile Library.	↓ Mobile Libraries	↓ 2. Municipal Corporations
	↓ Village Libraries	↓ 3. Municipalities
	↓ Book Deposit Centres	↓ 4. Panchayats
		↓ 5. Co-operative Societies

Grandhalaya Parishad

The A.P.Government on 2nd December, 1988 issued an ordinance for constituting a state level body called the A.P. Grandhalaya Parishad. According to the provisions of the amended APPL Act I960, through an ordinance during 1988, the State Library Committee was ceased to exist with effect from 2-12-1988, and the constitution of the Grandhalaya Parishad was under active consideration of the A.P. Government.

The Andhra Pradesh Public Libraries (Amendment) Act, 1989 (Act No. 11 of 1989) was passed in April 1989 which replaced the ordinance of December 1989, for the purpose of constituting the Andhra Pradesh Grandhalaya Parishad. The Education (Libraries) Department issued G.O.Ms. No. 236 in 10-7-1989, constituted the Andhra Pradesh Grandhalaya Parishad (Under Section 3 and 7 of the Act) consisting of 9 members as a compact body.[18]

Composition of the A.P.G.P.

(*a*) Chairman may be appointed by the Government, from among the persons who has rendered eminent service for the cause of education and library movement.

(*b*) Director of Public Libraries (Member - Secretary).

(*c*) Seven Members nominated by the Government of whom :

(1) One expert having specialized knowledge of library science.

(2) Two members who have rendered service for the development of library movement.

(3) One person representing aided libraries.

(4) One from Chairman of Zilla Granthalaya Samsthas.

(5) One from Secretaries of Zilla Granthalaya Samsthas, and

(6) Chief Librarian, State Central Library, Hyderabad.

Objectives of the Parishad

(1) Organise and promote library service.

(2) Establish, equip, maintain and develop an integrated, comprehensive and efficient library service in the State.

(3) Augment supply of books and periodicals to library.

(4) Develop infrastructural facilities like building, furniture, equipment etc. to public libraries.

(5) Raise finances and regulate their usage.

(6) Undertake other related activities.

(7) Suggest ways and means for raising additional resources; and

(8) Prepare long-term and short-term plans for providing library service.

Functions of the Parishad

(1) Evolve perspective plans.

(2) Prepare consolidated programmes with the guidelines issued by the Government and RRR Library Foundation and implement the programmes.

(3) Approve the budget estimates of the Parishad and Granthalaya Samsthas.

(4) Sanction opening of libraries, deposit centers, etc. and creation of full-time posts with the approval of the Government.

(5) Accord administrative and financial sanction for (*i*) Construction of buildings. (*ii*) Additional staff; and (*iii*) Shifting of regional and mobile libraries.

(6) Accept gifts or endowments.

(7) Approve and submit to the Government every year the audited statement of accounts and utilization certificates of its funds.

(8) Approve annual audited statements of accounts of the Granthalaya Samsthas.

(9) Approve Annual Report of the working of public libraries to be placed before the legislature.

(10) Decide policy for selection and purchase of books.

(11) Organize and conduct library seminars, meetings and conferences.

(12) Coordinate all activities concerned with the library service, and

(13) Prepare consolidated programme in accordance with the guidelines issued by the Government.

(14) Advice the Government on all matters arising under this act. It shall meet atleast once in two months.

The Chairman shall preside all the meetings. The Chairman and every member of the Parishad, other than the ex-officio Members, shall hold office during the pleasure of the Governor.

Department of Public Libraries

The Government shall constitute a separate Department of Public Libraries and appoint a Director for the Department. The Director so appointed shall subject to the control of the Government.

(1) Supervise the State Central Library and its branches.

(2) Superintend and direct all matters relating to public libraries.

(3) Declare libraries eligible for aid from the Government.

(4) Direct and control the work of all the Granthalaya Samsthas.

(5) Report to the Parishad on the working of libraries.

(6) Publish a bibliography of all books published in the State, and

(7) Arrange centralized classification, cataloguing, inter library loan, coordination, book selection and maintenance of copyright registry.

Regional Library System in U.S.A.

The American Public Library movement belonging about 1900, saw an increasing emphasis on the development of largest units of library including country and regional libraries. In 1930 the first regional library in the world was organised in the Fraser Valley of British Columbia. The term 'Regional Library is' used as synonymous with 'multi-county library'. In a majority of cases, regional libraries are formed as federations of a co-operating libraries on regional basis, with network of libraries. Generally Regional Libraries have been organized by combining two or more county libraries or other large governmental units. The regional board composed of representatives from each county libraries in the region. The cities and county libraries of a region transfers all their library funds to the regional board for regional co-operation of the library system. Members of the regional board understand the Geographical and socio-economic profiles of these and plan a programme to meet their regional needs. It is their concern to develop a unified system of public library service for all people of the country.[19]

Objectives and Functions of Regional Library Centre

* To coordinate library activities in the region and provide materials and services to the local libraries.
* To acquire books to meet the needs of the region with an effort to secure maximum use of each volume.
* Centralized purchase and processing of books, providing in-service training programme for local librarians.
* If any book or few number of books, are identified as idle, the local librarian sends it back to the regional library, where it may be sent on to another community to use. Thus, this process of putting them in active one, of these idle books, assuring a live and useful collections in each local library.
* To maintain consultant services such as adult service and children's service consultant, etc.
* To provide book mobiles service to local libraries and small rural communities.
* Offering professional help by regional staff to the library trustees and librarians.

* The regional centre and its local libraries as an unified system in which limited resources are used to the best advantage of the users, the regional centre can buy the variety of titles, and can assure that the small stock of each library and book mobile station is changed frequently to promote with new collections.
* Services are extended to local public libraries through the librarians.

Regional Library System in U.K.

The regional library concept in England developed because of the effects of Carnegie United Kingdom Trust which following upon the recommendations of Michel (1924), the Board of Education Public Libraries Committee (1927), and the Kenyan Report and Wright (1928) encouraged the establishment of co-operative efforts in one after another by ensuring incentive funds to meet the heavy expenditure in organizing and compiling a Union Catalogue. The Kenyan report held that: "we shall not be satisfied by mere participation in area of co-operation, but it will be treated this as the foundation. The trust wants to see that the library services must be improved by linking these co-operative groups into larger co-operating groups and centered on some great library, which may be described as regional library, as per the norms of the report.[20]

From 1929 onwards many libraries, have voluntarily grouped together into ten geographical regions, in order to make their resources available to the public. The National Committee on Regional Library Co-operation', which met in every quarterly and co-ordinate their efforts in linking them with the National Central Library with the executive committee of four representatives. The National Central Library in 1949 appointed one-man committee in 1950 to examine the working of the national interlending system. And the other suggestions were incorporated and issued by the Joint Working party during 1954, to implement them.

The Robert Committee urged that regional libraries should have statutory recognition, and the local authorities should bear the expenditure of these libraries. The enactment of the Public Libraries and Museums Act of 1964, was empowered the Secretary of State in the Department of Education and Science to establish statutory bodies and to govern the regions were to be fixed and the composition, scope and activities have been laid down. The regional libraries in United Kingdom are working under close co-operation with clearly defined objectives are as follows :

* To act as centers for the holding of rare books.
* To act as agencies to facilitate loans among one another, and
* To act as repositories for historical records of the region.

Regional Libraries in India

The Regional Library System is not a new feature to the Public Library System in India. The Regional Library System is of recent, in the development of public library services. States like Maharashtra, Assam and Karnataka also have Regional Libraries established as early as the 1940's. Before Independence the Bombay government appointed a Sri A.A.A. Fyzee Committee in the year 1939-40 for the purpose of exploring the possibilities of establishment of provincial central library in Bombay as well as three Regional Libraries at Ahmedabad, Poona and Dharwar. As per the committee, the functions of the Regional Libraries will also approximately resembles that of Central Library with limited powers to its region, and it will be under the general guidance of the Central Library and play a role in developing the library movement in the district.

The regional library at Vidarbha region at Nagpur, stands as an example for collaborating the principle of regionalism. Dr. S.R. Ranganathan, the Father of Library Science in India, had suggested Regional Libraries only for bilingual states. Mrs. S.K. Rait had described the formation of the Regional Libraries in Great Britain along with the one National Central Library should be a model for India. The public library development programme was also incorporated in the 4th and 6th Five Year Plans. The state of Andhra Pradesh is now having 7 Regional Libraries, covering the three regions of the State i.e. Telangana, Rayalaseema and Andhra.

Regional Libraries and Library Advisory Committee

The Library Advisory Committee was appointed by the Government of India in the year 1958 and recommended the establishment of Regional Libraries. And "the District Central Libraries in turn, linked to the Regional Libraries and through the regional libraries will be connected to National Central Library. The Committee also recommended that the establishment of regional libraries are for bilingual states. The regional libraries will serve the needs of a particular linguistic groups and will discharge some functions of the State Central Library. The committee has not drown clear guide lines about the uniformity in functioning and in standardizing the activities of the regional libraries.

Regional Libraries in Andhra Pradesh

In 1953 Andhra State was formed by carrying out the eleven Telugu Speaking districts from the composite Madras state. The Madras state had the Public Libraries Act of 1948. It also applied to the eleven telugu speaking districts of Madras state. When they were separated and were included in the state of Andhra Pradesh, they brought along with other laws, the Madras Public Libraries Act 1948 to the Andhra state. Since the State Central Library was situated at Madras, the State of Andhra has to establish under the Act, a State Central Library, and consequently the State Central Library was established at Visakhapatnam in 1954-

55. In November, 1956, however, the Telangana part of the former Hyderabad state comprising of the city of Hyderabad and nine districts were integrated with the Andhra area and thus Andhra Pradesh was formed on November 1, 1956.

The state of Hyderabad also had enacted a Library Law in 1955. The Telengana area was covered by the said Act and took itself the said library law along with it and joined Andhra Pradesh. The State Central Library for the former Hyderabad state was at Hyderabad. Thus when two regions came together, they had two separate library enactments and had two State Central Libraries. There could only be one State Central Library. According to APPL Act 1960 the Andhra State Library situated at Hyderabad was declared to be the State Central Library for the State of Andhra Pradesh. After the formation of Andhra Pradesh, the State Central Library at Visakhapatnam was converted as the State Regional Library. That is how first Regional Library was established at Visakhapatnam. In 1958 the Visakhapatnam State Regional Library was shifted to Guntur and this was the only State Regional Library functioning in the state till the end of 1963.

Establishment of these Regional Libraries and the Districts in which they are expected to spread with effective library service is as shown below :

APPL Act, 1960 and Regional Libraries

As per the 1960 Act, [Section 2(12)] "State Regional Library means a Library established by the government under the APPL Act 1960, as a Sate Regional Library". The Act is completely silent with regard to its functions and its place in the organizational structure of the state library services. It also does not mention about its relationship with the State Central Library or other libraries in the district.

The Act clearly envisages only one State Central Library, but it is silent as to whether there would be only one Regional Library or many such Regional Libraries. It is true

Establishment of Regional Public Libraries in Andhra Pradesh

Name of the library and location	*Date of Establishment*	*Districts to be served*
1. Regional Public Library, Visakhapatnam.	6-9-1965	Visakhapatnam, Vizianagaram and Srikakulam.
2. Regional Public Library, Rajahmundry.	19-2-1966	East Godavari, West Godavari and Krishna.
3. Regional Public Library, Guntur.	4-1-1955	Guntur, Prakasam and Nellore.
4. Regional Public Library, Tirupati.	9-1-1964	Chittoor, Cuddapah and Ananthapur.
5. Regional Public Library, Warangal.	4-2-1964	Warangal, Khammam, Nalgonda and Mahbubnagar.
6. Government Regional Library, Nizamabad.	4-8-1966	Nizamabad, Adilabad, Medak, Karimnagar and Hyderabad including city.
7. State Central Library/ Government Regional Library, Hyderabad.	Originally Established in Feb., 1891.	Hyderabad, Secunderabad and Rangareddy.

that Section 8 empowers and this APPL Act, 1960. At present, there are seven regional libraries in the state and out of these seven regional libraries, the Government Regional Library at Hyderabad is known as state central library also. For the purpose of the present study the State Central Library at Hyderabad is also taken as a Government Regional Library. The Director to "Supervise the State Central Library and the Branches of such library. As per the APPL Act 1960, under Section 8, the branches were not clearly defined and the powers, functioning of the regional libraries are also not clear. Hence, it is felt that APPL Act 1960, in general and the section of the Act should be modified to improve the Regional Library Functions and Services.

Towards formulation of Objectives and Functions

It is also noticed that the APPL Act I960, has not laid down any specific features of the regional libraries, through this act. The regional libraries and their relationship with state central library is also not very clear. During the implementation period of the legislation, a number of recommendations were made through various committees, seminars and conferences to amend and update the status of the regional libraries i.e. the functions and its relationship with state central library and lay down the clear objectives and functions for the regional libraries to provide better services to the public. The present study made an attempt to analyse certain areas of importance to improve the regional library through these committee reports and conferences.

* **The State Library Committee,** at its meeting held on October 27, 1969 decided to determine the functions of these libraries and then requested the Government to take necessary action to develop the specific functions. The in action of the State General on this issue is a big set back to the public library system in the State/particularly to the regional library system.
* **The first Andhra Pradesh Libraries conference** was held in August, 1972, at Hyderabad recommended that the Regional Libraries should have a close cooperation and link between administrative relationship between the State Central Library and the Zilla Grandhalaya Samsthas. It was also resolved that the Regional libraries should share the library functions of the

State Central Library to provide better services to the public. As well as the following services should be organised by the regional libraries.

* To have a good text-book collections and reference books which can not usually acquired by the local libraries.
* The regional libraries should under take the bibliographical services in coordination with state central library.
* To encourage the inter library lending books to other libraries, which fit are fall with their close jurisdiction, to extent the library facilities, for a which few districts may be allotted for each Regional Library.
* To create uniformity and standardization the regional libraries should supervise the technical work of the district central libraries, and other branch libraries in the district.
* The librarian of the regional library should as certain himself as Regional Officer for the local libraries of the district.

In actual practice the Regional Libraries have failed miserably in the implementation of their objectives. As per the Government's expectations each Regional Library has to expand its library services atleast to five districts. There may be District Central Library of the Zilla Grandhalaya Samstha functioning in each District headquarters and the branch libraries in the rural areas. As these Regional Libraries were established at the district headquarters to supplement the services of the District Central Library.

The regional libraries should show 'high standards of service' to stand as a model to guide the district central libraries. In reality these regional libraries were unable to show any leadership to the District central libraries. Neither these regional libraries are unable to collect and preserve the manuscripts to develop local history collections, nor providing any facilities to the research scholars and historians. Even the basic reference collections in these libraries are of poor quality.

Bhoji Reddy Sub-Committee, 1973

The state library committee at its meeting held on October 18, 1973 appointed a sub-committee of three members to go into the working of the Regional Libraries and to suggest measures for their reorganization so as to bring them into the public library system. The members of the subcommittee were Sri M. Bhoji Reddy, Sri Abdul Mahamood and Sri Kodati Narayana Rao.

The committee submitted an elaborate report in 1974. Their principal recommendations were as follows :

* The State Central Library shall be the apex library at the State level.
* The State Regional Libraries shall be "the branches of the State Central Library".
* All the five State Regional Libraries shall be allotted certain districts as mentioned in the report.
* All the five State Regional Libraries shall be allotted certain districts as mentioned in the report.
* The State Central and the Regional Libraries should concentrate on reference collections and research materials particularly about the state of Andhra Pradesh.
* They should make exhaustive collections of publications of both state and Central governments.
* They should public bibliography annually of all the books published in the state.
* They should provide technical guidance to all the departmental and private aided libraries in their regions.

* They should arrange inter-library loan within their region, the State Central Library arranging between the regions.
* They should prepare regional union catalogue of the region.
* They should also do the documentation work.
* They should organize book reviews and other literary and cultural meets.

The libraries directly managed by the Government in Andhra Pradesh happen to be the State Central Library, Hyderabad and five Regional Libraries at Tirupathi, Guntur, Visakhapatnam, Warangal and Nizamabad including mobile library at Eluru. The criticism about the role played by these six libraries in the library system of the state in serving the public. These libraries have failed to deliver the goods, by not playing their legitimate role and also in the absence of clear goals and objectives. All these libraries, simply duplicating the services of the Samastha Libraries at the District level.

Ekbote Committee, 1977

In February 1977 the Government of Andhra Pradesh had appointed a Committee with Sri Gopala Rao Ekbote, retired Chief Justice of Andhra Pradesh as its Chairman to review the working of the Andhra Pradesh Public Libraries Act, 1960 and to suggest amendments to the Act.[21]

The committee visited all these regional libraries. It was observed that except Guntur, no other regional library has sufficient number of books to warrant the characterizing it as a regional library. All these libraries are almost duplicating the work of the District Central Library. None of these libraries is carrying out the work, which is expected from them. The reference collections in these libraries are particularly far from satisfactory. It is necessary to note that each Regional Library was allotted certain districts. What they were expected to do with these districts are not elaborated clearly.

The committee suggested the following broad functions to be performed by the Regional Library.

* Collection and preservation of manuscripts, rare books, available in the region should be mentioned by the regional libraries. All the necessary reference books must be provided in the library.
* Organise inter-library co-operation including inter-library loan.
* Set standards for Zilla Grandhalaya Samsthas and their branches, book deposit centers and mobile library services.
* Compilation of bibliography for the region as well as the preparation of union catalogue for the region.
* Inspection and supervision of Zilla Grandhalaya Samsthas in the the region and to provide them technical advice and assistance.
* Serve as an essential link between the State Central Library on the one hand and Zilla Grandhalaya Samsthas in their region on the other.
* To stock all reference books and non-book materials and special materials such as films, filmstrips and music records, etc.
* To serve principally as reference library and not lending library at all to individuals.
* Dr.Velaga Venkatappaiah has thought that instead of making a good number of amendments and make the Act so unwidely, it is better to prepare a fresh draft for an integrated, comprehensive and efficient library service, by clearing almost all the lacunae, by "infusing new thoughts suited to the changing times of modern India.

Functions of Regional Libraries Comprehended from the Recommendations so Far Made

Considering the various recommendations made by different committees, commissions and seminars and basing on a careful analysis of the observations, the functions and objectives of a regional library are conceptualized and expected to be in the following lines.

* The regional libraries must be given importance to fit into the state library system.
* The regional libraries should be given lead role to foster the cooperation among libraries.
* A clear cut functions and objectives should be developed to improve the regional library system.
* The legitimate functions should be carried out by the State Central Library with the help of Regional Libraries to improve the library activities in the state.
* Collection, maintenance and preservation of rare books and manuscripts available in the region.
* Provisions for research facilities and collection of books and other materials relating to the region.
* Organization of inter-library cooperation including loan. Inter-library loan need not be confined to the libraries functioning in the region but may be extended to those outside it.
* Setting up of standards for the District Libraries and the branch libraries book deposit centers and mobile library service.
* Preparation of a catalogue of the region and the offering of assistance in preparing and maintaining union catalogue for the state and the nation.
* The cooperative efforts of classification and cataloguing in the region are very helpful to improve the processing.

* Inspection and supervision of libraries in the region and arrangement for the provision of technical advice and assistance.
* Serving as a link between the State Central Library on the one hand and all kinds of libraries in the region on the other.
* Preparation and submission of annual reports of the working of the regional library, district central libraries and other libraries in its region to the State Central Library.
* Performance of any other duty entrusted to it by the State Central Library.
* To be the spokesman for all libraries in the matters concerning the region.
* To serve principally as reference library.

The above functions visualized in this study should of course be determined by the Government and conferring on it a statutory status. It is also felt that the territorial jurisdiction could be limited to the districts within its region to avoid un-necessary problem in the future.

References

1. Somasekhara Rao, K. : Junior College Libraries - Perspectives, trends and Challenges (Ph.D. Thesis), 1992.
2. Narayana Rao and Ramachandra Rao, T. : Rise and Growth of the Public Library Movement in India. Eluru, Iyyanki Library awards Committee, 1981.
3. Mukherjee, S.K. : Development of Library and Library Service in India, Calcutta, Wald Press, 1969.
4. Khanna, J.K. : Library and Society. Kurukshetra, Research Publications, 1987, p. 121-130.
5. Esdalle, Arudalle : National Libraries of the World, London, Library Association, 1957.
6. Books for the Millions at their Doorsteps : Information Manual, 5th Ed., RRRLF, B.B.Co., Calcutta, 1997.

7. Khanna, J.K. : Library and Society, Kurukshetra, Research Publication, 1987.
8. Bandhopadhyay, A.R. : The Delivery of Books Act, 1954 : Suggestions for fresh book. ILA Bulletin, 34(3), Oct.-Dec., 2000, p. 69.
9. UNESCO Public Libraries Manifesto, 1994. NISSAT News Letter, 13-14, Oct.-Dec., 1994.
10. UNESCO Public Library Manifesto, ILA Bulletin, 9(1), Jan.-March 1973, p. 30-32.
11. Rao, S.R. : Public Library System. Asia Publishing House, Bombay, 1972.
12. Great Britain, Reconstruction (Ministry of __). Adult Education Committee, 1919, Final Report (HMSO).
13. Ramanayya, I.V.: Role of the Public Library in Adult Literacy Work. Herald of Library Science, 16(2), 1977, pp. 204-208.
14. Ramachandra Rao, P. : Significance of the Library Movement in Andhra Pradesh, 1900-1948. Library Herald, 20(2-4), July 1981 - March 1982, p. 151-154.
15. Government of Andhra Pradesh : Review Committee for the working of the A.P. Public Libraries Act 1960 and to suggest amendments to the Act. Report of the Review Committee. Hyderabad, Deptt. of Public Libraries, 1978.
16. Majeed Khan, MA : A.P. Public Libraries Act, 1960 - as modified upto April, 1989 (with amendments and communications). Published by A.P. Public Library Association, 1990.
17. Kapoor, A.L. : A.P. Public Libraries Act, 1960. Library Herald, 5(2), July 1962, pp. 81-96.
18. Andhra Pradesh Library Act (Amendment), 1989. Hyderabad, Govt. of A.P., 1989.
19. American Library Association and Public Library Association Standards Committee. Minimum Standards for Public Library System, 1966. Chicago, ALA, 1967.
20. Murrison, W.J. : The Public Library, its origins, purpose and significance, 2nd ed., London, George, G. : Hamap & Co., 1971.
21. Ekbote, Gopalarao: Public Library System. Hydeabad, Ekbote Brother, 1987.

2

Review of Earlier Studies Study Design and Methodology

The invasion of Information Technology into the area of Library and Information Science has been received well by the professionals working in the field of Library Science, as they will have scope for catering the needs of the users in a more accurate, systematic way especially in a relatively less period of time. However, aspects like providing necessary infrastructural facilities like automation, skill development of the manpower involved etc. are to be taken into consideration while expecting the desired results. Although, the process of automation and providing technical training to the professionals has been initiated, the situation is not uniform in the Regional Libraries in the State of Andhra Pradesh as these Libraries were set up in different periods of time.

Review of Earlier Studies

It is thought pertinent to present an account on the different studies conducted in this area of research.

For any research work review of available literature is the most important aspect. Review of literature is a measure, stating the recent output on a particular area of research and organised in a helpful sequence to strengthen the present research techniques. The main objective of the review of literature is to understand the research activities that have taken place in a particular discipline in general, and the area of research in particular. As the present study is aimed at understanding the functioning of Regional Public Libraries in Andhra Pradesh, all the available relevant literature was reviewed here. The contribution of academicians, information scientists, research scholars, and library professionals on this topic in various dimensions has yielded invaluable set of research output.

Thus, the reviewed literature is arranged under the following aspects of public library under each heading, the articles are further arranged in ascending chronological order.

1. Culture and Development
2. Public Libraries funding
3. Staff Training
4. Library Legislation
5. Public Library Services
6. Collection Development
7. Community Information Services
8. Extension Services
9. Mobile Libraries
10. Management
11. Development
12. Cooperation and Automation
13. Networking
14. User needs and User Education
15. Regional Libraries

Culture and Development

Debeij, J.[1] (1997) described, one-third of the population of the Netherlands are registered library members, while half make occasional use of library services. The importance of public libraries was recognized by Aad Nuis, Dutch minister for Education, Culture and Social Welfare, in referring to libraries as dynamic institutions...of immeasurable value for the life and functions of society.

Epstein, R.[2] (1998) examines, the United National Educational, Scientific and Cultural Organization

(UNESCO) Manifesto in its Public Library Manifesto of 1994 advocated lifelong learning for all and universal access to resources not only to schoolchildren and educational institutions but to adults as well. Argues that the public library is not there to fulfill the role of the school library or education department and that the daily routine of public librarians is being compromised by the demands of these sectors. Suggests that additional staffing from other sectors be brought into: liaise with teachers; instruct teachers how to use the library; train students in library use; and identify and address the need for materials and equipment. Argues that only with this support will public libraries be able to carry out their role in the creation and development of a culture of reading.

Veeranjaneyulu, K., Rao, T.S.[3] (1999) outlines the importance of public libraries as instruments and evaluates the main objectives of Indian library systems in terms of their being inheritors and repositories of past culture and civilization and their role as agents for political awareness and social development.

Buragohain, A.[4] (1999) describes the socio-cultural background to human resource development in India and the role that public libraries are expected to play in continuing education. Identifies the major drawbacks to the existing Library Acts of Indian states and proposes a solution in the form of the Panchayati Raj system and the future of comprehensive multipurpose public library system for social and cultural renaissance in India.

Agnoli, A.[5] (2002) contribution to a special section devoted to libraries in Italy. Reports the encouraging Italian trend towards renovating and expanding children's sections in public libraries, a phenomenon due not just to the widespread interest in reading among young people, but also to the poor state of school libraries - badly organized, funded and staffed. In north Italy, children and adolescents now make up 40 percent of public library users, even though 0-14 year-olds are only 15 percent of the population. Describes the improved public library facilities for children.

Public Libraries Funding

Kumar, R. P.; Nagpal, S. P.[6] (1980) stresses the importance of the public library service in supporting adult education in India. Suggests several ways in which libraries could improve their adult education services, and argues that need for special funds to carry out these improvements.

Govind, Vijai[7] (1988) said, Public libraries in India are financed mainly by Library Cess (tax) and a government subsidy. Discusses the inadequacy of cess, remittance problems, and the adequacy of government contributions.

Ramaiah, L.S.[8] (1993) describes information as an important resource for national development. States that every nation should develop an information infrastucture for its present and future needs. Public libraries and community information centers are very important intermediaries for the tansfer of knowledge to the people and may be regarded as the people's universities. Stresses that public libraries require mandate by law and adequate finances for their efficient functioning and points out that our of 25 states in India, only 8 states have enacted library legislation. Ordinary people in the villages are not getting even a semblance of public library service, even though they are paying for it. At present growth rates it will take 100 years to provide minimum library services to all the villages in India and for the fast development of the public library system, adequate sources of finance must be found. Discusses various methods of financing public libraries and suggests a proportional method be adopted which allocates a certain percentage, either of the education budget or the regular state budget. This allocation must be made by each constituent state of India under the mandate of the Public Library Act.

Jambhekar, N.[9] (1995) examines the place of public libraries in India's 5 year plans since independence in 1947, with particular attention to finance. The 1951-56 plan established district libraries in each state and model library systems in 29 areas. The 1956-61 plan doubled the number of libraries. National libraries were established in Delhi, Calcutta, Bombay and Madras during the 1962-67 plan. The 1969-74 plan provided 17.3 million dollars for information services of which 2.66 million dollars went to libraries.

Kaula, P.N.[10] (1996) discusses the growth of the public library system in India, their relatively low priority in government funding and the potential of computerization and networks in assisting Indian public libraries in the fulfillment of their goals.

Bolles, C.[11] (1996) Idaho is 1 of only 10 United States that does not have direct state aid for local public libraries, derived from state taxation. Reviews the current impact of finance from federal and state sources for public library development and speculates on the continued viability of these sources for the improvement of library services in Idaho.

Bhattacharjee, R.[12] (1999) describes the main objectives of the Raja Rammohun Roy Library Foundation (RRRLF), and the main projects it has undertaken, in the promotion of the public library movement in India through the drafting of the National Policy on Library and Information System and the pattern of financial assistance provided to public libraries in the country.

Thomas, V.K.[13] (1999) points to the way in which the Raja Rammohun Roy Library Foundation (RRRLF) has funded and promoted 22,000 public libraries in India, over a 25 year period. Analyzes the financial contribution of RRLF to public library development in India by considering the specific schemes of assistance in detail and examining the performance of the schemes in aggregate.

Kraft, 1, Geist, C, Frohss, W., Leutemann, C, Walther, B.[14] (1999) During German reunification the national government gave generously to help preserve the new federal states' cultural heritage, including libraries. 10 years later, most state subsidies have been reduced; municipalities have to shoulder increased responsibilities as state government contributions decline. Criteria applied to fund allocation varies among the states; generally allocations concentrate on libraries providing regional services.

Stanton, I[15] (2001) Councils and state governments across Australia expend considerable funds on library stock. The problem arises as to how those who are responsible for the expenditure of these funds can know what value for money users are receiving and how collection development staff can know whether their stock selections are performing well, long after they have been acquired. Examines how it may be possible to quantify the saving to the community that this expenditure represents. Describes experimental calculations and benchmarks which attempt to quantify value for money in library collection development.

Daines, G.[16] (2001) the second half of the 1990s was a period of low morale in UK public libraries, with falling budgets, reduced opening hours and staffing levels and unfavourable government attitude. However, there were brighter aspects to the situation, such as the creation of the consortium EARL (Electronic Access to Resources in Libraries), new emphasis on users and on cooperation with other cultural institutions, and a rediscovery of the role of libraries in the promotion of reading novels. The election of a Labour government in 1997 saw a return to optimism with a political commitment to encouraging reading and efforts to end social exclusion and the information divide. Practical measures have included the requirement for librarians to submit annual plans, the modernization of standards, and 5-yearly inspections. The financial provision is still not satisfactory in that although 200 million pounds is to be made available for Internet linking, funds for renovating buildings and maintaining services remain very modest.

Staff Training

Kanakachary, M.; More, S.[17] (1992) explains the main components of computerization of library and information systems. Stresses the need for and necessity of manpower. Emphasizes in-service training. Suggests a methodology for conducting training programmes for computer applications in public library systems.

Minai, H.[18] (1999) Japanese public libraries are facing great changes. They must improve their direct contact with users and provide better guidance on books and reference services. In staffing, there must be clearer distinctions between professional and nonprofessional work. Training needs to be improved including provision of courses in management with changes to professional education. Library research must be encouraged. The Nihon Toshokan Kyokai (Japan Library Association) must reconsider its activities and organization, with more emphasis on its regions, and on public relations.

Boscheinen, C.[19] (1999) In libraries the question of professional education and development is becoming important within the context of administrative reforms, increased workplace demands and reduced financial resources. A survey conducted in 1999 among 105 large German public libraries showed that while personnel development is considered important, its implementation is far from routine. Shortages of staff, time and money may cause problems.

DeCandido, G.A.[20] (1999) a commencement address delivered to new graduates at the School of Information

Science and Policy, State University of New York, Albany, USA. Gives advice to graduating librarians, communicate with colleagues, pursue continual education, take advantage of opportunities, nurture a sense of humour, be open to users, keep your life and work in balance, accept change develop a sense of self and professional worth, write for publication, view librarianship as a way of connecting people to ideas.

Chavez, G.T.[21] (2001) reports on a study to survey the levels of workforce training and development programmes in selected public libraries throughout the State of Oregon, and to consider staff training and development efforts as a basis for enhancing library services. The study targeted all public libraries in the State with service populations ranging from 1,000 to 15,000. Findings indicated varying levels of workforce training and suggested a need for improvement, concluding that services would be enhanced through more staff training and development. Makes recommendations aimed at library directors and governing bodies.

Library Legislation

Mangla, P.B.[22] (1984) examines the characteristics of a developing county. The role of the public library is discussed in the context of continuing education the dissemination of information and the problems of mass illiteracy. The advantages of a public library system are discussed along with the usefulness of public library legislation. The need for suitable reading material and for professional manpower is emphasized. Provides a resume of the public library situation in India.

Inamdar, N.B.[23] (1992) describes *3* periods in the development of public libraries in Andhra Pradesh, India: the pre-independence period (1800-1947); post-independence development (1948-1960) and library legislation; and developments since 1960. discusses the Andhra Pradesh Public library system since 1960 focusing on: financial resources; personnel; reading materials, their selection and use; audiovisual and extension services; and library services to special groups, in urban areas and in rural areas. Expresses concern at the low per capita expenditure, poor coverage of rural areas and the limited role played by the public libraries, and voices reservations about the latest amendments to the Library Act.

Raju, A.A.N.[24] (1993) Paper presented at the 19th All India Conference of IASLIC, Calcutta, India, 26-29 Dec., 1993. The enactment of the Andhra Pradesh Public Libraries Act I960, India created the Grandhalaya Parishad as the principal policy making body for the public libraries in the state. Presents the structure of public library system consisting of 8 government libraries, 2,303 Zilla Grandhalaya Samstha Libraries (ZGS), and 2,277 aided libraries and cities the provision in the Act for the selection and acquisition the delay in bringing out book lists, paralyzing acquisitions and refers to the solutions suggested by the Ekbote Committee. The Parizhad has to play crucial role to revamp the existing policy with the cooperation of professional experts to help develop balanced, up to date and useful collections.

Hamby, P. and Najowitz, I.[25] (1998) the Public Libraries Act of 1850 provided the catalyst for British public library development. Discusses and analyzes the background and relevance of this seminal piece of legislation. The utilitarian and idealist views held by middle class social reformers in early Victorian Britain are evaluated in terms of their effect on the debate and passage of the Act. Concludes that: the social concerns of middle class reformers were instrument in the development of the UK public library movement; utilitarianism and idealism were the guiding social philosophies; and the framers of the Act envisioned public libraries primarily as an agency for both social control and betterment of the working class.

Khan, M.A.M.[26] (1999) points out the neglect of public libraries in Andhra Pradesh, India, once a leading state in

Indian public library development. Stresses the need for amendments in the Public Lirbaries Act 1960 and the implementation of the recommendations of the Ekbote Committee Report and the suggestions of library experts.

Kaula, P.M.[27] (2000) refers to India's cultural renaissance and movement for the revival of work on the country's culture and heritage. Discusses the role of public libraries as institutions of the masses and the growth of movements for national awakening from Andhra Pradesh. Highlights the work of lyyanki Venkta Ramanayya who is regarded as the 'Architect of the Public Library Movement in India'. Presents a brief account of adult education and literacy specifying the National Adult Education Programme. Describes the plans for the network of libraries through enactment of legislation in ten states stressing the emphasis on rural libraries. Outlines the various schemes and methods to develop information services at grass roots level urging also the need for promoting the reading habit, book culture and publication of books for the rural masses.

Deshpande, K.S.; Hungund, B.B.[28] (2001) the Raja Rammohun Roy* Library Foundation (RRRLF) was established by the Government of India in 1972 to reactivate the public library movement in the country, and fund public libraries in various states. Suggests that despite this, much has been left unattended, such as persuading those states without library legislation to introduce it, strengthening existing library laws by amendments, and reviewing and critically evaluating the work of beneficiaries of the RRRLF funds. Recommends a study of IFLA standards for adoption in Indian public libraries: also that the RRLF should publish documents relevant to public library scenarios and undertake surveys on personal libraries and reading habits, as part of a programme to transform India into a land of libraries.

Public Library Services

Finhegan, Gerry[29] (1975) the author is a former member of the West Belfast Community Development Team. Deals with the problems of providing an effective and meaningful library service to deprived neighbourhoods. Looks at some efforts made through community development and government departments to diagnose and treat social ills, e.g. throughout Britain, the Home Office has designated specific areas of social need as Community Development Project Areas. Shows the close affinity between the standards of the community worker and those of the outreach librarian and suggests how the rich resources of the library can best assist community groups. In disadvantages areas, librarians should be positive, innovating and adventurous.

Kaminska, Halina[30] (1978) as more public libraries in Poland have record collections there is a need to utilize them to the best advantage. Four countries (Finland, Sweden, France and England) which have record libraries already are examined to discover the problems involved. The biggest problem is whether to have home loans or listening facilities in the library. Finland and Sweden have comfortable listening areas with headphones. France and England have loans for home listening; a charge is generally made but amounts vary with yearly subscriptions, changes per record and fines for overdue loans. In Oct., 77 the Polish Library Association organised a conference at Szezecin Public Library to discuss future record facilities in Polish Libraries; no firm agreements were reached. Some of the arguments presented are examined.

Mackenzie, Christine[31] (1990) the public libraries are now expected to make their collections accessible to all members of the community. Most libraries already have material that is useful to, or useable by, people with disabilities. Marketing these resources to those people who require them, but who are probably not aware of what is available at their local public library, needs to be a public library objective. Discusses the services offered by Danenong Valley Regional Library Service one of the largest regional libraries in Victoria.

Eichhorn, S.[32] (1996) demonstrates the possibilities and discusses the supply of and experience in the use of CD-ROM to support enquiry service in public libraries. Explains how the use of CD-ROM can improve library service and can be integrated at different levels of service and outlines organizational and financial considerations. Offers selection criteria and explains the legal implications which are of importance for public libraries. Provides a list of CD-ROM products which are suitable to public libraries and discusses public relations, training, maintenance, and the technical possibilities of presentation.

Roberts, W.[33] (1998) founded in 1998 and based in the Hague, FORCE supports all initiatives aiming to improve access to information for people in developing countries with a reading handicap. Dutch librarians have proposed the creation of a resources centre for libraries in these countries and the ex-USSR specializing in reading handicap as an alternative to well meant but inappropriate donations of old Braille books. FORCE cooperates with IFLA, the World Union of Blind People and Unesco. Activities planned include a website, regional workshops and technical aid for setting up new libraries.

Naidu, G.H.S.; Narasimhulu, A.; Rao, V.S. ; Ramesh, L.S.R.C.V.[34] (1999) reviews the range of user services provided by public libraries in India, including document services, information services, current awareness services, location type services, reference services, backup services (repographics, translations, audiovisual materials) and computerized information services.

Itou, S., Kato, H., Kawata, T., Sato, T., Muraoka, K., Murabayashi, M., Yamamoto, A., Wakisaka, S.[35] (1999) numerous misleading statements and theories about public library services are currently circulating in Japan and they are damaging the development of public libraries. Examples are given and counter-arguments put forward. Areas addressed include: the library's role is to preserve, guide and edify; library freedom is unimportant; children's library services should preserve children's innocence, borrowing, request services, duplicate copies, interlending are unimportant; biased views of library uses; complacent book selection, inaccurate views of prefectural libraries.

Wigell-Ryynanen, B.[36] (2000) Finnish public library facilities were surveyed during the summer of 1999 to ascertain their adequacy in terms of size, condition and location. Presents results of the survey. Concerning size, 27 percent of municipalities have library facilities that fall short of the minimum. Concerning the condition and modernity of the facilities, 40 percent of libraries were built or renovated during the 1980s and 40 percent during the 1990s. Also gives details regarding the location of libraries. In addition, library staff were asked for a general estimate of their facilities. Respondents rated their facilities as follows: 5 percent very poor, 12 percent poor, 31 percent satisfactory, 37 percent good, and 15 percent excellent.

Collection Development

Tait, H.M.[37] (1981) describes New Zealand public library developments in the areas of regional service; 'free and rental' service; standards; computerisation adult literacy; hospital and housebound services; service to minority groups; school community libraries; and the National Library. A public library enquiry (possibly by a visiting expert) could provide the key to future development. In any case, librarians must present costed documented proposals for action and must learn how to make them irrestible to politicians and public.

Agrawal, S.P.; Walia, Meena; Lal, Manohar[38] (1986) outlines the objectives and the functions of public libraries. Examines the growth of public libraries in India focusing on 7 public libraries at national level. Briefly discusses the lack of a public libraries infrastructure and the uneven development of public libraries at village, city, district and state levels. Describes the following aspects of a plan of action; administrative infrastructure, library legislation, library resources, utilization of resources, depository libraries, resource sharing, fulfilling the needs of the public library clientele, the role of private organizations, staffing pattern, facilities for career development, and financial resources.

Baliarsingh, R.K.; Mahapatra, M.[39] (1993) paper presented at the 19th All India Conference of IASLIC, Calcutta, India, 26-29 Dec., 1993. Assesses the usefulness of the general public's reading interest in the collection development of public libraries in the Puri District of Orissa, India. Concludes that the public library's collection, especially in rural areas, should not be hampered by the economic recession. Stresses the overall emphasis on the public library to select, collect, and organize need based literature to suit the public's reading interest.

Robinson, W.C.[40] (1995) questionnaires were sent to public library systems in the 200 largest cities in the US to learn more about the role of price in the selection of materials. A 34 percent response rate yielded 67 usable responses. When ranked on a scale from 1 to 7, with 7 being least important, list price had a median ranking of 4, while likely community demand was ranked 1. When faced with price increases, these collection developers tended to select fewer duplicates, fewer periodical and annual publications, and fewer non-book items. About 26 percent of those responding had adopted an informal or formal piece ceiling for selections. About 66 percent of these librarians were likely to be more price conscious when selecting non-book items.

Jong, J.D.[41] (1996) in the Netherlands government policy towards public libraries is aimed at encouraging maximum use of the collections with reduced funding. As a result libraries are committed to stocking popular titles. A recent independent report commissioned by the Ministerie van Onderwijs Cultuur en Wetenschappen (Ministry of Education, Culture and Science) and the Nedelands Bibliotheek en Lekturr Centrum (Dutch Centre for Libraries and Reading) concluded that too little was known about library acquisition policies. A national programme for cooperative acquisition is required to make optimum use of available resources.

Ostendorf, J.E.[42] (1997) argues that libraries needs Internet policies analogous to collection development policies to help them decide what services and degrees of access should be provided. Drafts some suggested details that could be incorporated into a typical Internet Acceptable use Policy. Concludes with a selection of public library web sites displaying typical Internet use policies.

Stephens, A.K.[43] (1998) Thematic issue devoted to public library collection development in the information age. From planning and budgeting, to exploring new methods and resources for building and evaluating collections, to education and training for improved collection development - the articles illustrate and emphasize the importance and use of information and information technologies in current collection development efforts.

Wang, M.I.[44] (2000) discusses collection development in public libraries in Taiwan. Firstly, explores the missions and functions of modern public libraries in the advent of the 21st century. Secondly, studies the definitions and theories of collection development in public libraries. Based on statistical data, gives detailed descriptions of the collections of public libraries in Taiwan. Also reviews recent collection development programmes and activities of these libraries.

Community Information Services

Musib, S.K.[45] (1989) attempts to find out the main information needs of and the sources for obtaining information by the villagers surrounding a rural public library in Banakura, India. Results show that persons from different groups need more information on problems regarding consumer, educational, employment, and medical issues. To solve such problems they gather information from traditional sources i.e. family members, friends, neighbours, relatives. The library plays a very less significant role as a source of information.

Manghani, P.[46] (1999) the London Borough of Merton in the United Kingdom is currently devising a community development strategy and in the process is re-evaluating its role, function and image within the local community. It is asking how the public library can contribute to community development, what role is played by the public library in the local community and how the library service is perceived by the local community. Reports a training course on community development and public libraries for staff working in the borough in which the following issues were discussed: how communities would satisfy their information needs in a world without libraries; and what shape or form a library would take in a world without tangible libraries. Argues that the challenge for libraries is to see how, where and when they can assist and actively enhance local community development in terms of improving connectedness, sustainability and empowerment. Looks at some practical examples that are already underway in Merton arguing that the public library services should beat the core of the local community.

Parker, S.; Banwell, L.; and K. Ray[47] (1999) presents the findings of the LOGOPLUS project, whose aim was to ascertain to what extent the move to unitary authorities during the 1995-1998 reorganization of UK local government was seamless for public library users and staff. The following areas were investigated: politics, finance, integration, cooperation, staff, communication and users. Success factors which contributed to seamlessness were: councilors and managers who were committed to the provision of excellent services; transitional finance sufficient to cover the process of the change; effective leadership; clear definition of mission and goals; multiskilling where appropriate; and supportive users. However, some libraries have suffered because of a lack of these success factors.

Extension Services

Gour, P. N.[48] (1980) describes the role of public libraries in adult education in the West, and argues the case for the advancement of adult education programmes in India through the public library. Discusses the National Adult Education Programme (NAEP) and pleads for its integration with public library services.

Waizer, N., Gruidl, J.J.[49] (1993) explains how public libraries can play a significant role in community economic development. In 1993, the Illionis Institute for Rural Affairs, with State Library funding, conducted a series of workshops for local librarians to help them better understand this role. Reports on the findings of a mail survey of libraries which participated in these regional workshops and follow up activities. 39 rural librarians responded to the survey, mailed in Nov., 1996. The results demonstrate the extent to which the libraries were actively engaged in local economic development efforts and how they perceive the benefits.

Sciacca, J.[50] (1998) describes the outcomes and impact of a Library Services and Construction Act (LSCA) funded project 'Economic development and the public library' carried out by the Lincoln Trail Libraries System in 1988-89. Its main goals were to conduct a market survey of the issues surrounding public library involvement in economic development activities in their local communities. The 'Economic Development Activity (EDA) Score' was developed and administered to 100 randomly selected Illinois public libraries. Lists the resulting recommendations for increased involvement by libraries in economic development.

Guerin, C.[51] (1998) the media centre, part of policy to humanize the hospital, provides education, cultural and information services, with a formal acquisitions budget and its own dedicated location. Books provide an escape for the patient from illness, and wider activities such as talks and exhibitions for those who are mobile help vary the monotony. Bedside visits with carefully selected materials allow patient and librarian to become friends. For staff unable to visit the public library, the hospital library provides both professional and cultural resources.

Yilmaz, B.[52] (1999) public libraries have been changing in line with social developments. This in turn can create new problems for public libraries. It can be useful to make international comparisons amongst public library systems and services. Describes research in which Turkish public library systems and services were compared with those in the UK, the Netherlands and Austria. As a result, some important deficiencies in Turkish public libraries have been brought to light.

Landry-Hyde, D.[53] (1999) contribution to an issue devoted to library outreach, partnerships, and distance education in the USA. Bell Library at Texas AandM University at Corpus Christi has reached beyond its walls to utilize as well as to enrich the diverse community resources in its midst. Explains how this has been done in terms of distance education library support, consortium arrangements and other initiatives.

Neigel, C.[54] (2000) The South Fraser Health Region of British Columbia, Canada is comprised of 4 hospitals, continuing care, public health and mental health facilities. A needs assessment of health care professionals was commissioned to determine clients' perception and use of library resources was designed to allow the Regional Librarian to take an informed approach in developing an effective strategic plan for the region. Reports the objectives of the survey. Also reports on the results of a review of the literature and the findings of a questionnaire designed to focus on those most likely to utilize library resources and to determine the general information seeking behaviours of the respondents. Lists the recommendations of the study.

Winston, M.D., Neely, T.Y.[55] (2001) to investigate the effect of participation in leadership development programmes on leadership activities for public libraries, participants in the Snowbird Leadership Institute were surveyed. Although it is difficult to identify a direct relationship between participation in a leadership development programme and greater participation in leadership activities, the respondents report increased levels of the types of leadership activity that are described in the literature as important for public libraries.

Mobile Libraries

Ude, C.C.[56] (1983) the development of public library services in Nigeria has been greatly influenced by Unesco which held the 1st conference on public libraries in Africa in Ibadan, Nigeria's capital, in 1953. Nigeia's 1st public library was opened at Enugu in 1956 and the 1st mobile library service began in 1958 as part of a Unesco regional project. Following Nigeia's independence in 1960 the importance of public libraries in the fight against illiteracy was recognized. In addition to conventional mobile library vehicles a number of library boats are operated in less accessible areas and the number of both has increased from 8 in 1966 to 22 in 1981. At present 65 percent of the population have access to a library service.

Khanna, S.N.[57] (1994) the Delhi Public Library, India, has 6 mobile libraries, 5 for general library use and 1 for the visually handicapped. The general library mobile vans cover 67 service points weekly at a scheduled day and time; the braille mobile library serves 16 institutions for the blind within the union territory of Delhi. Mobile library use statistics are given for the year 1991-1992; 7,403 registered borrowers borrowed 92,018 books during the year.

Goedel-Hoche, G.[58] (1994) cooperation between schools and public libraries is important; it must improve as must public library facilities for primary schools. Library staff must learn from teachers about school learning programmes. Cooperation requires adequate space in a suitable location or the provision of a mobile library. Children need facilities for finding information and for browsing. Primary school children learn best through practical activities. Public libraries should provide modern non-fiction for children.

Rustomfram, I.P.[59] (1998) Indicates the role of mobile libraries in the USA and summarizes issues relating to bookmobiles, such as financial viability and the impact of automation, as reflected in the literature. Presents a case study of the bookmobile programme at the Memphis and Shelby Country Public Library (MSCPLIC) and Information Center which has been operating since 1935, describing traditional services and users, non traditional services such as JOBLIN and the Training Wheels unit which is equipped with cycles and designed to be a classroom with an observation area for carers and staff. Outlines future plans for MSCPLIC and briefly describes mobile services in Chattanooga-Hamilton and Knox Country.

Osborne, L.[60] (1998) discusses the provisions of mobile libraries and mobile library services to rural areas of Australia with particular reference to the experiences of the Maroochy Mobile Library, Queensland.

Nyeng, P.[61] (2000) with the acquisition of a minibus 2 years ago and the new large media bus, Randers Libraries,

Denmark have realized their plan for a more flexible mobile library service. The 13 metre long trailer was developed by the French mobile library company Gruau together with the Danish Norfrig. It has space for a wide range of materials and a computer system as well as seating and exhibitions. There are 4 computers for the public and 2 for staff with access to the library system BOOK -IT and the Internet via a radio system Bib 2000. It will visit 15 large localities stopping 4 hours at a time.

Library Management

Lee, W-n.[62] (1994) public library services are closely related to the lifelong education of citizens. The role played by public libraries in Taiwan is of great importance in the continuing education process. Effective management of public libraries in terms of facilities, collections, finance rules, promotion, staffing and objectives will have a crucial effect on citizens' willingness to seek knowledge and education. Thus, public library management must catch up with technology, social needs, and international developments. Public libraries should constantly adjust their management objectives and update their equipment in accordance with social trends, and also play a leading role in laying emphasis on knowledge in Taiwanese society. Original abstract-amended.

Dante, G.P.[63] (1999) in recent years information professionals have increasingly used management techniques and tools in the course of their everyday work. Looks at the literature on management techniques and tools in the Library and Information Science Abstracts (LIS Plus) database in an attempt to identify emerging themes. These include: library management, strategic planning; information management; management of human resources; quality management, total quality management, reengineering and benchmarking; marketing; economic evaluation; optimization and investigation of operations; and project management. Looks at some themes identified by

M.E.D. Koenig and suggests some elements which form part of the concept of knowledge management which will be very much in the forefront of management thinking in the future.

Umlauf, K.[64] (1999) guiding principles, long used in private industry, have been applied only recently to the public sector. Libraries have tended to formulate theirs on unspecific and unsuitable external models. Libraries should develop their own to show the public what to expect, the maintaining authority why money is needed, the staff how to act. Central Instruments for guiding principle implementation are internal communication, marketing and external public relations.

Das, I.V.[65] (1999) describes the establishment of public libraries in the Kerala region of India, including the Travancore, Cochin and Malabaar regions. Outlines the growth of an extensive library movement which helped in the Total Literacy Campaign of 5,000 libraries. Refers to the holding of conferences and the formation of the Kerala Granthasala Sangham and its activities, including the UNESCO Award, presented to the Sangham in 1975. Concludes with notes on attempts made to enact library legislation, including drafts prepared by Dr. S.R. Ranganathan and the adoption of the Kerala Public Library Act in 1989.

Venkatappaiah, V.[66] (1999) describes the public library system in Kerala state, India and sets out the special features of the Kerala Public Libraries (Kerala Grantahasala Sanghom) Act 1989. Considers the lessons that can be learned from Kerala's experiences applicable to other Indian public libraries.

Proctor, R. and Simmons, S.[67] (2000) reports on management issues arising when authorities decide to close public library service points. The data come from 2 British Library funded projects. Concludes that there are no criteria, which can justify closure to library users. Consultation is often mininmal due primarily to the short budget timescales. The process of closing libraries can be traumatic, the public backlash often deterring local politicians from agreeing to further cuts. A key issue in preventing the closure of libraries is the way the authorities conventionally measure their success. Authorities need to recognize that the local library has a wide ranging social value, besides being a source of reading material.

Development

Khan, H.A.[68] (1976) paper presented at the Indian Library Association Conference, New Delhi, Jan. 76. The present picture of public library development in India, after 30 years of independent rule, is an unhappy one. Only 4 of the 22 states have a public library law and there are serious deficiencies in organization, investment, qualified personnel, resources, bibliographic control and government interest. The level of literacy in India was 30 percent in 971, representing an increase of only 15 percent over the 2 preceding decades. Some urgent measures required to establish public library services are: the basics in building and equipment; librarians with drive and enthusiasm, specifically trained to meet public library requirements; standards; the acquisition of book and non-book material in all regional languages; and adequate government funding.

Singh, P.A.[69] (1994) paper presented at the All India Public Library Conference on the 8th Plan: perspective of public library development, New Delhi, 24-5 Feb., 1989. Describes the administrative structure, staffing pattern, financial resources and book collection development during 1984-85 and 1988-89 in the Maniur Public Library System. Discusses the various public library services and training facilities, assistance received from the Raja Rammohun Roy Library Foundation, and gaps and deficiencies in the development of public libraries.

Adak, T.[70] (1994) paper presented at the All India Public Library Conference on the 8th Plan: perspective of public library development, New Delhi, 24-5 February 1989. The Union Territory of Andaman and Nicobar Islands, India, comprising 306 islands of which 38 are inhabited, has one State Library, 10 zonal libraries and 8 information centers providing a variety of services. Describes services provided by the State Library and assistance provided by the Raja Rammohun Roy Library Foundation during 1986-88.

Lianzama, C.[71] (1994) paper presented at the All India Library Conference on the 8th Plan: perspective of public library development, New Delhi, 24-5 February 1989. Describes the history, staffing pattern, administrative structure, financial resources, and collection development activities of public libraries in Mizoram, India. Draws attention to assistance by the Raja Rammohun Roy Library Foundation and discusses difficulties experienced in library development.

Justa, H.R.[72] (1994) paper presented at the All India Public Library Conference on the 8th Pan: perspective of public library development, New Delhi, 24-5 Feb., 1989. Discusses the administrative structure of public libraries, staffing patterns, financing of public libraries, training and assistance from the Raja Rammohun Roy Library Foundation.

Kaula, P.N.[73] (1995) paper presented at the All India Public Library Conference on the 8th Plan: perspective of public library development, New Delhi, 24-25, February 1989. Describes the history, staffing pattern, administrative structure, financial resources, and collection development activities of public libraries in Mizoram, India. Draws attention to assistance by the Raja Rammohun Roy Library Foundation and discusses difficulties experienced in library development.

Das, H.[74] (1999) paper presented at the Pica Congress, 25 October 1999 in the Netherlands. Despite gloomy predictions for the future of libraries new technology represents a challenge to the library service. The use of ICT is essential in a library's basic processes to enable librarians to match specific needs of target groups to resources. Libraries should be reorganized in 3 parts: (i) the physical collection, (ii) an online library with Internet access and (iii) an intranet library. To win users back to the physical collections a new profile is required for libraries with readings by authors and social debates.

Bernier, G.[75] (2000) reflects on the impact of various technologies on the future development of public libraries. Defines the mission of the public library and describes the various changes under way that simultaneously affect the collections, services, premises, staff, budget and readership of public libraries.

Cooperation and Automation

Minai, Hideki[76] (1984) public library circulation statistics prove that literacy works absorb more interest than those in other fields and excellent bibliographies of literacy works are therefore of vital importance to public libraries. Compares and evaluates 7 bibliographies published since 1959, 4 compiled by public libraries, 1 by the National Diet Library, 1 by a special library and 1 by a commercial publisher. Concludes that nationwide planning and close cooperation among the compilers of bibliographies are indispensable for improving standards.

Beer, E.; Flemming, A.; Glaubrecht, S.; Gratz, M; Hamann, H.; Kaspar, A.; Natusch, M.; Schneider, G.; Schumann, A.; Ullrich, U.; Wagner, E.[77] (1995) describes the development of the following former East German public libraries between 1989 and 1994: Arnstadt, Chemnitz, Dessau, Dresden Erfurt, Frankfurt an der Oder, Gera, Jena, and Schwerin. Considers the situation before and after reunification in the following areas: buildings; staff; acquisitions; collection building; services to the public; automation; and organization.

Witwer, M.[78] (1996) traces the development of interlibrary loan in the Colorado, USA, regional library service system. The system routes requests from local library, to system headquarters to the Denver Public Library, which acts as the Colorado Resource Center. Interlibrary loan peaked in the early 90s, but declined after 1994 as increased demand led to slow turn around, as staff resources had not been increased. Use of technology has also increased with development of the Access Colorado Library Information Network. Interlibrary loan staff now focus on training, support and technology assistance.

Schaefer, M.T.[79] (1998) CD-format disc drives are undergoing rapid change. Industry trends include: short product life cycles, writable versions of CD format drives, continued popularity of disc towers and automated libraries, and Asian predominance in the manufacture of optical disc drives. Highlights the benefits of CD use in libraries and assesses the implications of industry developments for library CD use. Covers: network configuration, Web CD-ROM servers, CD recordable and CD Rewritable, CD-ROM longevity, preserving CD-ROM quality and the recently released standards for writable optical discs.

Schulman, S.[80] (1998) traces the changes in selection criteria for new or replacement library automation systems as they have been influenced by the rapidly developing technology. Now the greatest emphasis is placed on ease of use an the availability of end user functionality, analysis the reasons for this and iscusses how to develop end user selection criteria.

Salmon, R.[81] (1999) analyses the essential ingredients for successful small rural libraries. Suggests success requires a blend of energetic fund raising, cooperative initiatives at community level, outreach projects, and contributions by individual librarians and volunteers within a sometimes political arena. Cities as illustrations of grass roots endeavour libraries in Nebraska; Northern California, Scottish islands in the UK; Arkansas; and Salzhausen, Germany. Highlights differing commitment levels in other examples. Discusses pioneering developments in Illinois; Sufolk, in the UK and the cost cutting Cape Libraries Automated Materials Sharing (CLAMS) cluster in Massachusetts. Further examples illustrate community and teenager involvement.

Karun, B.[82] (1999) describes the intensive development of Slovene public libraries in the last 8 years since joining COBISS (Cooperative Online Bibliographic System). COBISS connects all types of Slovene libraries (national, university, special, school and public) via an online cataloguing and uniform database access system, supports the automation of local functions and enables access to various databases via the internet. The needs of users and the possibilities offered by a high level technical base, including access to the Internet, spawned many new public information services in public libraries.

Raju, K. A.[83] (1999) describes the impact of developments in information technology and other electronic information handling techniques and communication technologies on public libraries in India. Considers the social mission of public libraries, the needs of general users and the expectations regarding public libraries. Focuses on the Indian public library developments such as the Andhra Pradesh and Maharashtra projects, library automation, public library networking and the interconnection of Mandal libraries through telecommunications accessibility in rural India with the need for adequate finance for this development.

Babu, T.A.[84] (1999) stresses the importance of computers for public libraries and surveys the various library software packages with criteria for their selection, with particular reference to the specific needs of public libraries in India. Points to the constraints in automating public libraries and reviews some of the public library networks operating in India.

Revesz, B.[85] (2001) Local and regional development is today regarded in Latin America as crucial to the strategic management of democracy, a role in which public libraries play no small part. Emphasizes the library's function in facilitating universal access to the information highway; and the expertise that librarians can offer as knowledge mediators. Public policies in Latin American states should seek to strengthen community information and services at local level, agreeing on joint programmes with other organizations. A priority should be the preservation and expansion of existing library collections, while at the same time reducing the 'digital divide' by supporting telecentres and promoting IT training for users.

Yang, C., Chen, C., Lin, L.[86] (2002) in China, public library automation systems are still at the planning stage. Eventually, they will promote the exchange of information and resources between public libraries. Once the development of networks is n the rise, libraries will be able to receive more information and resources from other libraries around the world. Physical distance between a user and a library will not restrict its use. Developing a public library automation system is necessary in order to keep up with the rapid growth of information and to improve library services. It will also boost the national information infrastructure and encourage more people to use the Internet. Proposes a reference model for a general public library digitization system.

Kisimu, F.N.[87] (2002) discusses the financial crisis faced by the Kenya National Library Service and the corresponding stress it has brought on the Acquisition

Librarian in the quest for collection development. Outlines some solutions to the problems such as the introduction of cooperative stores of information and networking both through inter-loans and computer networking. Discusses some of the attributes which can be borrowed from colleagues in the library field to make a vibrant collection development strategy.

"Biswas, S.[88] (2003) provides information about the lack of a public library in India, and describes how information professionals are attempting to use the Internet to bridge the information divide. Computer literacy and Internet usage have become widespread, especially in urban India. Because public and even school libraries are sometimes non-existent, India students are increasingly using the Internet to meet their information needs.

Networking

Ito, Satoru[89] (1989) the rural library service in Kitami, north Japan is noted for its pioneering achievements. In 1987 local libraries formed a network study committee to plan for the 21st century. Topics flagged were bibliographic databases, computerization developments, including local software development support facilities, and standardization. The libraries are now using the CD-ROM bibliographic data base J-BISC, which has proved easy to use. Data is exchanged between libraries on floppy discs but a telecommunications network should be established soon. Libraries must respond to the demand for 'lifelong learning'.

Romer, Gerhard[90] (1989) the conference, held in Nov., 88, concentrated mainly on the regional library's tasks from a scholar's viewpoint. Planning for the future includes the construction of large networks, although this is limited in West Germany. A few libraries must expand into large research centers, existing beside many smaller libraries which can serve as independent local research centers. Regional libraries must review their role. Nobody disputes their position as deposit libraries and providers of research literature in their respective regions. The term 'regional' should be redefined and decisions made about which material should be collected in which library. Regional libraries must collect non-commercial material.

Hiese, P.[91] (1991) contribution to an issue devoted to cooperation and library networks among public libraries in Scandinavia. Describes the relationship between country libraries and local or municipal libraries in the public library system in Denmark Explains some of legal requirements with regard to service provision and financing which govern relationship and how these are changing.

Panda, B.D.[92] (1998) paper presented at the 5th National Convention for Automation of Libraries in Education and Research (CALIBER-98), at Bhubaneswar, 4-5 March 1998. Networking is a major concern for public library services in Orissa. Provides an action plan for a networking programme for the state, which would provide public libraries with network facilities using LAN and WAN technology.

User Needs and User Education

Veatch, Julian Lamar[93] (1979) Study of selected environmental design factors and their application to the planning of public library buildings. Seeks to identify information which might be useful to the provision of such facilities in terms of human needs.

Miranda, Antonio[94] (1979) examines the public library as a means of continuing education and cultural integration. Advocates legislation defining federal, state and local responsibilities; state financed training of librarians for under-developed areas; the establishment of 'Friends of the Library' societies to promote user interests; the integration of public and school library services; and the development of library networks to diminish costs and facilitate access to information.

Vermeulen, C. H.[95] (1981) the controversy concerning the relative importance of the public library of the user versus the non-user of the library service is considered. The implication is that the library can be effective only if it applies its resources towards meeting the cultural needs of the whole community. South Africa in the main lacks research on community needs relevant to library services. Research on the non-user in the UK, the USA and South Africa is briefly reviewed.

Onadiran, G.T.; Onadiran, R.W.[96] (1981) results of a user study conducted over a 6-day period of 7 public libraries of Nigeria using questionnaires are presented. It has been found that 51.5 percent of users do not use the library daily, because the library does not open daily. 48.7 percent of users can not use the library daily because of long distance. 51.2 percent of the users come to the library on foot and 38.9 percent take about 40 minutes to reach the library. It has been recommended that libraries should be brought closer to the people and efforts should be made to attract more people to the library.

Harmse, R.[97] (1989) the public library is experiencing a financial crisis due to the limitations of and inflation's effects on the sources of income of its controlling body, the local authority. Sketches the mission of the local authority as 3rd-level government and administration. Explains the nature and origin of the finances needed to render the many essential services, which it should offer in fulfillment of users' needs. Due to shrinking budgets, rising costs and amended priorities, the public library as rates supported, free service has recently become increasingly less able to afford to rely on the financial goodwill of local authorities.

Kumbar, M., Biradar, B.S.[98] (1998) reports results of a questionnaire survey to assess the use of mass media (newspapers, radio and television) compared with the use of public libraries by the people of the rural Singanamane

Gram Panchayat area of Shimoga district Karnataka, India. The study revealed that a majority felt that library opening hours were insufficient and that the location of the library was inconvenient. Based on the study findings, suggests that: awareness should be created among the public about the importance of public libraries through user training programmes library collections should be improved in both quality and quantity film and picture shows should be arranged and television sets installed in public libraries" and minimum facilities and services should be provided to change the adverse opinion of the public about the library. Concludes that, with proper initiatives and care taken, public libraries stand as equally competitive to other mass media.

Linley, R.[99] (1999) a recent research project at Sheffield University's Centre for the Public Library in the Information Society, in Sheffield, U.K., used focus group techniques as part of a research project on the social impact of public libraries which looked at the value, impact and outcomes of library activities in relation to stated local authority objectives. The research was conducted in 2 contrasting local authorities (Newcastle upon Tyne and Somerset) and involved cross-checking perceptions of elected members, library staff and groups of library users and non-users. Reports the key issues and difficulties with using focus groups to obtain the views of users and non-users.

Heitzman, J.; Asundi, A.Y.[100] (2000) describes the development of the public library system in the state of Karnataka, India, several exercises conducted in its evaluation during the mid - 1990s and the current direction of its planning. After outlining the system in the rural district of Chikimagalur, concentrates on the system in the city of Bangalore, the state capital and India's 'Silicon Valley'. Quantitative and qualitative survey data portray the demographics of library users, their information needs, their rating of library materials, facilities and library staff and the relationship between their evaluations and the preliminary stages of automation.

Barreau, D.[101] (2001) in public libraries computers and information systems are increasingly important tools for selectors because they offer alternatives for assessing user needs, gathering information about published materials and obtaining them quickly.

Regional Libraries

Brezova, Lydia[102] (1986) the Department of Bibliographic and Information Services of the Regional Library in Trencin was established in 1982. The main aim of the work of the Department, which has 3 sections, is to develop an effective system of regional bibliography in Western Slovakia. Discusses the work of the Department which at present concentrates its attention on the production of regional bibliographies. The bibliographies compiled so far include: periodicals of Western Slovakia 1981-1982. Newspapers and magazines 1983; Periodicals of Western Slovakia 1982-1983; Handbooks 1984, and Western Slovakia in the press.

Dolinska, E.[103] (1986) discusses the work of the regional library of Zvolven, which was opened on 1 Jan. 1986 and which employs 42 staff. Among the areas on which the new library will focus its attention are: methodology, acquisition coordination of bibliographic work, training of personnel, processing of statistical data and of political literature.

Prucess, J.[104] (1995) the Tampines Regional Library is a product of Singapore's Library 2000 Review Committee and was planned to meet the changing needs and interests of present and future users. Committee recommended that it become the first of 5 regional libraries and that it serve as a prototype to test services designed for the upcoming generation demanding computer literate uses. Concentrates of the library's facilities in terms of management; interior design; library collection; innovative library services; Internet services; online information retrieval and CD-ROMs, and community links.

Borm, J.V.[105] (1995) paper presented at the LIBER annual conference, Leuven, Belgium, 1995. Presents an overview of regional library cooperation among research libraries in Belgium. Information is given on the federal, regional and community structure of the country which is richly diverse in history, language and culture. Research libraries in the Flemish region have created a cooperative structure in which all types of libraries are included, helped by generous government funding. In contrast, cooperative activities in the French speaking Wallon region have not developed due to a lack of government funding to support the infrastructure required for the creation of a modern library and information service. It is hoped that this will improve in the near future so that the 2 communities do not develop at different speeds and can through cooperation, achieve greater effectiveness and a better position in Europe.

O'Hara, W.[106] (1996) following a survey in 1994 of 8 community groups and services, it was decided that there was a great need for adult literacy resources in the region of Victoria, Austrialia. The Regional Library Service offered the Echuca Adult Literacy Group facilities to house its collection and hold meetings, bar-coding the materials enabled a better loan service to be provided and funds were raised to provide a computer, CD-ROMs and discs for patrons to progress is being made in providing a small collection for young people.

McAllister, N.; Curry, A.[107] (1997) Presents the results of a survey of Canada's 98 country and regional library systems, which covers such areas as staff, services, circulation, technology and budgets, and which attempts to discover if an annual survey would be fruitful and useful. These libraies lack the national profile they deserve, but the publication of information such as that revealed in the survey would help to raise their profile. Unlike with the large urban libraries, there is no annual survey of regional and country libraries.

Boadi, B.Y.[108] (1998) presents historical sketches of 2 regional library associations: the West African Library

Association (WALA) and the East African Library Association (EALA), both of which were formed in the 1950s but were later dissolved. However, whereas a Federation of West African Library Associations, proposed as a replacement for WALA has still not materialized, the Standing Conference of Eastern, Central and Southern African Librarians (SCECSAL), the replacement for EALA, has become a reality and has provided a forum for a practical learning experience in regional library cooperation. Describes its structural set up and the performance of SCECSAL as a regional cooperative scheme, viewed against some basic principles of cooperation. Concludes that, although SCECSAL's achievements are highly commendable, a lot more could still be achieved if the basic tenets of cooperation, especially that of a willingness to accept responsibility, were given more serious attention.

Leskien, H.[109] (1999) an attempt to show regional library problems en route for the future with special reference to Bavaria. Most regional libraries were founded in the early 19th century. Since then their stocks, rich in historic material, have influenced their work. Meanwhile the situation in the tertiary sector has changed. To protect their future, regional libraries could become centers of competence for historic stocks. In support of university libraries, they could be linked into a network and given modern infrastructure.

Delcourt, T.[110] (1999) Article in a series of accounts of intranet experiences. Computerisation at Troyes began in 1996. System were chosen to cohere with the new regional library opening in 2001, where multimedia documents will be on open access, organised by subject not support. A basic service opened in 1998 offering intranet access to the municipal and university library catalogues. Catalogue use has greatly increased and in 1999 the CD-ROM collection and bibliographic Intranet sites will be added. Lack of space in the present building prevents developing the full multimedia network.

The role of Public libraries for development of society is rightly realized in India and other countries. The paucity of funds in public libraries is almost universal phenomena. A special provision for development and conduct of adult education programme through public libraries is suggested.

The legislation of public libraries in India is functioning and yielding results far from satisfaction. Therefore, Government has to take necessary steps to improve the functioning of public library system in India. The services rendered by RRRLF are noteworthy. The development and funds problem of public libraries in Australia is good. The funds position of public library system in Andhra Pradesh is not promising.

Training on computer applications for professionals in public libraries is suggested. In developed countries, the use of computers in public libraries is excellent and the user is given with exact information. Keeping this fact in mind, the library professionals are given training.

The importance of public library legislation and national development is well discussed. The growth and development of public library legislation in India is mapped systematically. The networking of public libraries through legislation is suggested. The information services available in Indian Public Library system is still embryonic stage.

The collection development of public library system is not upto the mark and the situation in rural library is still grim. Necessary steps be initiated to develop rural libraries and their book collection. Many studies were conducted to understand the community information services offered by public libraries.

In order to meet the social needs of the people, the public library management must catch up with technology and other development. The Kerala Public Library Act and it activities which support public library management are outstanding.

The development of public libraries in India is not promising. The development of public libraries during the VIII plan period were discussed.

The inter library loan facilities of public libraries of west was discussed. The influence of technology and the application of library automation in the public library are explained.

The community services of public libraries are commendable in developed countries. The Indian Library System mostly confined to adult education and related areas. The 'mobile library service' service at doorstep is available in Indian public libraries. The Delhi public Library is doing a commendable job.

The importance of public library networking is elevated. The need for user education in public libraries is realized. The growth and development of regional libraries in other countries was presented.

It is evident from the review of literature a good number of foreign scholars made effort to understand the Public Library System. The effort made by Indian scholars is far from satisfaction, particularly on automation of Public Libraries, financial sources for public libraries, professional attitude etc. The Government of Andhra Pradesh is very keen to apply Information Technology in Public Libraries, through even user requirement could be met to a great extent. To find out a possibility to offer various kinds of information service the present topic is selected for research.

Study Design and Methodology

After a careful review of the earlier studies, the present study has been planned keeping in mind the constraints of budget and time. As far as possible, the study was designed to be elaborate within the scope and limitations of the objectives set.

Study Design

After a careful review of the earlier studies in this study area, it is decided to take-up this study on the functioning of the Regional Public Libraries (RPLs) in Andhra Pradesh. Next important aspect of the study. design is to identify the study area. In the present study, it becomes imperative to cover the Regional Public Libraries in the state of Andhra Pradesh.

It is noticed that there are seven libraries in the state which belong to this category, i.e., the Regional Public Libraries. They are:

The State Central Library, and Six - Regional Public Libraries (located in different cities).

Hence, it is decided to cover all these libraries in order to understand the functioning of these Regional Public Libraries and the study is designed to be taken-up with the following objectives.

Objectives of the Study

Main objectives of the present study are :

(*i*) To study the facilities and services available in these Regional Public Libraries at present.

(*ii*) To understand the opinion of the librarians as well as users regarding the functioning of these libraries.

(*iii*) To identify the felt needs of the users in utilizing the services of these libraries.

(*iv*) To collect the opinion of the librarians and users on the areas in which interventions for development are required, and

(*v*) To obtain suggestions from these respondents for making recommendations for strengthening public library system in the state.

Coverage Planning

Keeping in mind the objectives of the study, it should be carefully decided - what institutions should be covered and what are the respondent groups that are to be covered and the study should be accordingly planned.

Coverage is of two types - complete coverage and sample coverage. Complete coverage is always important as it gives valid inferences from the analysis. But, in a large scale study,

COVERAGE

I.	Institutions	Complete coverage
	One-State Central Library Six - Regional Public Libraries	Since the number of institutions in the State is only seven, a complete coverage of these has been done.
II.	Library Professionals	Complete coverage
	Six Librarians of RPLs One Librarian of the SCL & Commissioner, Public Libraries, Andhra Padesh.	Since, these categories of respondents is small, a complete coverage of these eight respondents has been done.
III.	Users/Readers	Sample coverage
	Heterogeneous group Large in number From the six RPLs and one SCL	User group is taken as a single unit and a sample of users in excess of 150 from each of the 7 libraries has been done.

coverage of a sample selected following appropriate procedures is more popular. The inferences made from the analysis of the observations made from a truly representative sample are also very important and useful for making comparisons as well as for making any formulations for interventions. In the present study, both these types of coverage are employed as detailed below :

As already mentioned, in order to meet the objectives set for the study, three areas are to be covered for obtaining the needed information.

(*i*) Institutions - i.e., the Regional Public Libraries.

(*ii*) Library Professionals - Librarians and the higher authorities i.e., the Commissioner, Public Libraries, Andhra Pradesh.

(*iii*) Users - users or readers of these libraries.

The following is the schematic presentation of the coverage procedures followed in the present study.

Procedure Followed for Selection of Sample from the User Group

For a homogeneous and comparatively large sample, it is more suitable to draw a random sample. The process of random sampling is also not an easy task and it requires very elaborate preliminary arrangements, which are not often possible. In such situations, some crude and readymade methods have to be employed. However, in order to maintain random users it should be ensured that there is no personal bias or prejudice on the part of the investigator.

No need to mention that the user or reader community in case of the Regional Public Libraries is heterogeneous comprising of students, employees, businessmen, retired people, women and children. All these people visit the libraries according to their convenient timings and selecting a strictly random sampling is a difficult task.

Hence, in the present study, each library was visited for 6 - 7 days for covering the user sample. Each day one hour in the morning and one hour in the evening these users were covered and each day, the interviews were done at different timings. The interviews were done in the form of exit interviews - i.e., during the fixed one-hour, some of the users who are leaving the library were selected for interviews irrespective of their status. Each day 20 - 25 interviews were conducted during the selected two hours time in the two sessions.

Sample size is another which is important to decide as the margin of error would depend on the sample size. If the size of the sample is too small, the margin of error may be large and the results will have no significance. Hence, it is decided to collect information from users in excess of 150 from each of the seven selected libraries following the above procedure.

Methods Employed and Research Tools Used

Direct personal interviews and obtaining information through structured questionnaires are the two methods employed for data collection in the present study.

Structured questionnaires have been used for obtaining information regarding the functioning of the library and also for obtaining user information. For getting the views and suggestions from the librarians and higher-ups, direct personal interview (using a check list of aspects on which questions are to be asked) is employed.

Keeping in mind, the purpose of the study and objectives of the study, the two types of questionnaires were constructed and pre-tested. After the pre-testing, they were modified incorporating necessary modifications. Then the finalized questionnaires were used for obtaining the needed information.

Analysis of Data

The information elicited from the structured questionnaires were analysed using the SPSS package (Version 8.0) on personal computers.

Simple statistical methods have been used in the study keeping in mind the purpose of the study. Mostly comparisons were made using the percentages and chi-square values were computed for notifying the significance of differences among the groups.

Limitations of the Study

The seven Regional Public Libraries are situated at Visakhapatnam, Rajahmundry, Guntur, Tirupati, Warangal, Nizamabad and Hyderabad. The Hyderabad Regional Public

Library is also known as State Central Library. Hence in the present study, Hyderabad Regional Public Library (State Central Library) is also taken into account. This study is mainly aimed at studying the functioning of the Regional Public Libraries situated in Andhra Pradesh.

It should be mentioned here that, the present study is purely aimed to understand whether the present Public Library System and Services in Andhra Pradesh is able to meet the goal set for the Regional Libraries are not. This study is limited to few areas of importance to assess the functioning of the Regional Public Libraries, viz. the facilities, sources, services, functions and objective of these libraries, to identify the weaknesses and gaps among the selected areas. However, it should be mentioned here that, the present study is purely aimed to understand whether the present public library system and services in Andhra Pradesh is able to meet the goals set for these libraries are not. Since automation is not initiated in all these libraries, the areas of automation and the opinions of the users on related issues were not included in the present study. The prime surmise of this study is to provide a platform for further research through revealing the existing status of the Regional Public Libraries in the state.

Organization of the Report

The thesis has been organized into 5 Chapters. They are :

Chapter-I: **Introduction**

Chapter-II: **Study Design: Review of Earlier Studies and Methodology**

Study design including review of earlier studies in the present area of research, study area, coverage details, sampling, methods employed, research tools used, procedures used for analyzing the data and organization of the report are the aspects discussed in this Chapter.

Chapter-III: Profiles of Regional Public Libraries (RPLs) of Andhra Pradesh.

A brief sketch of RPLs with their objectives, functions, services, staff position, book collection, circulation, A.V. components, etc. has been presented in this Chapter.

Chapter-IV: Analysis of observations and discussions.

Observations made from the present study are presented and discussed in this Chapter under three sections - viz Section - (*i*): Information on functioning of the Regional Public Libraries, Section - (*ii*): User's perception on the functioning of the Public libraries, Section - (*iii*): Views of the Librarians and Commissioner of public libraries on the functioning of these libraries.

Chapter-V: Summary and Conclusions

Summary of the study and conclusions made from the observations along with some suggestions for improving the functioning of these libraries has been presented in this Chapter.

References

1. Debeij, J. A golden future for libraries in the knowledge society. BibliotheekBlad, 1(9), 1997, p. 12-13.
2. Epstein, R.: Openbare biblioteke en skole [Public libraries and schools]. Cape Librarian, 42(3), 1998, p. 14-15.
3. Veeranjaneyulu, K.; Rao, T.S.: Role of public library in development of culture and civilization: an overview. Herald of Library Science, 38(1-2), 1999, p. 39-42.

4. Buragohain, A.: Public Library scenario in India - Problem and Prospects, Herald of Library Science, 38(1-2), 1999, p. 5-14.
5. Agnoli, A.: L'emergence des bibliotheques pour la jeunesse. The emergence of chihldren's libraries. Bibliotheque(s), (1), 2002, p. 49-51.
6. Kumar, R.P.; Nagpal, S.P.: Public libraries: a pivot to adult education. International Library Movement, 2(1 and 2), 1980, p. 45-48.
7. Govind, Vijai: Financing public libraries. Lucknow Librarian, 20(1), 1988, p. 1-6.
8. Ramaiah, L.S.: Public libraries and public finances in India. A critical perspective. Herald of Library Science, 32(3-4), 1993, p. 171-80.
9. Jambhekar, N.: National policy on public libraries in India. Third World Libraries, 5(2), 1995, p. 8-21.
10. Kaula, P.N.: Some hints on the development of college and public libraries. Herald of Library Science, 34(1-2), 1995, p. 92-7.
11. Bolles, C: Federal and state support for public library development. Idaho Librarian, 48(3), 1996, p. 61-64.
12. Bhattacharjee, R.: Role of Raja Rammohun Roy Library Foundation in the promotion of public library movement in India. Herald of Library Science, 38(1-2), 1999, p. 14-20.
13. Thomas, V.K.: Public library financing: analysis of RRRLF schemes of assistance. Herald of Library Science, 38(1-2), 1999, p. 27-39.
14. Kraft, J., Geist, C., Frohss, W., Leutemann, C., Walther, B.: Bibliotheksforderung im Land Brandenburg, Die Forderung Offentlicher Bibliotheken in Thuringen. Das sachsische Kulturraumgesetz and die Bibliotheksforderung. Library development in the state of Brandenburg. The development of public libraries in Thuringia. Saxony's culture laws and library development. Buch and Bibliothek, 51(4), 1999, p. 224-229.
15. Stanton, J. Measuring value for money in public library collection development. Australasian Public Libraries and Information Services, 14(2), 2001, p. 58-61.

16. Daines, G.: New Ambitions for public libraries in the United Kingdom. Bulletin Des Bibliotheques de France, 46 (1), 2001. p. 121-3.
17. Kanakachary, M.; More, S.: Computerisation of public libraries in India: manpower development through in-service training. Lucknow Librarian, 24(4), 1992, p. 133-7.
18. Minai, H.: What is necessary for public library development? Issues and trends for 5 years hence. Toshokan Zasshi (The Library Journal), 93(10), 1999, p. 866-869.
19. Boscheinen, C.: The role of personnel development in public libraries: results of a survey. Buch und Bibliothek, 51(10/11), 1999, p. 632-636.
20. DeCandido, G.A.: Ten graces for new librarians. Trends in law Library Management and Technology, 10(5), 1999, p. 1-2.
21. Chavez, G.T.: Workforce training and development in selected public libraries throughout the State of Oregon: patterns and implications. Rural Libraries, 21(1), 2001, p. 25-49.
22. Mangla, P.B.: Role of the public library in developing countries with particular reference to literacy. Journal of Library and Information Science (India), 9(1), 1984. p. 1-15.
23. Inamdar, N.B.: Development of public libraries in Andhra Pradesh. Granthana, 3(2), 1992, p. 115-31.
24. Raju, A.A.N.: Government's books acquisition policy: its impact on collection development in the public library system in Andhra Pradesh. Proceedings of the 19th All India Conference of IASLIC, Calcutta, India, 1993, p. 43-8.
25. Hamby, P. and Najowitz, I.: The Public Libraries Act of 1850: utilitarian pragmatism and idealist humanitarianism in action. Public and Access Services Quarterly, 2 (4), 1998, p. 73-88.
26. Khan, M.A.M.: Some observations on public library service in Andhra Pradesh, Herald of Library Science, 38(1-2), 1999, p. 106-8.
27. Kaula, P.N.: A study of public library development and services for rural upliftment. Herald of Library Science, 39(3-4), 2000, p. 184-190.

28. Deshpande, K.S.; Hungund, B.B.: Raja Rammohun Roy Library Foundation and its role in galvanizing the public library movement in India. SRELS Journal of Information Management, 38(3), 2001, p. 179-200.
29. Finnegan, Gerry: Public library and community development. Library services to the disadvantaged edited by William Martin. Hamden, Conn., Linnet Books and London, Clive Bingley, 1975, p. 32-46.
30. Kaminska, Halina : Udostepnianie plty we bibliotekach publicznych za granica. Record facilities in public libraries abroad. Poradnik Bibliotekaza, 30(11-12), 1978, p. 244-247.
31. Mackenzie, Christine: Library services to people with disabilities at Dandenong Valley Regional Library Service. Australasian Public Libraries and Information Services, 3(2), 1990, p. 84-88.
32. Eichhorn, S.: Enquiry service on new ground: CD-RM in public libraries. Bibliothek Forschung und Prasis, 20(1), 1996, p. 50-94.
33. Roberts, W.: The FORCE Foundation : A new international organisation in the field of visual handicap. Bulletin d'lnformations de Association des Bibliothecaires Francais, 181, (4th Quarter), 1998, p. 54-56.
34. Naidu, G.H.S.; Narasimhulu, A.; Rao, V.S.; Ramesh, LS.R.C.V. : User services in modern public libraries towards improving readership. Herald of Library Science, 38(1-2), 1999, p. 70-5.
35. Itou, S.; Kato, H.; Kawata, T.; Sato, T.; Muraoka, K.; Murabayashi, M.; Yamamoto, A.; Wakisaka, S.: These wrong thoughts arrest the development of public library. Toshokan-Kai (The Library World), 51(2), 1999, p. 110-119.
36. Wigell-Ryynanen, B.: Library facilities in Finland. Scandinavian Public Library Quarterly, 33(2), 2000, p. 21.
37. Tait, H.M.: Current developments in public libraries - New Zealand. LAA NZLA conference proceedings, 1981, p. 548-553.
38. Agrawal, S.P.; Walia, Meena; Lal, Manohar: Development of public libraries in India: review and projections. International Library Movement, 8(2), 1986, p. 82-99.

39. Baliarsingh, R.K.; Mahapatra, M.: Public's reading interest in the collection development of public libraries. Proceedings of the 19th All India Conference of IASLIC, Calcutta, India, 1993, p. 99-102.

40. Robinson, W.C. : Price of materials and collection development in large public libraries. Library Acquisitions: Practice and Theory, 19(3), 1995, p. 299-312.

41. Jong, J.D.: Verscharling of versterking? Collectievorming in de OB ter discussie. Reducing or improving services? A review of collection development in public libraries. Open, 28(5), 1996, p.123-125.

42. Ostendorf, J.E. : Internet policies for Public Libraies, Georgia Librarian, 34(4), 1997, p. 4-7.

43. Stephens, A.K. : Public library collection development in the information age. Acquisitions Librarian, (20), 1998, p. 1-202.

44. Wang, M-l: Collection Development of Public Libraries in Taiwan. Bulletin of the Library Association of China, (65), 2000, p. 29-43.

45. Musib, S.K.: Community analysis and the library collection building: a survey report. IASLIC Bulletin, 34(3), 1989, p. 121-127.

46. Manghani, P.: Community development and the public library service: an innovative training course in the London Borough of Merton. Assignation, 16(4), 1999, p. 18-21.

47. Parker, S.; Banwell, L., and K. Ray: The LOGOPLUS Project - A Seamless transition? Library Management, 20(5 & 6), 1999, p. 273-82.

48. Gour, P.N.: Public library services in India and National Adult Education Programme: a plea for their integration. Indian Library Association Bulletin, 16(1-2), 1980, p. 3-9.

49. Waizer, N.; Gruidl, J.J.: Rural Public libraries and community economic development. Illinois Libraries, 79(4), 1993, p. 178-181.

50. Sciacca, J.: Economic development and the public libraries: perspectives on the impact of an LSCA funded research project. Illinois Libraries, 80(2), 1998, p. 80-83.

51. Guerin, C: Del'importance de la mediatheque en milieu hospitalier [About the importance of the media centre in the hospital milieu]. Bulletin d'lnformations de 'Association des Bibiothecaires Francais, 181(4th quarte), 1998, p. 63-65.
52. Yilmaz, B.: Halk Kutuphaneleri uzerine guncel bir karsilastirma. [A recent comparison on public libraries]. Turk Kutuphaneciligi/Turkish Librarianship, 13(1), 1999, p. 28-39.
53. Landry-Hyde, D.: Outreach at a public, academic, regional libray - Texas AandM University at Corpus Christi. Reference Librarian, (67/68), 1999, p. 289-98.
54. Neigel, C.: A blue-print for action: a needs assessment for the South Fraser Health Regional Library. Bibliotheca Medica Canadiana, 21(4), 2000, p. 51-6.
55. Winston, M.D.; Neely, T.Y.: Leadership development and public libraries, Public Library Quarterly, 19(3), 2001, p. 15-32.
56. Ude, C.C. : Mobile library services in Nigeria. Bibliotheek en Samenleving, 11(1), 1983, p. 12-17.
57. Khanna, S.N.: Mobile library service with a special reference to Delhi Public Library. Resource Sharing and Information Networks, 9(2), 1994, p. 119-26.
58. Goedel-Hoche, G.: Zusammenarbeit, eine Aufgabe for Schule and offentliche Bibliothek. "Cooperation, a task for school and public library". Schulbibliothek Aktuell, (2), 1994, p. 133-5.
59. Rustomfram, I.P.: Democracy on wheels: bookmobile services in Tennessee, part. Tennessee Librarian, 50(1), 1998, p. 22-23.
60. Osborne, L.: Driving the bush track to the superhighway: the Maroochy Mobile Library experience. Electronic Library, 16(5), 1998, p. 301-4.
61. Nyeng, P.: When Randers Regional Libraries inaugurated their new hit of a media bus. Biblioteckspressen, (8), 2000, p. 248-9.
62. Lee, W-n.: A library is a lifetime learning place [in Chinese]. Bulletin of the Library Association of China, (53), 1994, p. 35-41.

63. Dante, G.P. : Gestion, gestion de information, gestion del conocimiento, gestion del futuro [Management, management of information, management of knowledge, management of the future], Ciencias de la Information, 30(3), 1999, p. 43-52.
64. Umlauf, K. : Principle: content - Function - demands - development - implementation, Buch and Bibliothek, 51(2), 1999, p. 98-105.
65. Das, I.V.: Public Library movement in Kerala, Herald of Library Science, 38(1-2), 1999, p. 83-9.
66. Venkatappaiah, V. : Some observations on the public library system in Kerala State, Herald of Library Science, 38(1-2), 1999, p. 89-95.
67. Proctor and Simmons, S.: Public Library closures: the management of hard decisions. Library Management, 21(1 & 2), 2000, p. 25-34.
68. Khan, H.A.: Public library development: policies, problems and performance. Timeless Fellowship, (10), 1975-76, p. 20-33.
69. Singh, P.A.: Public library development in Manipur. Granthana, 4 (1 & 2), 1994, p. 69-74.
70. Adak, T.: Development of public libraries in Andaman and Nicobar Islands. Granthana, 4(1 and 2), 1994, p. 117-9.
71. Lianzama, C.: Status report of public library development in Mizoram. Granthana, 4(1), 1994, p. 75-8.
72. Justa, H.R.: Development of public libraries in Himachal Pradesh. Granthana, 4(1 and 2), 1994, p. 57-60.
73. Kaula, P.N.: Some observations on networking of public libraries. Herald of Library Science, 38(1-2), 1996, p. 62-8.
74. Das, H.: ICT and Libraries: a chance for an open goal. BibliotheekBlad, 3(23), 1999, p. 6-8.
75. Bernier, G.: The information resources of the public libraries of tomorrow. Documentation et Bibliotheques, 46(4), 2000, p. 173-8.
76. Minai, Hideki : Public libraries and bibliographies of literary works. Annals of Japan Society of Library Science, 30(1), 1984, p. 13-32.

77. Beer, E.; Flemming, A.; Glaubrecht, S.; Gratz, M.; Hamann, H.; Kaspar, A.; Natusch, M.; Schneider, G.; Schumann, A.; Ullrich, U.; Wagner, E.: The development of public libraries in the new German federal states. Bibliothek Forschung und Paxis, 19(3), 1995, p. 295-321.

78. Witwer, M.: Intelibray loán in Regional library service systems. Colorado Libraries, 22(3), 1996. p. 42-3.

79. Schaefer, M.T.: Changes in CD-ROM industry benefit libraries, "Information Retrieval and Library Automation, 34(1), 1998, p. 1-3.

80. Schulman, S.: Big changes in Library system selection criteria: now, its "end users rule!" when selecting automation products, Information Today, 15(9), 1998, p. 56, 58.

81. Salmon, R.: Growth and vitality for the library. Rural Libraries, 19(1), 1999, p. 7-29.

82. Karun, B. : Slovene Public Libraries. New Library World, 100 (1146), 1999, p. 20-3.

83. Raju, K.A.: Information technology and public libraries in 21st century. Herald of Library Science, 38(1-2), 1999, p. 52-62.

84. Babu, T.A.: Automation of public libraries. Herald of Library Science, 38(1), 1999, p. 47-52.

85. Revesz, B.: Politicas de information , bibliotecas publicas y desarrollo local y reginal. Information policies, public libraries, and local and regional development. Revista Interamericana de Bibliotecologia, 24(2), 2001, p. 45-63.

86. Yang, C.; Chen, C; Lin, L. : Development of a general public library digitization system. Bulletin of the Library Association of China, (69), 2002, p. 24-31.

87. Kisimu, F.N.: Collection development in the public library system in Kenya: constraints, solutions and the way forward. IFLA Journal, 28(2), 2002, p. 66-68.

88. Biswas, S. : Can the Internet and digital libraries compensate for the lack of pubic libraries in India ? New Zealand Libraries, 49(8), 2003, p. 280-2.

89. Ito, Satoru: Trial construction of Kitami regional libraries' network [in Japanese]. Toshokan Zasshi/Library Journal, 83(5), 1989, p. 253-255.

90. Romer, Gerhard : The Study Group on Regional Libraries. Autumn Conference in Oldenburg. Bibliotheksdienst, 23(1), 1989, p. 29-30.

91. Hiese, P.: Regional library work in Denmark. Scandinavian Public Quarterly, 24(3), 1991, p. 4-5.

92. Panda, B.D.: Public Library networking programme: some action plan for the State of Orissa. Informatin management in academic and research libraries. Proceedings of the 5th National Convention for Automation of Libraries in Education and Research (CALIBER-98, Bhubaneswar, India, ISBN: 81-900825-1-5, 1998, p. 319-321.

93. Veatch, Julian Lamar : Library architecture and environment design: the application of selected environmental design factors to the planning of public library facilities. Ann Arbor, Michigan, University Microfilms International, 1979, p. 298.

94. Miranda, Antonio: Aspects of the development of public libraries systems and networks in Brazil. Revista de Biblioteconomia de Brasilia, 7(2), 1979, p. 230-235.

95. Vermeulen, C.H. : What about the non-users of the public library? South African Journal for Linbrarianship and Information Science, 49(1), 1981, p. 10-14.

96. Onadiran, G.T.; Onadiran, R.W. : Public library development: an assessment of present tends in Nigeria. Annals of Library Science and Documentation, 28(1-4), 1981, p. 119-123.

97. Harmse, R.: The public library as alternative source of income for local authorities. Mousaion, 7(2), 1989, p. 2-33.

98. Kumbar, M.; Biradar, B.S.: Use of mass media and public library by the rural community: a study. Annals of Library Science and Documentation, 44(3), 1998, p. 86-92.

99. Linley, R.: Use of focus groups in a public library research project. Assignation, 16(2), 1999, p. 11-13.

100. Heitzman, J.; Asundi, A.Y.: Evaluation of public libraries in India. Information Development, 16(3), 2000, p. 142-53.

101. Barreau, D.: Information systems and collection development in public libraries. Library Collections, Acquisitions, and Technical Services, 25(3), 2001, p. 263-279.

102. Brezova, Lydia: A visit to the Department of Bibliographic and Information Services of the Regional Library in Trencin. Citatel, 35(10), 1986, p. 376-377.

103. Dolinska, E,: A visit to the regional library in Zvolen. Citatel, 35(6), 1986. p. 234-235.

104. Prucess, J.: Tampines Regional Library, Singapore. Asian Libraries, 4(3), 1995, p. 8-12.

105. Borm, J.V.: Regional Library cooperation in Belgium. European Research Libraries Cooperation, 5(4), 1995, p. 373-82.

106. O'Hara, W. : Literacy service at the Echuca Regional Library. Linkup, 1996, p. 17-18.

107. McAllister, N.; Cury, A.: Canada's country and regional library systems: a national survey. Feliciter, 43(2), 1997, p. 30-3.

108. Boadi, B.Y.: SCECSAL: a lesson in regional library co-operation. Libri, 48(2), 1998, p. 116-23.

109. Leskien, H.: Regional libraries on the way to specialization. Zeitschrift for Bibliothekswesen und Bibliographie, 46(4), 1999, p. 297-309.

110. Delcourt, T.: Internet et intranet a la bibliotheque municipale a vocation regionale de Troyes. "Internet and intranet at the Troyes municipal library with regional remit. Bulletin d'lnformations de I'Association des Bibliothecaires Francais, 184-185 (3rd and 4th Quarter), 1999, p. 217-218.

3

Profile of the Regional Public Libraries in Andhra Pradesh

Profile of the Regional Libraries

Introduction

The composite Madras State (now Chennai) of which formed part of Andhra Pradesh, took lead for the whole country in passing the Madras Public Libraries Act, 1948. Subsequently the erstwhile Hyderabad state followed suit and passed the Hyderabad Public Libraries Act, 1955. After the formation of the enlarged State of Andhra Pradesh in 1956, the two acts were integrated and named as Andhra Pradesh Public Libraries Act, 1960, and it came into force with effect from April, 1960. A separate and independent Department of Public Libraries was set up in January, 1961 for organization and administration of Public Libraries and for the first time a separate Director was appointed in January, 1967.

Regional Library Concept

The concept of regional library is not of recent origin in our country. Before reorganization, states on linguistic base the need for establishing Regional Libraries to meet the needs of the linguistic groups was felt by the then State Governments. Even before Independence the Government of Bombay appointed a Committee headed by Shri A.A.A. Fyzee in the year 1939-40 for the purpose of exploring the possibilities of the establishment of provincial Central Library in Bombay as well as three Regional Libraries at Ahmedabad, Poona and Dharwar obviously for the three regions to develop library services and facilities in this province.

The committee recommended that the functions of the Regional Library will be approximately the same as that of Central Library with the difference that its sphere of action will be limited to its region; it will be under the general guidance of the Central Library and it will essentially have to develop the library movement in the districts.

The Library Advisory Committee appointed by the Government of India in the year 1958, recommended the establishment of Regional Libraries as one of the links in the National Library system. It recommended that "the District Libraries would in turn be linked up with the Regional Libraries and through them with the National Central Library culminating in a link-up with the library system of the world".

Regional Libraries in Andhra Pradesh

After the break-up of the old Madras State, the Andhra State (which was formed in 1953) was left without a State Central Library and so it set up a library at Visakhapatnam to serve as State Central Library. Later in year 1954, this library was shifted to Guntur. After the formation of large state, incorporating the Telugu-speaking districts of Hyderabad state, the library at Guntur has been declared as State Regional Library. Till the end of 1963 this was the only State Regional Library functioning in the state catering to the needs of the coastal districts. But the two other regions of the State viz., Rayalaseema and Telangana were without a State Regional Libraries. In order to provide efficient library service in these two regions and also to northern coastal districts of the State, six more regional libraries were opened at the educational centers such as Visakhapatnam, Rajahmundry, Tirupati, Warangal, Nizamabad and Hyderabad.

Director of Public Libraries (PPL)

State Central Library (SCL)	*Zilla Grandhalaya Samasthas*
State Regional Libraries	District Central Libraries
(Govt. Regional Libraries (GRL=7)	(DCLs = 23)
1. Visakhapatnam 2. Rajahmundry 3. Guntur	Coastal Andhra
4. Tirupati	Rayalaseema
5. Warangal 6. Nizamabad 7. Hyderabad	Telangana

State Regional Libraries

The scope of the present study was limited to the only seven Government Regional Libraries, situated at Visakhapatnam, Rajahmundry, Guntur, Tirupati, Warangal, Nizamabad and Hyderabad. The State Regional Library at Hyderabad, otherwise known as State Central Library, is one among the seven is also considered for the study. The State Regional Libraries are popularly known as 'Regional Public Libraries' (RPL), here RPLs, SRLs, and GRLs are used interchangedly. The Zilla Grandhalaya Samasthas and District Central Libraries are out of the scope of this present study. Regarding the Government Regional Libraries, the act simply gives the definition of the term 'State Regional Library', without mentioning anything of its functions, its place in the organizational structure of the state library services, and its relationship either with the State Central Library (SCL) or with the Zilla Grandhalaya Samasthas in its regions.

The researcher has also collected the primary data besides the data collected through the questionnaires. The primary and secondary data in the form of Annual Reports,

Administrative Reports, Published reports and budget estimates and few programme pamphlets. This Chapter on Profiles of Regional Public Libraries are developed on the basis of the data available through the above documents.

Regional Public Library, Visakhapatnam

Government Regional Library, Visakhapatnam is established in the year 1965 as a research and reference library to cater the educational and informational needs of the North-Coastal districts of Andhra Pradesh viz., Visakhapatnam, Vizianagaram and Srikakulam. It is supposed to serve the Public of this region along with other public libraries which are under the control of Zilla Grandhlaya Samsthas.

Presently this library is situated on the upstairs of Municipal Elementary School, Dwarakanagar near Nehru Bazar. It works 6 hours in a day at two spells 8.00 AM to 11.00 AM and 4.00 PM to 7.00 PM. Weekly holiday is on Thursday and it remains closed on all government holidays and second Saturday of every month. At present, this library is having the book stock of nearly 50,000 and subscribing to periodicals. There are 5300 registered borrowers. The strength of the staff is 9 out of which 2 posts are vacant. There are good number of reference books which include Dictionaries, Encyclopaedias, year books and biographical sources. There are good number reference books which include biographical sources. There is a rich collection of history language, literature and other social sciences. There are some standard books of science and technology including Telugu Academy Books.

There is a separate competitive exam cell in which all types of competitive books are kept for reading in the library itself. Along with newspapers and magazines in Telugu and English some competitive exam materials and monthlies including employment news were also subscribed. For future reference it is preserving the daily newspapers. The Hindu and Eenadu, the weekly English India today and the Telugu monthly Yojana and English monthly competition success review are the important ones to mention. There is a Xerox facility in this library and the readers are permitted to take the necessary information they require by paying nominal cost.

This library is following open access system in which readers are directly permitted to the book stacks and can select the books of their choice for reading in the library and for taking home. Books will be issued for home reading only to the members. One can become a member of the library by depositing refundable deposit of Rs. 85/- out of which two books will be issued to the tune of Rs. 150/- and for a period of fortnight after which a fine of 0.05 paise per day will be collected for late return. Once in two years a member has to renew his membership with fresh application without paying any amount. Once issue system followed in this library is browne charging system. Books are classified and arranged according to Devy Decimal classification system and catalogued as per classified catalogue code.

Along with regular duties such as enrolment of members issue and return of books, displaying latest periodicals, reference service, classification, cataloguing and keeping books in order with dust free, book selection and accessioning this library is also conducts social education activities, arranges book exhibitions occasionally and conducts National Library week every year in the month of November.

Since its establishment, this library is running in rented buildings at different places from 1965 to 1989 near Nehru Bazar, in 1990 official colony near Amba Mahal, 1991 to 1995 at Jagannadhapuram in Akkayyapalem and from 1996 to date is on the building of Dwarakanagar Municipal Elementary school. Many trials were made since 1982 for acquiring suitable land for construction of own library building but were not materialized till the year 2002.

During 2002, with the initiation and trials of incharge Librarian Sri G. Krishna Reddy and the efforts of MLA Dr. Pinninti Varalakshmi the District Collector allotted a land near R.K. Mission comprising of 2000 sq. yards to this library for construction of library building. The foundation stone was laid by the Minister of School Education Sri M. Venkateswara Rao on 2-8-2003. It is expecting the funds from the Government for the building with all amenities to complete for better service the Library Development Committee members who are behind in acquiring the land are also decided to raise funds through donations committees. To fulfill the aim of its establishment the library needs the annual budget to be increased, vacant posts to be filled and additional staff to be sanctioned by increasing the working hours. It is the need of the hour to computerize the library to meet the demands of the library users.

Committees of the Library

There are 3 committees in the Library for strengthening the libray resources and services (1) Book Selection Committee, (2) Library Development Committee, and (3) Readers forum.

Book Selection Committee

Comprises Joint Collector as Chairman, District Educational Officer (DEO), Deputy Director of Adult Education, Andhra University, Head of the Department of Library and Information Science and other two professors from the University as the members. The books approved by this committee only are purchased by the library every year depending upon the availability of funds.

Library Development Committee

As per the directions of the District Public Library a Library Development Committee was constituted with the local professionals such as Librarians, retired professors, literacy persons, Doctors, Journalists and other interested in the library field. At present, the following are the members of the committee :

- Dr. Moturi Sri Rama Krishna
- Dr. A.G. Prasada Rao
- Sri Gandhikota Brahmaji Rao
- Dr. G.V.S.L. Narasimha Raju
- Sri G.V. Ravi Raju, Contractor
- Sri G.S.P. Prabhu
- Sri V. Amarnath
- Sri V.M. Sarma, and
- Sri N. Nageswara Rao

With the help of the above members chairs and book racks were provided to the library. For construction of the library building the development committee members are trying to raise the funds though local institutions and philanthropists. The National Library week celebrations are also being organized with the help of the members.

Readers Forum

Readers forum was constituted among the members and readers of this library for giving suggestions in selecting books providing amenities to the leaders and strengthening the library collection by donating books and other material. At present there are 5 members, of whom only two are active participants and the rest are seldom visiting the library. It is proposed to revise the forum by introducing new members who can pay interest in the development of the library.

Objectives

(1) To serve the general public.

(2) To encourage students in the use of competitive books employment information etc., for career development.

(3) To Create interest in the use of public libraries through conducting quiz, competitions, drawing, songs, essay writing, elocutions,...etc., and to improve the reading habit.

(4) To increase readership and membership.

(5) Development of book collection from philanthropist.

(6) To meet the educational needs to the readers to provide news papers, journals, magazines and reference service.

(7) To provide information at free of cost with open access system.

(8) To improve public participation in library activities and development.

(9) To provide reference service.

(10) To Issue books on membership.

Functions :

(1) Providing information for self employment schemes through computer books, interior decoration, stitching, etc., with reference tools.

(2) Creating entertainment through film shows, cricket match, etc., with help of TV service.

(3) Creating inspiration to public by conducting book-exhibitions, photo-exhibitions and numismatics (coins) exhibitions, etc.,

(4) To offer children, young people, men, women opportunity and encouragement.

(5) Acquire book pamphlets, magazines, newspapers, maps, pictures, films, recordings and to their use.

(6) Keeping all sections neat and clean.

(7) Arranging the books in classified order.

(8) Enrollment and withdrawal of membership.

(9) Involving public in the community development programs like janmabhoomi, clean and green, cultural and literacy schemes.

(10) Providing reference services from the available sources.

Sri Gowthami Reginal Library, Rajahmunry

Sri Gowthami Regional Library, Rajahmundry started functioning as a Regional Library in 1979. It's original establishment was in 1898 as a private library. Sri Gowthami Library's role part in the Andhra Library Movement has a century old history.

The library is functioning from 8 a.m. to 11 a.m. and from 4 p.m. to 7 p.m., Thursday is weekly holiday. On weekly holiday the paper section only is kept open. The book stock of the library is 70,375 and subscribing for 75 periodicals. The number of the registered borrowers is 3,133. The number of daily readers on average is 550 and researchers of academic and non-academic fields use this library.

A children section has been functioning in an old asbestos shed of the library to which the Raja Ram Mohan Roy Library Foundation is giving assistance by way of providing books and furniture. The library is located in the centre of the town and serve the needs of readers, students, scholars and the public at large in the district. The services are also extended to researchers at national and international level.

Objectives

1. To serve the general public and research concerned.
2. To provide information at free of cost with open access system without any restriction.
3. To make available to all citizens access to refer all kinds of documents, periodicals, manuscripts, palm leaf manuscripts, maps, microfilms, copper plates, rare book material and to extend full cooperation to scholars.
4. To encourage students in the use of competitive books, journals, employment information etc.
5. To create interest in the use of public libraries to high school students through conducting Quiz

competitions, drawing, songs, essay writing, elocutions etc., and to improve the reading habit.

6. To increase readership and membership.
7. Book collection from donors.
8. To increase public participation in library activities and development.

Functions

1. Providing information for self-employment schemes through computer, books, small scale industry, interior decoration, stitching etc. with reference tools.
2. Creating entertainment through film shows, cricket match etc. with the help of T.V. Service.
3. Involving public in the community development programmes like Janmabhoomi, clean and green, cultural and literacy meetings.
4. Creating inspiration to public by conducting Book-exhibitions, photo exhibitions and Numismatics (coins) exhibitions etc.
5. Involvement of old committee members and their families.

Services

1. Charging and discharging
2. Enrolment of Memberships
3. Reference (Rare and Current)
4. Reprographic
5. Interlibrary loan
6. Micro films
7. Periodicals (Old and New)
8. Yoga for Male (early hours)
9. Wall newspaper (News on black board)

Future vision of the Library

1. It is suggested by the local public that the regional library should be changed as "National Library".
2. Net work of all libraries in the state (providing internet facilities).
3. Construction of complete building as per the plan approved.
4. To fulfill the basic requirements of the library such as racks, furniture and useful items through public donations and also government.

Accommodation (as on 31-3-2002 and 31-3-2003)

Own Building - 3100 sq. yards

Main building - (old) consists of social education wing and periodical section.

New Building - (Ground floor)

Stock area consists of

Binding sec. (Tech.)

Reference section & Rare book section 1st floor

Issue counter, Reading hall and stock area (requires extension wings & upstairs)

Librarian, Lending and Ladies Sections (North wing)

Periodical section (South wing) and 1st floor of above these wings.

Book stock - Increase in book stock during 2002-2003

Net book stock in the beginning of the year	69,386
Books supplied under RRRLF Matching Scheme	
By the Director of public libraries	693
Books supplied directly by RRRLF from Kolkata	32
Books purchased from own funds (plan & non-plan)	9
Books received through donations	287
Total	70,375

Membership - Increase in Membership 2002-03

Description on the following :

Net membership at the beginning of the year 2002-03	2,952
New Membership added during 2002-03	181
Membership withdrawn 2002-2003	Nil
Net membership at the end of the year	3,133

Readership

Description on the following :

Total readership during 2001-02	1,43,859
Total readership during 2002-03	1,84,814
No. of Readers increased during 2002-03	40,955

Analysis of the Trend - there is an increase of 28.47% on 2001-02

Books Consulted

Description on the following :

Books consulted during 2001-02	78,875
Books consulted during 2002-03	1,20,943
Number increased during 2002-03	42,068
Types of books frequently consulted	Text books,

Competitive books, fiction, literature, general books, reference and rare books.

Books lent for home reading

Description on the following :

Books lent for home reading 2001-02	10,766
Books lent for home reading 2002-03	12,114
Increase in books lent home during 2002-03	1,348

Purchase and distribution of books to the libraries 2002-03

Plan/Non-plan

Description on the following :

Books purchased during 2002-03	9 (English books)
Amount	1,015-00
Budget allotted under non-plan for books & periodicals	68,000-00
Expenditure spent for periodicals 2002-03	21,476-00
Expenditure spent for Technical & Stationery 2002-03	25,500-00
Budget surrendered	20,000-00

Best Practices

Previously getting books from RRL Foundation through publishers and author publishers caused worry of thinking their problems and bringing them to the Director of Public Libraries.

The central purchase system solved many of such problems. Moreover it did not cause any loss of books or damages of parcels etc. The new system is being appreciated and the system became not only an experimental one but also proved fruitful on various aspects.

Development indicators

(*a*) Increase in net book stock during 2002-03 over 2002-02	989
(*b*) Increase in books consulted during 2002-03 over 2001-0	42,068
(*c*) Increase in books issued during 2002-03 over 2001-02	1,348
(*d*) Accommodation increase during 2002-03 over 2001-02	Nil

(*e*) Public donation raised (kind and money) during 2002-03 over 2001-02

1. Book binding for old periodicals 500-00
2. Mike set donated by Sahithi Vedika 1

Extension Services

(*a*) Participation in total literacy campaign - 2

(*b*) Participation in Janmabhoomi/clean & green:

1. Every 3rd Saturday of every month participated in cleans & green programme. Cleaning the premises and surroundings of the library and all other sections keep neat and tidy.
2. In Janmabhoomi programme "completed toilets constructions" with people participation.

Succession stories (2002-03)

1. Implementation of CERUs - Nil (Plan scheme not allotted)
2. Undertaking repairs to building to make them suitable for computerization of library services - No funds available to be repaired.
3. Implementation of various RRRLF schemes during the year - Storage material received.
4. Enforcement of targets and achievements made by individual employees.

Regional Public Library, Guntur

The State Regional Library was established in the year 1958 at Guntur. It is the second biggest government library in the state of Andhra Pradesh. At present this library is having 1.27 lakh book stack and subscribes to nearly 102 magazines/periodicals and receive 25 other periodicals as grants. It works from 8 a.m. to 8 p.m. and the text book section of this library from 8 a.m. to 12 mid night continuously with reading, lending, photo copying and all other possible facilities for the benefit of reading public.

Sri Gowthami Regional Library, Rajahmundry

On average daily 686 readers visit the library. The library had 12,981 registered borrowers who are permitted to lend books for their home reading. The admission to this library is open to all categories of people. The library specially caters to the need of college and school going pupils and other students who want to prepare for competitive examinations. Besides, it also serves other classes of people by providing general books and periodicals, as it is a public library.

One of the important features of this popular library is the preservation of old newspapers, gazettes and certain periodicals. Xerox facility is also an added advantage to the readers. Number of education activities like seminars/essay writing, elocution and drawing competitions, guide lectures by the selected candidates of competitions examinations are arranged to encourage the readers and to inculcate the habit of reading with competitive spirit. The location map of library showing the distance from railway station and RTC bus stand is also furnished.

Staff position (As on 1-4-2001 and 1-2-2002)

As to be covered in description :

(*a*) Category wise posts sanctioned and vacancy position.

(*b*) Filling up of S.C. and S.T. backlog vacancies: Nil

(*c*) Filling up of vacancies meant for disabled persons etc.: one post of watchman.

Book Stock increase in book stock during (2001-02)

Description on the following

* Net book stock in the beginning of the year (31-3-2002) - 1,15,007

* Books supplied under RRRLF matching scheme by the Director of public libraries: 694

* Books supplied directly by RRRLF from Kolkata : 543

* Books purchased from other funds : Plan and Non-Plan) : 327
* Books received though donations: 736
* Books weeded out: 2
* Availability of books language wise : As at table No. 6
* Periodicals subscribed language wise: Telugu 30, English - 43
* New Magazines subscribed during 2001-2002
* Any other point you wish to mention here under this item.
* No. of books loss/theft.

Membership

Description on the following :

* Net Membership at the beginning of the year 2001-2002 (31-3-2002)	9,875
* New members added during 2002-03	308
* Members withdrawn during the year 2002-03	Nil
* Net membership at the end of the year 2002-03	10,183
* Reasons for shortfall	Nil

* Steps taken to increase the Membership : relaxation of rules to enroll the new members.
* Any other information you wish to mention under this item.

Readership

Description on the following :

* Total Readership during 2001-02	1,63,141
* Total Readership during 2002-03	1,91,806

* Readers added or decreased during 2002-03 over 2001-02

Increased 28,665.

* Analysis of the trend · Increased
* Reasons for shortfall: This is not shortfall in this year.
* Steps taken to increase the readership: Purchased new competitive books.
* Any other point you would like to mention under this item: Nil

Books Consulted

Description on the following :

* Book consulted during 2001-02 3,47,270
* Books consulted during 2002-03 3,22,240
* Increase or decrease in books consulted during 2002-03 :

  Decreased 25,030
* Reasons for decrease: Due to power cut by the electricity dept. duing the year.
* Types of books frequently consulted: Reference, competitive books (new courses in telugu). Astrology, medicine, bio-chemistry, physiotherapy, food technology, hotel management, electronics and computer science subjects.

Books lent for home reading

Description on the following :

* Book lent for home reading during 2001-02 7,181
* Books lent for home reading during 2002-03 8,107
* Increase or decrease in books lent home during 2002-03:

  Increased 926
* Reasons for decrease:

* Books lent vs. members covered: 8,107 Vs. 5,228
* Types of books demanded by the members and other readers : Subject books like physic science, biological science, engineering books, computer and competitive books.
* Any other point you would like to mention under this item: More recent editions on these subjects may be purchased.

Purchase and distribution of books to Libraries Plan/ Non-Plan

Description of the following :

(*i*) No. of titles purchased, No. of books purchased and amount spent if purchased from Plan/Non-Plan funds separately (languagewise): From non-plan only.

(*ii*) Reasons for not purchasing the books during the year:

(*iii*) Total amount allocated under Plan/Non-plan budget for books/periodicals : 75,000/-

(*iv*) Allocation made for subscription of periodicals from the total budget allocated : 30,679/-

(*v*) Any other item you would like to mention under this item.

Performance during 2002-03

Performance indicators: Targets fixed and achievements during 2002-03: Target fixed for membership - 240. Target fixed for readership - 2,01,455.

(*a*) Comparative study with other Government libraries

(*b*) Statements on enrollment of new members, readers visited, as on 31-3-2002: Members - 308

(*c*) Analysis of performance of Librarians - Targets fixed and achievement. Competitive study among the librarians (high achievers, medium achievers, low achievers and zero achievers).

Development indicators (2002-03 over 2001-02)

(*a*) Increase in Net Book Stack during 2002-03 over 2001-02 : 2,298

(*b*) Increase in Books consulted during 2002-03 over 2001-02

(*c*) Increase in Books issued during 2002-03 over 2001-02: 926

(*d*) Accommodation increased during 2002-03 over 2001-02

(*e*) Public donations raised (kind and money) during 2000-01 & 2001-02

Innovative practices

1. Change of existing system to centralized supply of books under RRRLF to avoid loss in transport and also delay in making payments.
2. Participation of employees in Akshara Sankaranthi program.

Success Stories

1. Implementation of CERUs.
2. Undertaking repairs to building to make them suitable for computerization of library services.
3. Implementation of various RRRLF schemes during the year.
4. Enforcement of targets and achievements made by individual employees.

Regional Public Library, Tirupati

The Government Regional Library at Tirupati, a famous pilgrimage, was established in the year 1964 to cater the information needs of the people of Rayalaseema area in Andhra Pradesh. The Library was housed in a rented building having an area of 2,250 square yards. The library building comprises of two reading rooms, one stack room and one room for administration. The library has sufficient and

State Regional Library, Guntur

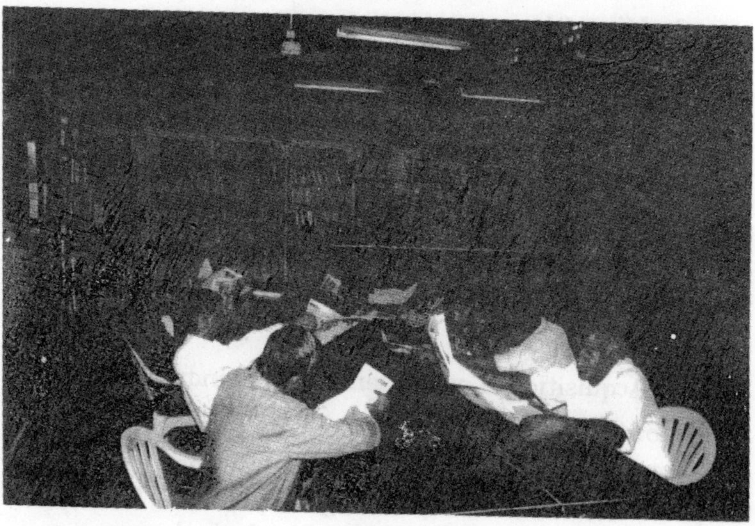

suitable furniture including audio-video equipment. This library is managed by a Gazetted Librarian and with other staff members.

Functions

1. Information to self-employment schemes small-scale industries etc.
2. Entertainment services through television.
3. Educate the public towards participation of social programme like clean and green and cultural meetings.
4. Conducting of book exhibitions, photo exhibitions etc.

Services

1. Charging and discharging
2. Enrolment of memberships
3. Reference (Rare and current)
4. Reprographic
5. Interlibrary loan
6. Micro films
7. Periodicals
8. Yoga for male (early hours)
9. Wall news - paper (on black board news)

Future vision of the Library

1. Connecting all libraries of the state to provision of Internet facilities in the libraries.
2. Construction of library building with all modern amenities in the facilities.
3. Acquisition of equipment use all kinds of materials.

Books Stack increase

In the year 2002-03 Net Book Stock in the beginning of the year - 54,046, additions during the year - 10,724, Net at the end of year - 55, 793, Number of books by language :

Telugu	29,084	
English	20, 112	
Hindi	4,123	
Urudu	1,000	
Other languages	1,474	
Total	55,793	

Books Category-wise

Children's section	15,562	
Reference Books	22,639	
Text Books	11,796	
Other fiction Books	2,320	
Other non-fiction books	3,476	
Total Books	55,793	
No. of books received from the RRRLF , 1971 onwards		19,137
No. of books received from RRRLF during the year		11,219
Daily papers		14
Other than dailies		58
Registered borrower		4,609

Categories of Borrowers

1. Professionals	332
2. Formers and Agriculturists	137
3. Businessmen	168
4. Students	1,885
5. House wives	227
6. Employees	553
7. Unemployees	288
Total	3,590

Number of books issued during the year	-	3,668
Number of books issued in children section	-	286
Other sections	-	3,382
Total	-	3,668
Number of non-fiction books issued	-	2,815
Number of fiction books issued	-	853
Total	-	3,668

Regional Public Library, Warangal

The regional library at Warangal was established in the year 1964. The library was housed in a rented building located near the Arts and Science College, Warangal. A separate functional building was constructed by the PWD (R&B) in the year 1983 and the library was shifted to the newly constructed building own building.

Objectives

1. The regional library is public library but this library services are totally academic and research library activities.
2. This library provides free service to readers.
3. This library rendering services for 4 districts i.e., Warangal, Karimnagar, Khammam and Adilabad (it also covers) instead of above district the library rendering services to the other districts of the state.

Functions

(*i*) Acquire book phamplets, magazines, newspapers, maps, pictures, films, music scores and recordings and guidance to their use.

(*ii*) To offer children, young people, men, women, opportunity and encouragement.

(*iii*) To educate themselves continuously.

(*iv*) To keep abreast of progress in all fields of knowledge.

(*v*) To aid generally in the advancement of knowledge.

(*vi*) Collection, organization, distribution, interpretation, and guidance of documents.

Services

The following are the services offered by this regional library.

1. Home lending or circulation service
2. Reference service
3. Reprographic service

Home lending service this includes lending of books and receiving them back. The circulation of the books involves the following jobs :

1. Registration of members
2. Lending of books to the members
3. Discharging of books when returned
4. Collection of over due charges
5. Renewal of books

Only registered members can borrow the books from the library.

Personnel in Regional Library

The personnel of regional library, Warangal can be categorized to :

(*a*) Professional (having B.L.I.Sc. or M.L.I.Sc.)

(*b*) Semi professional (having C.L.I.Sc.)

(*c*) Non-profession including skilled personnel (without any professional degree).

There are total 10 staff members in regional library Warangal with 3 professional having M.L.I.Sc./B.L.I.Sc. and

1 semi-professional remaining of are non-professional and skilled workers.

Library Hours

The regional library is kept open from 8 am in the morning to 8 p.m. in the evening.

However, it is closed on Thursdays and public holidays.

Entrants

1. Just like rule of law all the members of the library are allowed to avail the reading facilities in the librarian.
2. Members have to be abide and follow the rules and regulations and maintain strict silence in the library premises.
3. Special care is taken to prevent mischievous activities viz. eating nut power, chewing gums, smoking etc.

Finance

Finance plays a crucial role in the growth and development of the libraries. The sources of the finance available for the public libraries should be of recurring nature. The following are the finance for public libraries in general.

1. Libraries
2. Government grants
3. Endowment and private donations
4. Fees and fines
5. Rents

The library offers free library service to the community. The library collects only deposits (returnable) Rs. 60/- as and when the member wants to withdraw the membership the entire amount of deposits Rs. 60/- will be returned to the member.

Sections

1. Book acquisition
2. Technical processing
3. Stack
4. Periodical section

The regional library maintains different types of home lending textbooks reference books and periodicals. The regional library is providing text book series for the benefit of academic community. The library subscribers for periodicals in five major languages of the area - Telugu, English, Hindi, Urdu and Sanskrit. Out of which the collections in - Telugu language are maximum followed by those in English, Hindu, Urdu and Sanskrit in that order.

Technical Processing in Library

Technical processing is of two types: (1) Classification, (2) Cataloguing.

1. Classification work in regional library done by the librarian and Assistant Librarians, grade-I D.D.C. is followed for the classification work. D.D.C. 16th edition is being used with modification adopting some provisions from DDC 19th edition for the simplicity and for easy to the library users.
2. Cataloguing work is to help the users to know whether particular book is available in the library or not. The catalogue gives the details of books and its location in the library. ALA catalogue code 1949 is used in this library for the preparation of catalogue entries. The following entries are prepared for each document.

   (1) Main entry, (2) Author entry, (3) Title entry, (4) Subject entry.

Regional Public Library, Warangal

Government Regional Library, Nizamabad

Government Regional Library, Nizamabad was established in the year 1966. It serves the information needs of the public from Nizamabad, Karimnagar, Adilabad and Medak districts.

Objectives

To meet the educational needs to the readers particularly in research, general and competitive areas, (*ii*) to provide newspapers and magazines, (*iii*) to provide reference service, (*iv*) to issue books on membership, and (*v*) to increase the readership and membership.

Functions

Arrange the books in classified order, (*ii*) keeping all sections neat and clean, (*iii*) providing current and old periodicals to the readers, (*iv*) reference service from the available sources, (*v*) enrollment and withdrawal of membership.

The main objective of the public library is to create interest among all age groups in reading.

Accommodation

(*a*) Present (Own building - area 1,404 sq. meters)

* One Reading Room for Magazines
* Big stock room
* Small room for Technical section
* One room for Hindi and Urdu books
* Small warandah for paper reading

(*b*) Extension requires

* Big hall for book reading

* Stock room
* One big room for reference section
* One separate room for text books and competitive books.

Particulars of posts sanctioned and vacant as on 1-4-2002 to 31-3-2003

Category of post	*No. of posts*		*Date of vacancy*
	Sanctioned	*Vacant*	*with reasons*
1. Gazetted Librarian	1	1	24-12-1994 transfer to Hyderabazd Sri Mohd. Naimuddin
2. Assistant Librarian Grade-I	1	0	—
3. Card Writer	1	0	—
4. Attender	1	1	Vacant from 1-5-2002 due to superannuation retirement
5. Night Watchman	1	0	—
6. Sweeper	1	0	—
Total No. of posts	6	2	—

Book stock increase in book stock during 2002-03

Net Book stock as on 31-03-2002	...	47,227
No. of Books supplied by D.P.L. under RRRLF	690	
No. of books supplied from Kolkata by RRRLF	533	
No. of books received under grants	335	
		1,558
Net book stock as on 31-03-2003		48,835

Number of periodicals subscribers languagewise

Regional Library, Nizamabad	Periodicals subscribed language-wise 2002-03													
	Purchased				Donated by public			Gratis			Total			
	Daily	Weekly	Fortnighty	Monthly	Daily	Weekly	Monthly	Daily	Weekly	Monthly	Daily	Weekly	Fortnightly	Monthly
Telugu	5	5	4	9	0	0	0	0	0	0	5	5	4	9
English	4	5	0	5	0	0	0	0	0	0	4	5	0	5
Hindi	0	0	0	0	0	0	0	0	0	0	0	0	0	0
Urdu	0	0	0	0	0	0	0	0	0	0	0	0	0	0
Other languages	0	0	0	0	0	0	0	0	0	0	0	0	0	0
Total	9	10	4	14	0	0	0	0	0	0	9	10	4	14

Number of books available - languagewise as on 31-3-2003

Number of books available in Telugu	-	23,633
Number of books available in English	-	18,070
Number of books available in Hindi	-	5,466
Number of books available in Urudu	-	1,649
Number of books available in other languages	-	17
Total number of books available		48,835

Increase in Membership 2002-03

Net membership as on 31-3-2002	-	1,724
New Member added during 2002-03	-	22
		1,746
Members withdraw during 2002-03	-	11
Net membership as on 31-3-2003		1,735

Increase in Readership 2002-03

Regional Library, Nizamabad		*Year*	
	2001-02		*2002-03*
Readers visited to the library	65,295		65,651
No. of readers increased to the library		356	
Percentage of increase of readers		0.5	

Readership Analysis (2002-03)

	Periodical section	*Book section*	*Total*
Total No. of readers during 2001-02	19,275	46,020	65,295
Total No. of readers during 2002-03	45,516	20,135	65,651
Percentage of increase in readership Over 2001-02		0.5	

Purchase and distribution of books to the libraries Plan/Non-plan

Books not purchased during 20002-03

Budget allotted under Non-Plan for books and periodicals for the year 2002-03	Rs. 53,000/-
Expenditure (Spent for Periodicals)	Rs. 14,563/-
Budget surrendered	Rs. 38437/-

since Books Selection Committee not meet for purchase of books.

Number of Books received from Director of Public Libraries under RRRLF scheme and also from Director, RRRLF, Kolkata and as Gratis from the Public

Description on the following :

* Total 1223 books received under RRRLF scheme from the Director, Kolkata and D.P.L. worth of Rs. 1,86,580-00
* No. of books and titles received as gratis : 335 of Rs. 31,583-00

RRRLF Grants during the year 2002-03

1. Proposals submitted scheme wise - Nil
2. Reasons for not submitting under RRRLF schemes - Nil
3. Stage of utilization of grants released under various, submission utilization certificates for the grants released prior to 2002-03: No scheme implemented.

Development Indicators

(*a*) Increase in Net Book Stack during 2002-03 over 2001-02: 1,558

(*b*) Increase in Books consulted during 2002-03 over 2001-02: Decreased - 25,885

(*c*) Increase in books issued during 2002-03 over 2001-02: Decreased - 35, 627 (*d*) Accommodation increased during 2002-03 over 2001-02: Nil

(*e*) Public donation raised (kind and money) during 2002-03 over 2001-02: Nil

State Central Library, Hyderabad

The State Central Library is one of the institutions of learning which had its genesis in the year 1891 due to the sustained efforts of late Moulvi Syed Hussain Bilgrami (Nawab Imad nl Mulk Bahadur of H.E.H.) the Nizam's Government. The personal library of this great scholar formed the initial corpus of this great institution. It was then known as Asalia State Library after the name of the Asaf Jah Dynastry. The library was shifted to the present building in 1936 and the building was constructed at a cost of Rs. 5 lakhs.

Objectives

1. The main objective of the State Central Library is to collect all the literature on Science and Technology and allied subjects.
2. State Central Library is expected to be main source in the State for reference materials for research workers and scholars.
3. The main objective is to serve as focal point and an organizing agency for inter library loan of books.
4. The State Central Library in accordance with its objectives maintains a strong reference collection including State and Central Government Publications.
5. As a public library, State Central Library organizes book exhibitions and professional seminars and conferences and nation wide Library week celebrations.
6. One of the main objectives of the State Central Library is to create awareness and to inculcate

reading habit in the minds of the students. This is emphasized and highlighted during the National Library Week Celebrations.

7. The State Central Library provides literature for neo-literate research scholars and children of different age groups, students and readers of all standards including blind readers

Functions

The State Central Library as a Public Library plays an important role in supporting the formal education. Its role in imparting informal education contributes to the social and economic development in making or making the life of individual and community as a whole.

This library functions within the state under the State Library system by collecting printed and audio-visual library equipment needed to serve the public readers. As a public library with an open access system now makes accessible all its resources to be convenient and easy for use by the public.

The main functions lie in interpreting and guidance to the use of library reading materials in the set pattern of collection, organization and distribution of each of these elements is very important to aid of these public libraries to serve all the people keeping in view the fact that every person has a equal right to knowledge.

This encircles individuals and groups of all ages, education, philosophy, occupation and other conditions. There by the services of library reaches the individuals regard less of what he is and where he is. Though the budget is limited, this library has the responsibility to provide access to full library service through a suitable and effective structure. This can be best achieved by means of interlibrary loan which is a part and parcel of the library networking system.

The following sections functioning in this library

1. Technical Section
2. Circulation Section
3. Reference Section
4. Periodical Section
5. Children Section
6. Text Book Section
7. English Section
8. Telugu Section
9. Urdu Section
10. Hindi, Marathi and Kannada Section
11. Arabic and Persian Section
12. Rare Book Section
13. Binding Section
14. Reprographic Section
15. Social Education Wing
16. Administrative Office

Technical Section: This section works from 10:30 a.m. to 5:00 p.m. to attend the processing work of the books i.e. preparation of books list, receiving the books (purchase, grants, RRRLF & ROP etc.) Accessioning work, Classification, Cataloguing and Indexing. In this section one Assistant Librarian Grade-II, one Assistant Librarian Grade-Ill and one Attender are working.

Circulation Section: This section works from 8:00 a.m. to 8:00 p.m. in two shifts. Issue and receive the books to the registered borrowers, enrollment of membership, withdrawal of membership, collection of overdue charges from the defaulted borrowers and sending reminders to the defaulters are the main activities. One Assistant Librarian Grade-II is in-charge of this section.

Reference Section: This section works from 8:00 a.m. to 8:00 p.m. in two shifts. This section is providing ready reference service to the readers through Encyclopedias, Dictionaries, Years Books, Directories, Atlases etc. In this section one Assistant Libraian Grade-II and one Attender are posted in each shift.

Periodical Section: This section functions from 8:00 a.m. to 8:00 p.m. in two shifts. This section is working in three sub-sections i.e., Old Periodical section, Old Magazines Section (works 10:30 a.m. to 5:00 p.m. to provide the Old Newspapers). Current Periodical Section subscribes for 337 periodicals in different languages. In this section, one Assistant Librarian Grade-II is kept in-charge and attends the work of processing the Bills for claim, entering the magazines and periodicals and supervise the section. The Old Periodical Section works from 10:30 a.m. to 5:00 p.m. The Old Magazine section works from 10:30 a.m. to 5:00 p.m.

Children Section: This section functions in General Shift i.e., 10:30 a.m. to 5:00 p.m. to provide the Juvenile Literature which includes Children's Encyclopedias, Biographies of National and International Leaders and Scientists. Fiction Books in English, Telugu and Hindi languages and Juvenile Periodicals. In this section one Assistant Librarian Grade-Ill and one Attender are working.

Text Book Section: This section works from 8:00 a.m. to 12:00 p.m. mid night without a weekly holiday in three shifts. This library is providing recent editions of Text books for all classes, in all subjects from Intermediate onwards to Post Graduation Level and is providing all recent competitive books for all competitive examinations. In this section one assistant Librarian Grade-Ill and one Attender are posted in each shift.

English Section: This section works from 8:00 a.m. to 8:00 p.m. to provide the books to the reading public, having a good number of English language books in different subjects. This section is maintained with two stack rooms wherein the books published upto 1960 were kept for reading purpose. Books published after 1960 are kept in English section for reading purpose as well as lending. In this section one assistant Librarian Grade-II and three attenders are posted in each shift.

Telugu Section: This section functions in two shifts from 8:00 a.m. to 8:00 p.m. to provide the services through Telugu literature, Encyclopedias, Dictionaries, Almanes in all different subjects and is maintaining separate technical work i.e. Receiving Books from Gratis, RRRLF and ROP, Accessioning, Classification, Cataloguing. In this section one assistant Librarian Grade-II, one assistant Librarian Grade-Ill and one Attender are posted in each shift.

Urudu Section: This section functions in two shifts from 8:00 a.m. to 8:00 p.m. to provide the services through Urdu literature, Encyclopaedias, Dictionaries in different subjects and is maintaining separate technical work i.e. Receiving Books from Gratis, RRRLF and ROP, Accessioning, Classification. Cataloguing and is having independent lending service to the registered borrowers. In this section one Assistant Librarian Grade-III, one Library Attender and one Attender are posted in each shift.

Hindi, Marathi and Kannada Sections: These sections function from 8:00 a.m. to 8:00 p.m. in two shifts to provide the books to the reading public having a good number of Encyclopaedias, Dictionaries, Year Books, Text Books in different subjects and Literature and is maintaining separate technical work i.e. Receiving Books from Gratis, RRRLF and ROP, Accessioning, Classification, Cataloguing. One Assistant Librarian Grade-II is kept in-charge of these sections; one Assistant Librarian Grade-II and one Attender are posted in each shift in Hindi and Marathi Section.

Arabic and Persian Section: This section functions from 8:00 a.m. to 8:00 p.m. in two shifts to provide the services to reading public through books for consultation only and these books are not to be issued to the registered borrowers at any cost. This section is having very important and valuable rare books and are not available throughout the world. In this section in each shift one Attender is attending the work of dusting and cleaning, supervise the readers etc. This section is having 38 racks with books.

Rare Books Section: This section functions from 8:00 a.m. to 8:00 p.m. in two shifts having good number of rare books in all subjects in English published in 18th and 19th centuries to provide the precious information to the Research Scholars. In this section in each shift one Attender is attending the work of dusting and cleaning, supervise the readers etc. This section is having 24 racks with books.

Binding Section: This section functions from 10:30 a.m. to 5:00 p.m. to attend the book binding work of this Library Books and periodicals for preservation. In this section 4 senior binders and 2 junior binders are attending the binding work of library books at the rate of 40 books in a month and bound the periodicals, office files etc.

Reprographic Section: This section woks from 10:30 a.m. to 5:00 p.m. Having one Modi Xerox copier to provide the service to the reading public charging 0.50 paise per copy on requisition by the reader. One junior supervisor is attending Reprographic work.

Social Education wing: This section works from 10:30 a.m. to 5:00 p.m.. Having Audio Visual Equipment, Television and 16 mm Film Projector and this section deals with conducting meetings, seminars and national library week celebrations etc. One Library Attender is attending the work entrusted in the Social Education wing.

Administrative Office: This section functions from 10:30 a.m. to 5:00 p.m. to attend the work of library personnel such as service matters, their pay, allowances, supervise over the budget allotted and convening the meeting of book selection committee towards the purchase of books in all languages. There are, 1 Superintendent, 4 Senior Assistants, 6 Junior Assistants, 3 Typists, and 3 Attenders are working in the office.

Total Collection

1. Book Stack (as on 31-3-2002)

English	1,35,461
Telugu	1,33,032
Urdu	81,181
Hindi	40,523
Marathi	16,902
Kannada	15,004
Tamil	1,060
Sanskrit	3,195
Total	4,26,358

2. Total number of Periodicals received — 304

Dailies	29
Weeklies	65
Fortnightly	30
Monthlies	180

3. Total number of Registered Borrowers as on 31-3-2002 — 28,255

4. Average number of Readers per day as on 31-3-2002 — 641

Average number of books lent per day — 47

Average number of books consulted — 483

	Years		
	1999-00	2000-01	2001-02
5. Total expenditure incurred . towards purchase of books	Nil	Rs. 5,28,779/-	Rs. 6,86,311/-

Proposed Achievements

1. Computerization of the State Central Library, Hyderabad.
2. Digitalization of State Central Library, Hyderabad.
3. Strengthening of Text Book section of State Central Library, Hyderabad to provide books for I.A.S., I.P.S., I.F.S., and other competitive examinations.
4. Microfilming of Old Periodicals and Rare Book collections with the assistance of RRRLF, Koltata.

Resource Mobilization

Many of the Registered Borrowers are not able to get the reading material on home lending with a meagre amount of membership deposit and also are not permitted to take the books above the worth of Rs. 150/-. It is suggested to enhance the membership deposit amount upto Rs. 300/- to enable to read the required book by the registered borrowers. Enhance the overdue charges upto 0.25 paise per book per day. Introduction of Donor Scheme to get donations from donors (Non-Refunable) for investment in long term deposits and to the utilize interest amount only on purchase of books, furniture an equipment for this library. Lease amount is to be utilized for the development of the Library.

Reprographic Section

Readers are utilizing the services of the Xerox Copier Machine for the restricted time only i.e. 10:30 a.m. to 5:00 p.m.

Rare Books Preservation

This library is having good number of valuable and important rare books for the Research Scholars. These books may be preserved in CD's (Compact Disc) Microfilms etc., to safe guard for the future generation.

Expansion of Text Book Section Services

This library is having Text Book Section as well as a separate cell for competitive examinations. This library is purchasing the text books and competitive books for all competitive examinations both under plan and non-plan budget.

Internet Services

Being an Apex Library of the state, it is providing the Internet Services to the readers.

Summary

It is seen from the objectives, functions and services of all the Regional Public Libraries that all are having some common objectives, functions and services.

Common Objectives

1. To collect all the literature on Science and Technology and allied subjects.
2. To serve the general public and Research workers.
3. To provide information at free of cost with open access system.
4. To make available to all citizens to refer all kinds of documents, periodicals, manuscripts, palm leaf manuscripts, maps, micro-films, rare book material, etc.
5. To encourage students to use of competitive books and employment information i.e., these libraries act as employment information bureaus.
6. To create awareness and inculcate reading habit in the minds of school going children through conducting quiz competitions, drawing competitions, essay writing and elocution competitions.
7. To increase readership and membership.
8. To improve public participation in library activities and development.
9. To serve as focal point an organizing agencies for inter library loan of books.
10. To provide reference service.
11. To issue books on membership.

Common Functions

1. Arranging the books in classified order.
2. Keeping all sections neat and clean.
3. Providing information for self-employment schemes though reference tools.
4. Creating entertainment through film shows, cricket matches, etc., with the help of television services.
5. Providing current and old periodicals to the readers.
6. Providing reference services from the available sources.
7. Involving public in the community development programmes like Janmabhoomi, Clean and Green, Cultural and literacy meetings, etc.
8. Creating inspiration to public by conducting book-exhibitions, photo-exhibitions and numismatics (coins) exhibitions, etc.
9. Enrollment and withdrawal of membership.
10. Collection, organization, distribution, interpretation and dissemination of information.
11. Educating the public continuously by keep abreast of progress in all fields of knowledge.

Services

All these libraries are providing the following services at their convenience basing on the finances and infrastructure available at their end.

1. Enrollment of membership.
2. Charging and discharging.
3. Reference services of rare and current documents.
4. Reprographic services.
5. Inter library loan facility.
6. Micro films.
7. Provision of old and latest periodicals.

8. Providing yoga facility to male members in the early hours (some libraries only).
9. News clippings on Notice Boards/Black board news.

It can be concluded that all the Government Regional Libraries (Regional Public Libraries) of the State were established with certain aims and objectives mentioned as common objectives for all Regional Libraries, to fulfill the desire of government is serving the public better. Though some of these libraries are lagging in fulfillment of the objectives set, they are providing the services to the public with the available resources and staff. To prepare bibliographies in coordination with State Central Library and for preparation of Union Catalogue of books and periodicals at regional levels, further exercise is required at the level of State Central Library as well as at the Regional Libraries.

STATE CENTRAL LIBRARY: HYDERABAD: ANDHRA PRADESH

State Central Library, Hyderabad

4

Analysis and Discussion

Information gathered in the present study was analysed and discussed under three sections in this Chapter. In the first section, some background aspects physical facilities of these State Regional Public Libraries such as the establishment, library building and its location, space available, status of the Librarians, work hours, furniture available, staff position, income and expenditure, material available, library collection, maintenance of records, membership particulars, library committee, inter-library loan facility, publicity, extension and other activities, community information services and library automation were discussed in detail.

The second section deals with the observations made from the user's survey. Here, the presentation include aspects like types of user group, user information needs, duration and frequency of use of the libraries, purpose of visit and time spent, users' opinion on library collection, staff co-operation, their views on establishing computerized networking of all the Government Regional Public Libraries, establishing data banks, establishing links with DCL, opinion on the available facilities, services, furniture, equipment and available ook resources and their willingness to pay user charges.

The third section includes a presentation on the opinions of the Librarians from the six Regional Public Libraries, one State Central Library and also the Director/Commissioner of Public Libraries on aspects like staff development, public relations, community relations, community information services, establishing computerized networking between the

Regional Public Libraries, establishing data banks, establishing links with DCL, text books to be introduced, their views on using the services of voluntary workers, their background particulars and contribution so far for the development of the Regional Public Libraries in the state.

As the present study is a qualitative narrative and descriptive one, the analysis and presentation of observations were made accordingly.

SECTION-1: Physical Facilities, Service and Sources of the Regional Public Libraries

As already mentioned this section covers the background information relating to the different aspects of the existing infrastructure, services and other activities. Before discussing these details, it is important to have an idea of the different libraries covered in the study.

Altogether, there are six Regional Public Libraries (RPLs) and one State Central Library (SCL) functioning in the state of Andhra Pradesh under the public library system. Information relating to the establishment and location of these libraries is shown in Table - 4.1.

Table 4.1. Government Regional Public Libraries in Andhra Pradesh

Name of the Library	*Address*	*Year of Establishment*
1. Govt. Regional Library	Dwarakanagar, Visakhapatnam.	1965
2. Sri Gowthami Regional Library	Lakshmivarapupeta, Near Gokavaram Bus stand, Rajahmundry.	1979
3. State Regional Library	Guntur	1958
4. Govt. Regional Library	TUDA Complex, R.C. Road, Tirupati.	1964
5. Govt. Regional Library	K.M.C. Post, Warangal.	1964
6. Govt. Regional Library	Chandrasekhar Colony, Kanteshwar, Nizamabad.	1966
7. State Central Library	Afzulgung, Hyderabad.	1891

It can be observed that the State Central Library at Hyderabad is the oldest being established in 1891 during the British regime. Among the Regional Public Libraries, the one at Guntur is the oldest and is established in the year 1958. The remaining five have been established between 1964 and 1966 at Visakhapatnam, Rajahmundry, Tirupati, Warangal and Nizamabad. The distribution of Regional Public Libraries jurisdiction show, some regional justification as three were in the Coastal Andhra area, one in the Rayalaseema area and the remaining two RPLs and SCL in Telangana area. This indicates that some policy has been followed for the establishment of these public libraries, as the goals and objectives of these libraries are different from the academic ones and are more aimed at catering to the information needs of public. Needless to say, the word 'public' is a broad one comprising of a variety of heterogeneous groups with varying needs.

Status of the Librarians

Information relating to the status of the Librarians who are heading these Regional Public Libraries, such as their designation, qualification and scale of pay are shown in Table 4.2. It is noticed that the State Central Library is headed by a Chief Librarian and the Regional Public Libraries by a Librarian and all these were of Gazetted rank with a scale of pay of Rs. 6,950/- Rs. 14,425/-. Only two RPLs - one at Warangal and the other at Nizamabad have reported that Assistant Librarians (Grade-I) are incharge of these libraries at the time of the present study and their scale of pay is Rs.5,000/- Rs.10,600/-. Regarding their educational qualifications, it is reported that four of these seven librarians are having graduate degrees while the remaining three are post-graduates. On the other hand four of them are having MLISc., And the remaining three are having BLISc., degrees as professional qualifications. This shows that these public libraries are functioning under qualified and professional leadership.

Table 4.2. Details of the Librarians Working in the Regional Public Libraries (RPLs) Covered.

Regional Public Library	*Designation*	*Qualifications*	*Scale of Pay (Rs.)*
1. Regional Public Library, Visakhapatnam.	Librarian (Gazetted)	M.L.I.Sc.,	6,950- 14,425
2. Regional Public Library, Rajahmundry.	Librarian (Gazetted)	MA, M.L.I.Sc.,	6,950 14,425.
3. Regional Public Library, Guntur.	Librarian (Gazetted)	B.A., M.L.I.Sc.,	6,950 - 14,425.
4. Regional Public Library, Tirupati.	Librarian (Gazetted)	B.Sc.,M.L.I.Sc.,	6,950 - 14,425.
5. Regional Public Library, Warangal.	Assistant Librarian Grade-I	B.A., B.L.I.Sc.,	5,000 - 10,600.
6. Regional Public Library, Nizamabad.	Assistant Librarian Grade-I	B.Com.,B.LI.Sc.,	5,000 - 10,600.
7. State Central Library, Hyderabad.	Chief Librarian	M.A., M.L.I.Sc.,	6,950 - 14,425.

Library Building and its Location

Information regarding the library building and its location is presented in Table - 4.3.

Table 4.3. Details Regarding Location and Occupation of the Library Building

	RPL Visakha-patnam	*RPL Raja-mundry*	*RPL Guntur*	*RPL Tirupati*	*RPL Waran-gal*	*RPL Nizam-abad*	*SCL Hydera-bad*
(*a*) Location of the Library:							
Centrally located	—	Yes	Yes	—	Yes	—	Yes
On the main road	—	—	—	Yes	—	—	—
In a corner	—	—	—	—	—	Yes	—
In a lane	Yes	—	—	—	—	—	—
(*b*) Library Building:							
Own	—	Yes	Yes	—	Yes	Yes	Yes
Rented	Yes	—	—	Yes	—	—	—

	RPL Visakha-patnam	RPL Raja-mundry	RPL Guntur	RPL Tirupati	RPL Waran-gal	RPL Nizam-abad	SCL Hydera-bad
(*c*) Occupation of the Library in the building:							
Full	—	—	Yes	—	—	Yes	—
A Part	Yes	Yes	—	Yes	Yes	—	Yes

With the exception of Visakhapatnam and Tirupati, the RPLs at all the other four places and the SCL are having their own buildings. At these two places, some rented accommodation is being used for housing the library. It is also reported that, the RPLs at Visakhapatnam, Rajahmundry, Tirupati and Warangal, also the SCL, some part of the building is only used for the library while the RPLs at Guntur and Nizamabad have reported that they are using the full building for the purpose of running the library.

With regard to the location of these libraries, three RPLs - at Rajahmundry, Guntur and Warangal and also the SCL at Hyderabad have been reported to be centrally located so as to be accessible to public from all corners of the city or town. The RPL at Tirupati is said to be located on the main road and the one at Nizamabad was said to be located in a corner of the town/city. Interestingly, the RPL at Visakhapatnam is reported to be situated in a side lane. This may be because of procuring rented accommodation on main roads or so.

Details of space available

Details of library space available and its adequacy at present and for future are shown in Table - 4.4.

It is observed that the RPLs at Warangal and Nizamabad are having 7 rooms for the library while the RPL at Rajahmundry has 9 rooms. The oldest RPL at Guntur is having 12 rooms. The two RPLs at Visakhapatnam and Tirupati which are run in rented accommodation have reported availability of only 3 rooms for the library which is inclusive of a hall etc. The SCL is having big accommodation is relatively large compared to the different RPLs. The available space is said to be adequate for the present requirements by only 3 RPLs - viz., Visakhapatnam, Tirupati and Warangal. While it is reported to be not sufficient for present requirement by the other three RPLs and also SCL. It is very interesting to note here that the two RPLs in rented buildings where there are only 3 rooms - reporting that the space is adequate for the present needs of the library. However, only the RPL- Warangal has reported that the available space is sufficient for the future developments also. All the remaining libraries including the SCL are in need of additional space for future developments.

Table 4.4. Details of Space Available for the Library.

	Library space	*RPL Visakha-patnam*	*RPL Raja-mundry*	*RPL Guntur*	*RPL Tirupati*	*RPL Waran-gal*	*RPL Nizam-abad*	*SCL Hydera-bad*
(*a*)	No. of Rooms	2+1 hall	9	12	3	7	7	12 flrs.
(*b*)	Total area	347.49 sq. mtr.	3,100 sft.	54,587 sft.	2,250 sft.	1,516.28 yards	1,404 sq.mtr.	1,52,492 sft.
(*c*)	Stack area	—	295 sft.	5,100 sft.	750 sft.	118.5 sq.yards	150 sq.mtr.	243 sft.
(*d*)	Reading space	—	154 sft.	450 sft.	180 sft.	101.52 yards	120 sq.mtr.	32,424 sft.
(*e*)	Whether the space is sufficient for future development?	No	No	No	No	Yes	No	No
(*f*)	Whether the space is sufficient for the present requirements?	Yes	No	No	Yes	Yes	No	No

Accommodation for different sections in the Library

Information relating to organization of different sections in the library, which is linked to the available space, in the six RPLs and the SCL is presented in Table - 4.5.

Table 4.5. Availability of Separate Accommodation for Different Sections.

		RPL Visakha-patnam	*RPL Raja-mundry*	*RPL Guntur*	*RPL Tirupati*	*RPL Waran-gal*	*RPL Nizam-abad*	*SCL Hydera-bad*
Whether separate accommodation for different sections available		Yes	Yes	Yes	Yes	Yes	Yes	Yes
1.	Stack room	Yes	Yes	Yes	Yes	Yes	Yes	Yes
2.	Reference section	Yes	Yes	Yes	Yes	Yes	Yes	Yes
3.	Technical section	Yes	Yes	Yes	Yes	Yes	Yes	Yes
4.	Librarian's room	Yes	Yes	Yes	Yes	Yes	Yes	Yes
5.	Computer section	Yes	Yes	Yes	Yes	Yes	Yes	Yes
6.	Display section	No	Yes	Yes	No	No	No	No
7.	Circulation section	No	Yes	No	Yes	Yes	No	Yes
8.	Reading hall	Yes	Yes	Yes	Yes	Yes	Yes	Yes
9.	Reprographi section	No	Yes	Yes	No	Yes	No	Yes
10.	Any other	No	Yes (Meeting Hall)	Yes	No	No	No	Yes

All the seven libraries covered in the study have reported that they are having separate accommodation for different sections. All these have reported separate accommodation for Librarian's room, stack room, reference section and technical section. All the libraries, with the exception of RPL at Tirupati reported availability of accommodation for computer section. Only two RPLs - at Rajahmundry and Guntur are having display section. Separate accommodation for circulation section is not available in RPLs at Visakhapatnam, Guntur and Nizamabad and the RPLs at Visakhapatnam, Tirupati and Nizamabad are not having separate accommodation for reprographic section in their libraries. However, all these libraries have reported accommodation for the reading hall which is very important. Interestingly, the SCL has not reported availability of accommodation for the display section.

Normal Schedule of Work

Details like number of days of work in a week, number of holidays and the regular hours of work are shown in the Table - 4.6.

Table 4.6. Schedule of Work.

	Work schedule	*RPL Visakha-patnam*	*RPL Raja-mundry*	*RPL Guntur*	*RPL Tirupati*	*RPL Waran-gal*	*RPL Nizam-abad*	*SCL Hydera-bad*
(*a*)	Number of working days in a week	6	6	6	6	6	6	6
(*b*)	Number of holidays in a year (excluding weekly holidays)	20	20	34	20	24	32	20
(*c*)	Regular hours of work	80-11 (am) 4-7 (pm)	80-11 (am) 4-7 (pm)	8 am- 8 pm	8-11 (am) 4-7 (pm)	8 am- 8 pm	8-11 (am) 4-7 (pm)	8 am- 8 pm

All the six RPLs and the SCL have reported that they work for 6 days in a week and normally have 20 holidays in a year excluding the weekly holidays. Four out of the six RPLs, those at Visakhapatnam, Rajahmundry , Tirupati and Nizamabad are working for 6 hours a day in two shifts i.e. 8 a.m. to 11 a.m. and 4 p.m. to 7 p.m. The remaining two RPLs at Guntur and Warangal and also the SCL at Hyderabad are functioning for 12 hours a day on all working days between 8 a.m. and 8 p.m. This shows that there is no specific directive regarding uniformity in the working hours of these Regional Public Libraries.

Furniture available and future requirements

Information regarding the furniture available and the facility of electricity is shown in Table - 4.7.

It can be seen that all these seven libraries covered in the present study are having sufficient number of reading tables and chairs and bookracks as well as office furniture and also reported that all the libraries are having electricity and fans in their reading rooms.

Table 4.7. Furniture Available.

	RPL Visakha-patnam	*RPL Raja-mundry*	*RPL Guntur*	*RPL Tirupati*	*RPL Waran-gal*	*RPL Nizam-abad*	*SCL Hydera-bad*
(*a*) Furniture available:							
(*i*) Reading tables:							
Wooden	6	14	30	10	26	6	95
Steel	—	12		—	4	10	115
(*ii*) Chairs:							
Wooden	—	12		20	5	14	356
Steel	25	46	324	20	132	91	511
Fibre	42	—		40	—	—	—
(*iii*) Book racks:							
Wooden	—	136	244	—	—	3	418
Steel	43	112		35	74	84	218
(*iv*) Office furniture:							
Wooden	5	42	18	4	20	7	52
Steel	1	—		—	—	4	
(*b*) Electricity facility							
(*i*) Electricity:							
Available	Yes	Yes	Yes	Yes	Yes	Yes	Yes
Not available	—	—	—	—	—	—	—
(*ii*) Fans in Reading room:							
Available	Yes	Yes	Yes	Yes	Yes	Yes	Yes
Not available	—	—	—	—	—	—	—

Details of furniture and equipment required for future needs are shown in Table - 4.8.

Table 4.8. Equipment and Furniture Required for Future Needs

	Section	*RPL Visakha-patnam*	*RPL Raja-mundry*	*RPL Guntur*	*RPL Tirupati*	*RPL Waran-gal*	*RPL Nizam-abad*	*SCL Hydera-bad*
1.	Reading tables & chairs	Yes	—	—	—	—	—	Yes
2.	Books racks	Yes	—	Yes	Yes	Yes	—	Yes
3.	Internet facility	Yes	Yes	Yes	Yes	Yes	Yes	—
4.	Scanner	Yes	—	—	—	Yes	—	—
5.	Audio-visual equipment	—	Yes	—	—	—	Yes	Yes
6.	Gramphone records	—	Yes	—	—	—	—	—
7.	Film projector/films/slides	—	—	Yes	—	—	—	—
8.	VCR and ailied material	—	—	—	—	Yes	—	—
9.	Computer systems	—	—	—	—	—	—	Yes
10.	Electronic equipment	—	—	—	—	—	—	Yes

The major requirement mentioned by all the six RPLs is the Internet facility, while four of these RPLs at Visakhapatnam, Guntur, Tirupati and Warangal are in need of additional book racks. RPLs at Visakhapatnam and Warangal have reported that they are in need of a scanner. Reading room chairs and tables are required at the RPL - Visakhapatnam. Need for audiovisual equipment is reported by the RPLs at Rajahmundry and Nizamabad. In the same way, the need for a VCR and allied material is reported to be needed at RPL - Warangal. RPL at Guntur has reported the need for a film projector, with films and slides of educational importance. Gramphone records are said to be required at the RPL - Rajahmundry.

The SCL has reported that they need some additional tables and chairs for the reading room, bookracks, audio-visual equipment, some electronic equipment and also some more computer systems for use in their library.

Staff position

Details of the staff position at the time of conducting this study in the seven libraries are shown in Table - 4.9.

Table 4.9. Staff Position

Section	*RPL Visakha-patnam*	*RPL Raja-mundry*	*RPL Guntur*	*RPL Tirupati*	*RPL Waran-gal*	*RPL Nizam-abad*	*SCL Hydera-bad*
(*a*) Professional:							
Chief Librarian	—	—	—	—	—	—	1
Gazetted Librarian	1	1	1	1	1	1	1
Asst. Librarian Grade-I	1	—	3	1	1	1	—
Asst. Librarian Grade-II	—	1	—	1	1	—	—
(*b*) Semi-Professional:							
Card writer	—	3	—	1	1	2	9
Book clearers:							
Book keeper	—	—	1	—	—	—	7
Book bearer	—	—	2	—	—	—	20
(c) Non-Professional:							
Finance Officer	—	—	1	—	—	—	1
Head Clerk	—	—	1	—	—	—	—
Senior Assistant	—	—	—	—	—	—	3
Junior Assistant	—	—	1	—	—	—	6
Typist	1	1	1	—	—	—	3
Record Assistant	1	2	2	1	1	—	—
Binder	—	—	1	—	—	—	6
Attender	1	—	7	—	—	—	10
Watchman	1	1	1	1	1	1	1
Sweeper/Scavenger	—	1	2	1	1	1	4
Total Staff	6	10	24	7	7	6	72

Among the six RPLs, the number of staff working is more (24) in the oldest RPL i.e. at Guntur followed by 10 at RPL-Rajahmundry. The total number of staff is 7 in RPLs at Tirupati and Warangal while it is 6 in the remaining two RPLs at Visakhapatanam and Nizamabad.

Coming to the details, in all the six RPLs, there is one Librarian (Gazetted) and a minimum of one Assistant Librarian (Grade-I). In the RPL-Guntur there are three Assistant Librarians (Grade-I) and none in RPL at Rajahmundry. Assistant, Librarian (Grade-II) are positioned in RPLs at Rajahmundry, Tirupati and Warangal. In all, the strength of professional staff in the RPLs is 4 in Guntur, 3 in Tirupati and Warangal while only 2 in Visakhapatnam, Rajahmundry and Nizamabad.

Regarding the semi-professionals, 3 card writers are there in RPL-Rajahmundry, 2 in Nizamabad, 1 each in Tirupati and Warangal and none in Visakhapatnam and Guntur. Three book clearers were reported in RPL - Guntur. Thus the strength of semi professionals is 3 in Rajahmundry and Guntur, 2 in Nizamabad, 1 each in Tirupati and Warangal while nil in Visakhapatnam.

Except in RPL - Nizamamad, Record Assistants are functioning in all the remaining five RPLs. These are 2 each in Rajahmundry and Guntur , 1 each in Visakhapatnam, Tirupati and Warangal. Typist is reported to be working in only 3 RPLs - Visakhapatnam, Rajahmundry and Guntur. All the six libraries have reported the availability of a watchman and sweeper/scavenger are reported in five of the six libraries (exception being RPL - Visakhapatnam). There is one attender in RPL- Visakhapatnam while RPL - Guntur has reported availability of 7 attenders and they also reported the availability of a binder. Thus the strength of non-professional staff is 16 in 16 in RPL - Guntur, 5 in Rajahmundry, 4 in Visakhapatnam, 3 each in Tirupati and Warangal and 2 in Nizamabad.

The staff position at the SCL, Hyderabad is totally different from that of the RPLs. Altogether there are 72 staff members working in the SCL. There are two professional staff - one Chief Librarian and one Librarian (Gazetted), 36 semi-professional staff - 9 card writers and 27 book clearers and 34 non-professional or ministerial staff.

Staff position in these libraries i.e. the number of professionals, semi-professionals and non-professionals working at the time of this survey is diagrammatically presented in Fig. - 1.

Income and Expenditure for the year 2002-2003

Details of the income and expenditure for the year 2002-2003 as reported by the six RPLs and the SCL are shown in Table - 4.10. The major sources of income in these libraries is reported to be the annual grant released by the state government and the amount accumulated through subscriptions. While the major component under expenditure is mentioned to be the payment of staff salaries and other allowances. It is noticed that the income and expenditure are relatively more for the RPL - Guntur as well as the SCL due to the relatively more number of staff working.

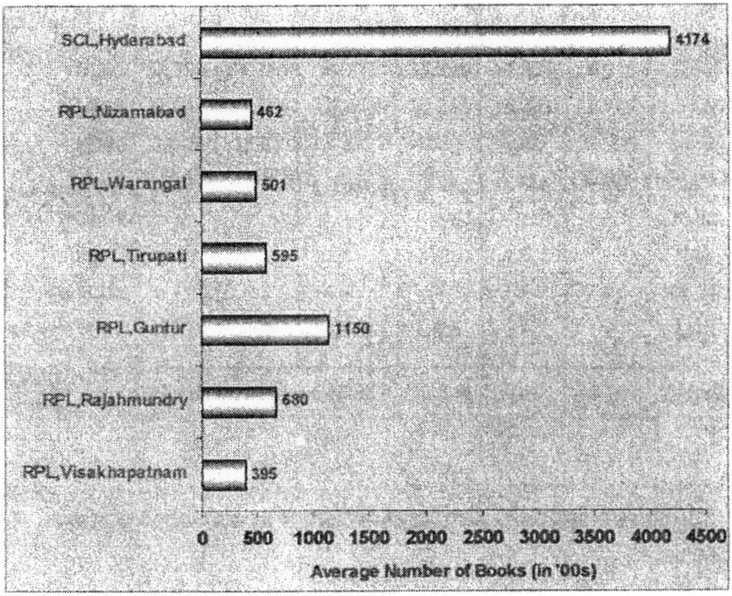

Fig. 1. Staff Position at the time of survey.

Table 4.10. Income and Expenditure for the Year 2002-2003.

Name of the Library	*Year 2002-2003*	
	Income (Rs.)	*Expenditure (Rs.)*
1. RPL, Visakhapatnam	8,54,405	8,02,210
2. RPL, Rajahmundry	12,00,358	11,32,252
3. RPL, Guntur	30,80,563	26,44,611
4. RPL, Tirupati	12,00,378	8,73,784
5. RPL, Warangal	6,25,521	6,08,415
6. RPL, Nizamabad	5,83,668	4,83,600
7. SCL, Hyderabad	1,00,96,950	93,86,327

Income and expenditure (in Rs. '000s) for the year 2002-2003 for all these seven libraries covered is diagrammatically shown in Fig. - 2.

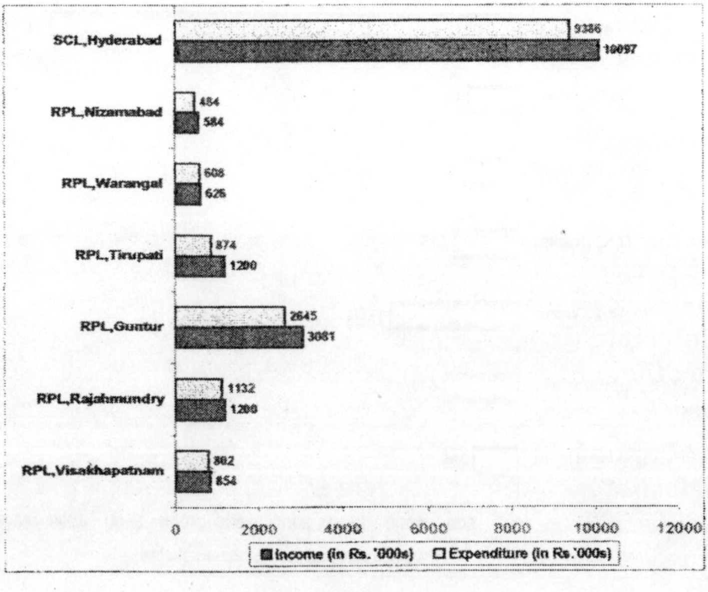

Fig. 2. Income & Expenditure of the Library.
(For the year 2002-2003)

Ways of Library Collection

Information relating to the different ways through which the collection of material is developed in these seven libraries is shown in Table - 4.11.

Table 4.11. Ways of Library Cololection

	RPL Visakha-patnam	*RPL Raja-mundry*	*RPL Guntur*	*RPL Tirupati*	*RPL Waran-gal*	*RPL Nizam-abad*	*SCL Hydera-bad*
(*a*) Haying a selection policy for collection of:							
Print materials	Yes	Yes	Yes	No	Yes	No	Yes
Non-print materials	No	No	No	No	Yes	No	No
(*b*) Methods of procuring the document and other library materials.							
Purchase	Yes	Yes	Yes	Yes	Yes	Yes	Yes
Gifts	Yes	Yes	Yes	Yes	Yes	Yes	Yes
RRRLF Scheme	Yes	—	—	—	Yes	—	—
(*c*) Whether received any periodicals free of cost/gifts/donation every year	Yes	Yes	Yes	Yes	No	No	Yes

It is stated that all the six RPLs and the SCL, with the exception of RPLs at Tirupati and Nizamabad, are having a set selection policy for the development of print materials while there is no such policy for the development of non-print materials. However, RPL - Warangal has mentioned that they do have a policy for non-print material collection also.

Regarding the methods of procuring the documents as well as other library materials, all the RPLs and SCL have mentioned that they do mostly purchase from the available grants or get them by way of gifts from other agencies or individuals. RPLs at Visakhapatnam and Warangal have also reported that they procured some material under the RRRLF scheme.

Except the RPL - Warangal, all other libraries have informed that they have received some periodicals free of cost or by way of gifts or by donation every year.

Type of Material Available

Details of different types of library material available are shown in Table - 4.12.

Table 4.12. Type of Library Material Available.

	RPL Visakha-patnam	RPL Raja-mundry	RPL Guntur	RPL Tirupati	RPL Waran-gal	RPL Nizam-abad	SCL Hydera-bad
1. Books	Yes	Yes	Yes	Yes	Yes	Yes	Yes
2. Seminar papers	No	No	No	No	No	No	Yes
3. Periodicals	Yes	Yes	Yes	Yes	Yes	Yes	Yes
4. Paper clippings	No	No	No	No	Yes	No	Yes
5. Reports	No	No	Yes	No	No	No	Yes
6. Newspapers	Yes	Yes	Yes	Yes	Yes	Yes	Yes
7. Cartographics	No	No	No	No	No	No	No
8. Non-Book material	No	Yes	No	Yes	Yes	Yes	Yes

All the six RPLs and SCL have reported the availability of book material, periodicals and news papers in their libraries. None of them have reported the availability of cartographic material. Seminar papers are not reported by any of the six RPLs. Availability of paper clippings is mentioned by RPL at Warangal and availability of reports by RPL at Guntur. Non-book material is said to be available with RPLs at Rajahmundry, Tirupati, Warangal and Nizamabad. Excepting the cartographic collection, all the other types listed in the table are available in the SCL.

Library Collection

Information relating to the library collection as on 1-4-2003 in the six RPLs and the SCL is presented in Table - 4.13. The total book collection ranged from 41,781 at Visakhapatnam to a highest of 1,27,672 at Guntur among the RPLs and it is 4,35,287 in the SCL. Text book collection is more at Warangal (15,379) and less at Guntur (2,000), while it is not reported by the RPLs at Tirupati and Nizamabad. The text book collection is 9,270 in the SCL. There is wide variation with regard to the collection of reference books. This collection ranged from a low of 4,130 in RPL - Visakhapatnam to a high of 25,000 in RPL-Rajahmundry and is only 8,750 in the SCL.

Table 4.13. Library Collection (As On 1-4-2003).

		RPL Visakha-patnam	*RPL Raja-mundry*	*RPL Guntur*	*RPL Tirupati*	*RPL Waran-gal*	*RPL Nizam-abad*	*SCL Hydera-bad*
1.	Books:							
	Total	41,781	70,735	1,27,672	62,439	52,919	48,835	4,[illegible]
	Text books	11,974	6,000	2,000	—	15,379	—	9,2[illegible]
	Reference books	4,130	25,000	4,000	15,000	8,907	4,500	8,750
2.	Periodicals	70	117	103	72	121	23	156
3.	Other periodicals, News papers, etc.							
	Dailies	12	20	15	14	13	9	28
	Weeklies	14	26	17	15	28	9	30
	Fort-night	5	71	-	—	—	4	14
	Monthlies	39	—	65	43	80	11	84
	Quarterlies	—	—	6	—	—	1	—
4.	Manuscripts	Nil	502*	Nil	Nil	Nil	Nil	Nil

*Includes 417 Sanskrit palm leaf scripts (in telugu lipi)

Collection of periodicals ranged from a low of 34 in RPL-Nizamabad to a high of 121 in RPL - Warangal. This collection is 156 in the SCL. These include dailies, weeklies, fort-nighties, monthlies and quarterlies.

RPL - Rajahmundry has also reported the availability of 502 manuscripts which include 417 Sanskrit plan leaf scripts (in telugu lipi) in their library collection. Manuscripts are not reported by any of the remaining five RPLs or the SCL.

In Fig. - 3, collection of total books (in 000's) and periodicals by these libraries as on 1-4-2003 are shown.

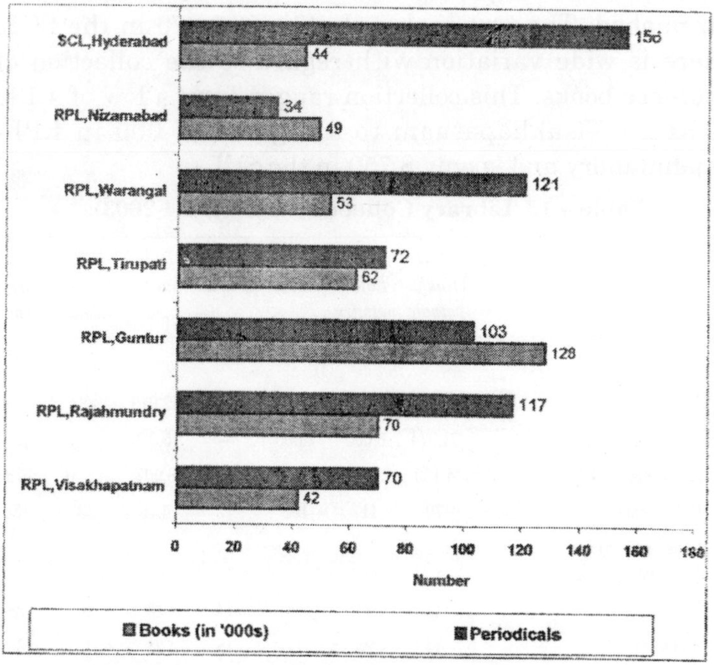

Fig. 3. Library Collection of Books & Periodicals.
(As on 1.4.2003)

Average Book Collection during the past 5 years

Average collection of books per year during the last five years by language of the books as reported by the six RPLs and the SCL are shown in Table - 4.14. The total average collection of books (in 000's) during the last five years is diagrammatically shown in Fig.-4.

It is observed that the total average collection of books per year ranged from a low of 39,519 in RPL-Visakhapatnam to a high of 1,15,011 in RPL - Guntur. This figure is 4,17,424 at the SCL. This book collection is RPLs mainly include books in Telugu, English, Hindi, Urdu and Sanskrit. Where as books in Marathi, Kannada and Tamil languages are also reported in addition by the SCL. Obviously the proportion of Telugu books is more in the collection followed by those in English, Hindi and Urdu among the RPLs. The collection of Urdu books is more than the Hindi books at the SCL. Collection of books in Sanskrit are nil in RPL - Warangal and very less in the RPL - Nizamabad.

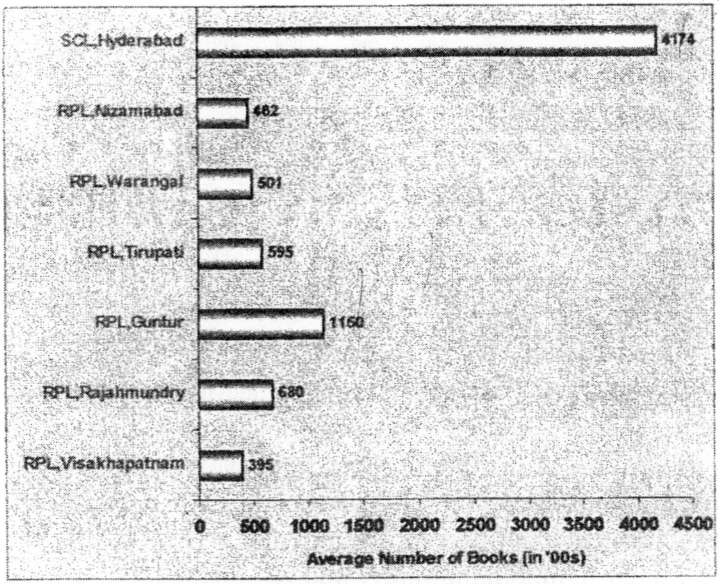

Fig. 4. Average Book Collection during last 5 years. (1999-2003)

Average collection of Periodicals during the past 5 years

In Table - 4.15, details of the average periodical collection per year basing on the information given by the six RPLs and the SCL for the past 5 years are presented.

Table 4.14. Average Book Collection during the Past 5 Years in Different Languages.

	RPL Visakha-patnam	*RPL Raja-mundry*	*RPL Guntur*	*RPL Tirupati*	*RPL Waran-gal*	*RPL Nizam-abad*	*SCL Hydera-bad*
Average Book coolection by language:							
Telugu	18,258	53,315	38,623	33,256	19,238	16,914	1,31,016
English	17,044	12,344	65,465	20,241	19,296	22,739	1,33,501
Hindi	3,818	1,585	7,278	4,151	6,597	5,118	38,931
Urdu	240	210	1,068	413	5,033	1,761	80,760
Marathi	—	—	—	—	—	—	16,421
Tamil	—	—	—	—	—	—	632
Kannada	—	—	—	—	—	—	14,243
Sanskrit and other	158	561	3,133	1,455	—	7	1,920
Total Average Book Collection	39,519	68,016	1,15,011	59,515	50,164	46,209	4,17,424

It is noticed that the average collection of periodicals among the six RPLs ranged from a low of 33 in Nizamabad to a high of 111 in Rjahmundry. This average collection is 205 in the SCL. When the periodicals by language are considered periodicals in Telugu are more in RPLs at Visakhapatnam, Rajahmundry and Nizamabad. While those in English are more in RPLs at Guntur, Tirupati and Warangal. Periodicals in English are more compared to those in Telugu or Hindi at the SCL. Periodicals in other languages are few in the RPLs. A sizeable collection of Hindi and Urdu periodicals are reported by the SCL.

In Fig. 5, the average total collection of periodicals during the years 1999-2003 is presented.

Table 4.15. Average Collection of Periodicals by Language during the Last 5 Years (1999-2003)

	RPL Visakha-patnam	*RPL Raja-mundry*	*RPL Guntur*	*RPL Tirupati*	*RPL Waran-gal*	*RPL Nizam-abad*	*SCL Hydera-bad*
Average coolection of periodicals by language:							
Telugu	42	70	42	30	43	21	48
English	21	39	57	31	47	12	114
Hindi	—	1	—	0.4	2	—	20
Urdu	—	—	—	0.6	2	0.2	17
Sanskrit	—	—	—	—	0.6	—	—
Tamil	—	1	—	—	—	—	—
Punjabi & Gujarathi	—	—	—	—	—	—	0.1
Marathi	—	—	—	—	—	—	3
Kannada	—	—	—	—	—	—	3
Others	—	—	—	4	0.6	—	3
Average Total Collection of periodicals	63	111	99	66	96	33	205

Availability and Maintenance of non-book materials

Information regarding the availability of non-book material and how they are maintained is presented in Table - 4.16. The non-book material collection includes cartographic material such as maps, globes and atlases, graphic materials such as charts, film clips and slides, other material such as manuscripts, audio-video recordings and microfilms.

Five out of the six RPLs, with the exception of RPL at Tirupati and also the SCL have reported the availability of all the three types of cartographic material viz., maps, globes and atlases in their libraries.

RPLs at Tirupati, Warangal and SCL have reported the availability of all the three types of graphic material - charts, film clips and slides. Only charts are available in RPLs at Visakhapatnam and Guntur while charts and film clips are available in RPLs at Rajahmundry and Nizamabad.

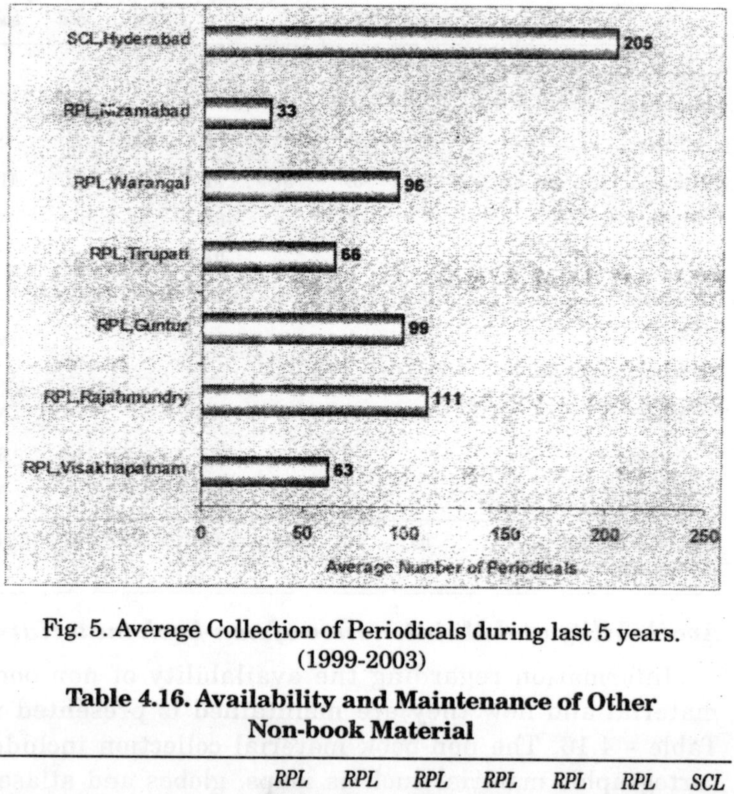

Fig. 5. Average Collection of Periodicals during last 5 years. (1999-2003)

Table 4.16. Availability and Maintenance of Other Non-book Material

	RPL Visakha-patnam	*RPL Raja-mundry*	*RPL Guntur*	*RPL Tirupati*	*RPL Waran-gal*	*RPL Nizam-abad*	*SCL Hydera-bad*
(a) Type of non-book material available:							
1. Cartographic materials:							
Maps	Yes	Yes	Yes	—	Yes	Yes	Yes
Globes	Yes	Yes	Yes	—	Yes	Yes	Yes
Atlases	Yes	Yes	Yes	—	Yes	Yes	Yes
2. Graphic materials:							
Charts	Yes	Yes	Yes	Yes	Yes	Yes	Yes

Film clips	—	Yes	—	Yes	Yes	Yes	Yes
Slides	—	—	—	Yes	Yes	—	Yes
3. Other materials:							
Manuscripts	Yes	Yes	—	—	—	—	—
Audio-visual recordings	—	Yes	—	Yes	Yes	Yes	Yes
Microfilms	—	Yes	—	—	—	—	Yes
(b) How the map collection is maintained:							
Displayed	Yes	Yes	—	NA	Yes	—	Yes
Kept in roll form	—	—	Yes	NA	—	Yes	—

NA: Not Applicable

Manuscripts, audio-video recordings and microfilms are reported to be available at RPL- Rajahmundry. Only audio-video recordings are reported by RPLs at Tirupati, Warangal and Nizamabad. None of these three items are available in RPLs at Visakhapatnam and Guntur. However, audio-video recordings and microfilms are available at the SCL.

Among the 5 RPLs and the SCL that reported availability of chart material, the charts are said to be displayed in 3 RPLs (Visakhapatnam, Rajahmundry and Warangal) and the SCL. In the remaining 2 RPLs the charts are kept in roll form.

Display of charts/models/posters and preservation of News Papers

Information on whether charts/models/posters and other exhibits that carry government or public interest are displayed, if yes on what interest and whether the newspapers are preserved, if yes for how long is presented in Table - 4.17. It can be seen that all the six RPLs and the SCL are displaying charts, models, posters and other exhibits that carry government and public interests. These display items are in general, carry messages regarding health awareness, family welfare, national book week and book exhibitions.

Table 4.17. Display of Charts/Models/Posters and Preservation of News Papers.

	RPL Visakha-patnam	*RPL Raja-mundry*	*RPL Guntur*	*RPL Tirupati*	*RPL Waran-gal*	*RPL Nizam-abad*	*SCL Hydera-bad*
1. Whether display charts/ models/posters/exhibits that carry Govt. and public interests.	Yes	Yes	Yes	Yes	Yes	Yes	Yes
2. The display is in the interest of:							
Health awareness	Yes	Yes	Yes	Yes	Yes	Yes	Yes
Family Welfare	—	—	Yes	Yes	Yes	Yes	Yes
National Book Week	Yes	Yes	Yes	Yes	Yes	Yes	Yes
Book Exhibitions	Yes	Yes	Yes	Yes	Yes	Yes	Yes
3. Whether the news papers are preserved?	Yes	Yes	Yes	No	Yes	Yes	Yes
4. Period for how long the news papers preserved (in years)	10	3	44 (Since 1960)	NA	3	1	5

NA: Not Applicable.

All the RPLs except the one at Tirupati and the SCL have reported that they are preserving the newspapers. RPL-Visəkhapatnam is preserving Newspapers for the past 10 years while the RPLs at Rajahmundry and Warangal are preserving newspapers for 3 years and the RPL - Nizamabad is preserving newspapers for one year. However, in RPL - Guntur newspapers from 1960 are preserved. The SCL has reported that they are preserving newspapers for five years.

Extent of Library Automation

Information regarding the extent of library automation as reported by the RPLs and the SCL is shown in Table - 4.18 and diagrammatically presented in Fig. 6.

Table 4.18. Extent of Library Automation.

		RPL Visakha-patnam	*RPL Raja-mundry*	*RPL Guntur*	*RPL Tirupati*	*RPL Waran-gal*	*RPL Nizam-abad*	*SCL Hydera-bad*
1.	Extent of Library Automation	No	Partial	Partial	No	Partial	No	No
2.	In case of partial automation, sections automated	NA	Technical and reference sections	Text Book Section, for readers (internet)	NA	Reader service (Internet)	NA	NA

NA: Not Applicable.

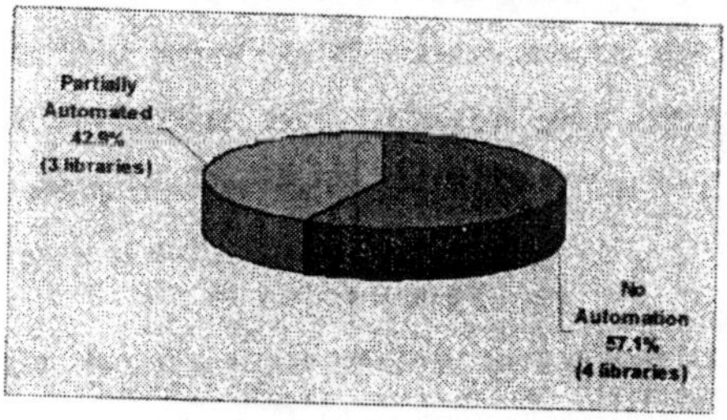

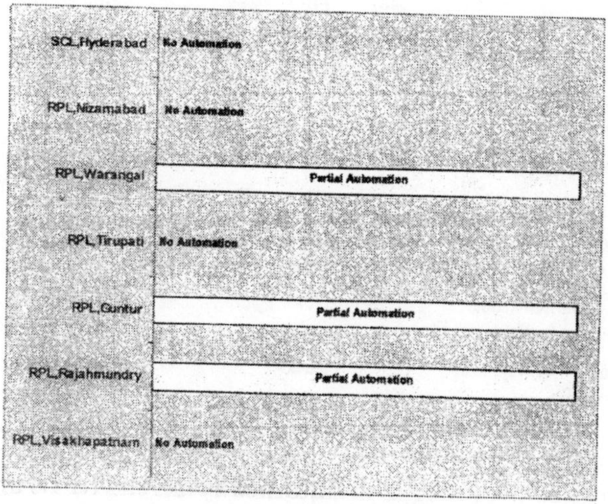

Fig. 6. Extent of Library Automation.

The observations in this regard are not encouraging as three out of the six RPLs (Visakhapatnam, Tirupati and Nizamabad) and also the SCL, were not so far automated. The remaining three RPLs are partially automated. Technical and Reference sections were only automated in RPL - Rajahmundry, Text book section and Internet (for reader) in RPL at Guntur and only readers service (internet) are automated in RPL at Warangal. This shows the need for automation in the public libraries which is very essential in these days of technological revolution.

Maintenance of Registers and frequency of stock verification

Details about maintenance of accession registers, staff list cards, frequency of stock verification, number of books found to be lost during stock verification and the personnel held responsible for such loss are presented in Table-4.19.

Table 4.19. Maintenance of Registers and Frequency of Stock Verification.

	RPL Visakha-patnam	*RPL Raja-mundry*	*RPL Guntur*	*RPL Tirupati*	*RPL Waran-gal*	*RPL Nizam-abad*	*SCL Hydera-bad*
(*a*) Maintenance of:							
Accession Register	Yes	Yes	Yes	Yes	Yes	Yes	Yes
Staff list cards	No	No	No	No	No	No	Yes
(*b*) Frequency of stock verification	Perio-dical	Perio-dical	Perio-dical	Perio-dical	Perio-dical	Perio-dical	Perio-dical
(*c*) No. of books lost (found in stock verification)	724	732	4,500	—	2,603	613	—
(*d*) Personnel held responsile for lost books	stack in-charges	stack in-charges	—	—	—	Recovery from the Librarian	—

Accession register is maintained by all the RPLs and the SCL while maintenance of staff list cards is reported by RPL - Guntur and the SCL.

All these libraries have stated that the stock verification is carried out only periodically but not on annual basis. About 4,500 books are found to be lost during stock verification in RPL - Guntur. Such loss is 2,603 in RPL - Warangal; 732 in RPL - Rajahmundry; 724 in RPL - Visakhapatnam and 613 in RPL - Nizamabad. No such loss is reported by RPL - Tirupati and the SCL. Stock incharges are the personnel held responsible for such loss in RPL - Visakhapatnamand, RPL- Rajahmundry where as RPL - Nizamabad informed that a recovery from the librarian is made towards the loss. This indicates that there is no specific rule or directive in this regard.

Access, classification and cataloguing

Information on the type of access system, classification and cataloguing procedures followed in the seven public libraries of the state is presented in Table - 4.20. All the RPLs and the SCL have reported that they are following the open access system and the RPL - Rajahmundry mentioned that access is closed for reference section in their library. All these seven libraries have also mentioned that the library collection is classified and they are following the DDC scheme for the purpose of classification.

A catalogue is reported to be maintained in all the six RPLs and the SCL. Regarding the type of catalogue used, there is some variation between these libraries. In the three RPLs - Visakhapatnam, Guntur and Warangal the catalogues is based on Author/Title/subject. In two RPLs - Tirupati and Nizamabad only the author catalogue is used while RPL - Rajahmundry, only subject catalogue is used. On the other hand, the SCL is following author/title catalogue. In all these seven libraries, the catalogue is maintained in card form. The entry arrangement in the catalogue is reported to be in classified order in RPLs - Visakhapatnam and Rajahmundry while the entries are made in dictionary order in RPLs - Guntur, Tirupati and

Warangal. The SCL is also following classified order for making entries in the catalogue. None of these seven libraries have reported the availability of any central catalogue facility.

Table 4.20. Classification and Cataloguing

	RPL Visakha-patnam	*RPL Raja-mundry*	*RPL Guntur*	*RPL Tirupati*	*RPL Waran-gal*	*RPL Nizam-abad*	*SCL Hydera-bad*
(*a*) Type of access system	Open	Open (Closed for reference section)	Open	Open	Open	Open	Open
(*b*) Classification:							
Whether all books classified	Yes	Yes	Yes	Yes	Yes	Yes	Yes
Scheme of classification	DDC	DDC	DDC	DDC	DDC	DDC	DDC
(*c*) Cataloguing:							
Whether cataloguing maintained	Yes	Yes	Yes	Yes	Yes	Yes	Yes
Types of catalogue	Author/ Title/ Subject	Subject	Author/ Title/ Subject	Author	Author/ Title/ Subject	Author	Author/ Title
Form of catalogue	Card	Card	Card	Card	Card	Card	Card
Entry arrangement in catalogue	Classi-fied Order	Classi-fied Order	Dictio-nary Order	Dictio-nary Order	Dictio-onary Order	Dictio-nary Order	Class-fied Order
(*d*) Is there any central catalogue facility	No	No	No	No	No	No	No

The scheme of classification and type of cataloguing followed in these seven libraries are diagrammatically shown in Fig. 7.

Membership

Details of membership as on 1-4-2003 and the average number of visitors and other transactions per day are presented in Table - 4.21.

Fig. 7. Scheme of Classification & Type of Cataloguing followed in the RPLs.

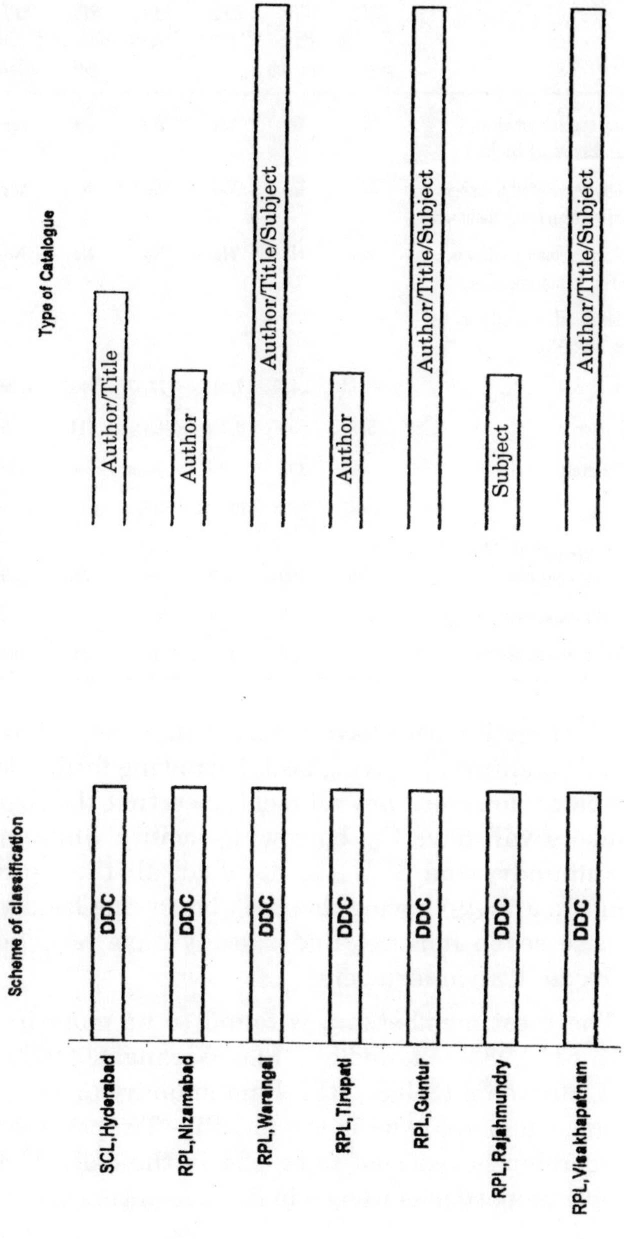

Table 4.21. Membership Particulars.

	RPL Visakha-patnam	*RPL Raja-mundry*	*RPL Guntur*	*RPL Tirupati*	*RPL Waran-gal*	*RPL Nizam-abad*	*SCL Hydera-bad*
(*a*) Any special conditions for borrowing books:	Yes	Yes	Yes	Yes	Yes	Yes	Yes
Only registered members	Yes	Yes	Yes	Yes	Yes	Yes	Yes
Only Permanent members	—	—	—	—	—	—	—
(*b*) Whether loan facility is given to non-members	No	No	No	No	No	No	No
(*c*) Membership details as on 1-4-2003							
Men	2,973	2,470	7,345	127	3,463	1,250	328
Women	515	530	3,208	28	514	350	137
Children	—	133	430	—	—	135	59
Total	3,488	3,133	19,983	155	3,977	1,735	524
(*d*) Average number of: Visitors per day	189	190	810	290	356	185	900
Books consulted per day	137	158	715	350	74	102	3,300
Books issued per day	117	160	124	40	24	45	90

All these libraries have reported that they follow some special conditions in giving book-borrowing facility to their members. However, they all mentioned that the registered members will have the borrowing facility while in RPL-Rajahmundry and SCL - Hyderabad, all the permanent members are also having this book borrowing facility. None of these seven libraries under study have reported loan facility to the non-members.

The total membership is found to be more in RPL - Guntur (10,983) followed by RPL - Warangal (3,977), RPL - Visakhapatnam (3,488), RPL-Rajahmundry (3,133), RPL - Nizamabad (1.735) and is low in RPL - Tirupati (155). The membership is reported to be 524 in the SCL. There are sizeable proportion of women in these members and children are also members in three RPLs at Rajahmundry, Guntur and Nizamabad and also the SCL.

The membership share of these seven libraries in the total membership is schematically presented in Fig. 8.

The average number of visitors per day is reported to be more (810) in the RPL at Guntur followed by 356 in RPL - Warangal, 290 in RPL - Tirupti, 190 in RPL - Rajahmundry, 189 in RPL - Visakhapatnam and 185 in RPL - Nizamabad. This average is 900 in the SCL. The average number of books consulted in a day ranged from 715 in Guntur to 74 in Warangal and this figure is 3,300 for the SCL. Regarding the average number of books issued per day, it is reported that as high as 160 books are issued per day on an average in RPL - Rajahmundry while this average is only 24 in the RPL - Warangal. In the SCL, the average number of books issued per day is reported to be 90.

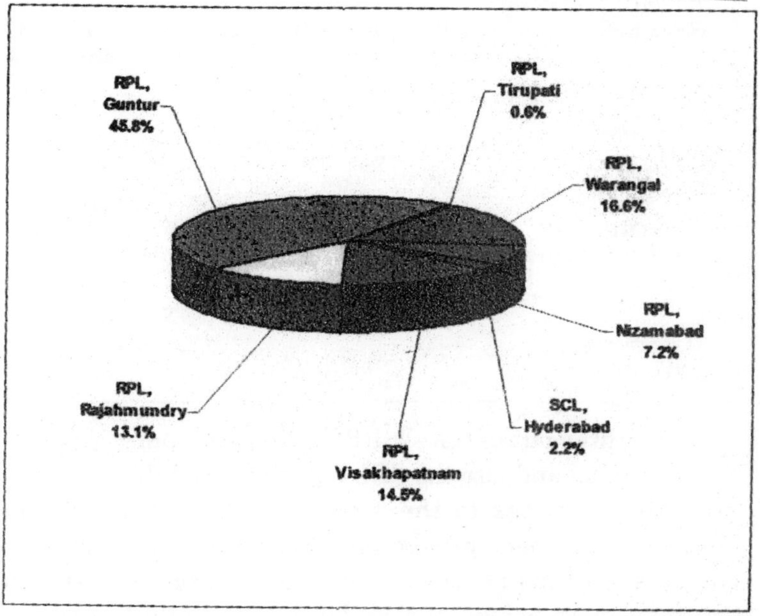

Fig. 8. Membership share of RPLs in Andhra Pradesh.

Book - borrowing Procedures

Information relating to the aspects of book borrowing are shown in Table - 4.22.

Table 4.22. Book Borrowing Procedures.

	RPL Visakha-patnam	*RPL Raja-mundry*	*RPL Guntur*	*RPL Tirupati*	*RPL Waran-gal*	*RPL Nizam-abad*	*SCL Hydera-bad*
(*a*) Whether providing services to non-resident borrowers:	No	Yes	No	Yes	Yes	No	Yes
Adults	—	Yes	—	Yes	Yes	—	Yes
Students	—	Yes	—	Yes	Yes	—	Yes
Children	—	—	—	—	—	—	Yes
(*b*) Whether lending material other than print material	No	No	No	No	No	No	No
(*c*) Lending period for:							
General books	14 days	14 days	14 days	15 days	15 days	14 days	15 days
Periodicals	—	—	—	—	—	—	—
Reference books	—	—	—	—	—	—	—
(*d*) Whether collecting any charges for late return	Yes	Yes	Yes	Yes	Yes	Yes	Yes
(*e*) Whether support user charges for the services	Yes Rs. 100/- p.a.	No	No	No	Yes Rs. 100/-	No	No
(*f*) Any other procedures for using/borrowing books	No	No	No	No	No	No	No

Only three out of the six RPLs - Rajanmundry, Tirupati and Warangal and also the SCL have informed that they are providing services to the non-resident borrowers who include adults (persons who have completed their studies), students (persons in school or college i.e. from 9th class to Graduation or above) and children (any child below 9th grade in school).

Reading material other than print material is not lent in any of these seven public libraries. In general, the general books are given for a period of two weeks and periodicals and reference books are not lent in any of these libraries. All these seven libraries have informed that they levy some over due charges for delay in returning the books borrowed. The charges are in a way very nominal as it is 0.5 paise per day and is uniformly followed in all these libraries.

When asked whether they support the idea of collecting some subscriptions from the users for using the library services, only two RPLs-Visakhapatnam and Warangal have responded positively and these two have suggested that an amount of Rs.100/- per annum can be fixed as user charges. The remaining four RPLs and the SCL have not supported this idea of user charges.

These public libraries have not reported any other procedures for using the library services or borrowing books.

Library Committee

Information relating to the existence of a library committee and other committees constituted and views of the librarians regarding the functioning of the library committee is shown in Table - 4.23.

Table 4.23. Library Committee

	RPL Visakha-patnam	*RPL Raja-mundry*	*RPL Guntur*	*RPL Tirupati*	*RPL Waran-gal*	*RPL Nizam-abad*	*SCL Hydera-bad*
(*a*) Whether there is a Library Committee?	Yes	Yes	No	No	Yes	No	Yes
(*b*) Other Committees:							
Book Selection Committee	Yes	Yes	Yes	Yes	Yes	Yes	Yes
Library Development Committee	Yes	Yes	—	—	Yes	—	Yes
Readers forum	Yes	Yes	—	—	—	—	—

Section	*RPL Visakha-patnam*	*RPL Raja-mundry*	*RPL Guntur*	*RPL Tirupati*	*RPL Waran-gal*	*RPL Nizam-abad*	*SCL Hydera-bad*
(*c*) Opinion on Library Committee:							
LC is helpful in smooth running of library activities	Yes	Yes	NA	NA	No	No	Yes
LC is extending all possible co-operation	Yes	Yes	NA	NA	No	No	Yes
Necessary to have a LC for looking after the affairs of the Library	Yes	Yes	NA	NA	No	Yes	Yes

NA: Not Applicable

Only three RPLs at Visakhapatnam, Rajahmundry and Warangal and the SCL at Hyderabad have reported that they have a library committee. In the SCL, the library committee is constituted by the state government under the provisions of A.P. Public Libraries Act 1980. This committee comprises of 12 members generally.

Other committees like book selection committee, library development committee, weeding out of books committee, and readers form are constituted at the local level involving the relevant persons from different fields. All the seven libraries have reported that they are having a book selection committee comprising of 5 - 7 members. The RPLs at Visakhapatnam, Rajahmundry and Warangal and also the SCL have reported the existence of a library development committee comprising of 9 - 12 members. The two RPLs at Visakhapatnam and Rajahmundry have mentioned that they have readers forum consisting of 5 - 8 members nominated by the librarian. The existence of a committee for weeding out books is mentioned by the SCL at Hyderabad.

The two Librarians of RPLs - Visakhapatnam and Rajahmundry and also the Librarian of the SCL expressed that the library committee is very helpful in smooth running of the different activities of the library and also felt that the library committee is extending all possible co-operation. To another question, Librarians of the RPLs at Visakhapatnam, Rajahmundry, Nizamabad and also the Librarian of the SCL have reported that it is necessary to have a committee for looking after the affairs of the library.

Inter - Library Loan facility

Details of the nearest library and inter - library loan facility available with the seven libraries covered are presented in Table - 4.24.

Table 4.24. Inter-Library Loan Facility.

	RPL Visakha-patnam	*RPL Raja-mundry*	*RPL Guntur*	*RPL Tirupati*	*RPL Waran-gal*	*RPL Nizam-abad*	*SCL Hydera-bad*
(*a*) Distance to the nearest public or aided library	1 km	4 km	3 km	1 km	4 km	4 km	13 km
(*b*) Whether borrow books from other libraries?	No	Yes	No	No	Yes	No	Yes
(*c*) With how many libraries having inter-library loan facility?	NA	4	NA	NA	State wide	NA	2

NA: Not Applicable

It can be seen that the nearest public or aided library is located at a distance of 1 km from the RPLs at Visakhapatnam and Tirupati, while at a distance of 4 kms from RPLs at Rajahmundry, Warangal and Nizamabad and at kms for RPL at Guntur. In the case of the SCL at Hyderabad, the nearest public or aided library is located at a distance of 13 kms.

When asked to mention whether they borrow books from other libraries, only two RPLs at Rajahmundry and Warangal and also the SCL responded in affirmative.

Regarding the number of libraries with which they are having inter-library loan facility, the RPL-Rajahmundry is reported to have inter-library loan facility with four libraries while the RPL at Warangal reported that they are having this facility with libraries all over the state. However, the SCL has mentioned that they are having inter-library loan facility with only two other libraries.

Proposals for extending co-operation among the RPLs

All the Librarians of the seven public libraries were asked to mention whether they are having any proposals for extending co-operation among the RPLs, whether they are contributing to the National Bibliography and whether they are developing a union catalogue and whether they are thinking of having some deposit centers. Their responses are shown in Table - 4.25.

Table 4.25. Proposals for Extending Co-operation among Other RPLs.

	RPL Visakha-patnam	*RPL Raja-mundry*	*RPL Guntur*	*RPL Tirupati*	*RPL Waran-gal*	*RPL Nizam-abad*	*SCL Hydera-bad*
(*a*) Whether having proposal for establishing co-operation among the RPLs.	No	No	No	Yes (at state (level)	Yes (at state level)	No	Yes (at state level)
(*b*) Whether contributing to the National Bibliography?	No	No	No	No	No	No	No
(*c*) Whether developing union Catalogue?	No	No	No	No	No	No	Yes * @
(*d*) Whether thinking of having deposit centers and having co-operation with social organizationsand educational institutions?	No	No	No	No	No	No	Yes

* of telugu books. @ of rare/scarce books.

It is reported that only two RPLs - Tirupati and Warangal and also the SCL at Hyderabad are having some proposals for establishing co-operation among all the Regional Public Libraries at the state level. None of these seven public libraries are contributing to the national bibliography. Regarding the development of a union catalogue, only the SCL reported that they are developing a union catalogue for Telugu books and also of books which are rarely/scarcely available. In the same way, only the SCL has reported that they are thinking of having deposit centers and having co-operation with social organizations and educational institutions.

Material available for Extension and other Activities

Details of the material available useful for the extension and other activities as reported by the seven public libraries covered in the present study are shown in Table - 4.26.

Table 4.26. Availability of Material for Extension and Other Activities.

	RPL Visakha-patnam	*RPL Raja-mundry*	*RPL Guntur*	*RPL Tirupati*	*RPL Waran-gal*	*RPL Nizam-abad*	*SCL Hydera-bad*
1. Audio-visual materials	No	Yes	No	Yes	Yes	Yes	No
2. Radio	Yes	No	No	Yes	Yes	Yes	No
3. Television	Yes	Yes	Yes	Yes	Yes	Yes	Yes
4. Tape Recorder	Yes	No	No	No	No	Yes	No
5. Film Projector	No	Yes	No	Yes	Yes	No	Yes
6. Films	No	No	No	Yes	Yes	No	Yes
7. Computers	Yes	Yes	Yes	Yes	Yes	Yes	Yes
8. Internet	No	No	No	No	Yes	No	Yes
9. VCD	No	No	No	No	Yes	No	No
10. Record Player/Records	No	No	No	No	Yes	No	No
11. Xerox	No	No	No	No	Yes	No	No
12. Scanners	No	No	No	No	No	No	Yes

It can be seen that computers and television are available with all the RPLs and the SCL. Availability of a radio is reported by RPLs at Visakhapatnam, Tirupati, Warangal and Nizamabad. Tape recorder is available with RPLs at Visakhapatnam and Nizamabad only. Film projector and films are reported by only two RPLs - Tirupati and Warangal and also the SCL. Internet, VCD, record player and records, Photostat or Xerox are reported by RPL - Warangal. Internet is also available at the SCL and also the SCL is having scanners. Availability of audio-visual material is reported by only four RPLs at Rajahmundry, Tirupati, Warangal and Nizamabad.

Publicity, Extension and Other Activities

Information relating to the different publicity, extension and other activities taken-up by these public libraries and also the number of activities conducted during the pat four years is presented in Table - 4.27.

Table 4.27. Publicity, Extension and Other Activities.

	RPL Visakha-patnam	*RPL Raja-mundry*	*RPL Guntur*	*RPL Tirupati*	*RPL Waran-gal*	*RPL Nizam-abad*	*SCL Hydera-bad*
(*a*) Whether celebrate National Library Week?	Yes	Yes	Yes	Yes	Yes	Yes	Yes
(*b*) Whether organize the following:							
Book exhibition	Yes	Yes	Yes	Yes	Yes	Yes	Yes
Popular lectures	Yes	Yes	Yes	Yes	Yes	Yes	Yes
Public meetings	Yes	Yes	Yes	Yes	Yes	No	Yes
Felicitation to renowned persons	Yes	Yes	Yes	Yes	No	No	Yes
Sports during festivals	No	Yes	Yes	Yes	No	No	Yes
Special activities for women	Yes	Yes	No	Yes	Yes	Yes	Yes
(*c*) Having any mobile library service unit?	No	No	No	No	No	No	No
(*d*) Number of activities conducted during:							
1999-2000	5	9	30	20	22	4	8
2000-2001	7	10	34	22	22	4	10
2001-2002	13	15	38	24	37	4	14
2002-2003	12	17	42	25	55	6	16
(*e*) Average number of activities organised per year?	12	40	48	20	55	18	22

It can be noticed that all these seven public libraries are celebrating the National Library week. All these libraries are organizing activities such as organizing book exhibitions, arranging popular lecturers and public meetings, felicitations to renowned persons, conducting sports during festivals and festive occasions and organizing some special activities for women. The SCL at Hyderabad has reported all these activities while conducting sports is not reported from RPLs at Visakhapatnam, Warangal and Nizamabad. In the same way, felicitation to renowned persons is not reported by RPLs at Warangal and Nizamabad and the RPL-Nizamabad has not reported any public meetings. The RPL at Guntur has not reported conducting any special activities for women.

None of these seven libraries have reported the availability of a mobile library service unit. The average number of activities organised by these libraries ranged from a low of 12 in RPL-Visakhapatnam to a high of 55 in RPL - Warangal and this average is 12 in the case of the SCL When the number of activities conducted during the past four years is observed, it can be seen that there is a steady increase in the number of activities from 1999-2000 to 2002-2003 which is welcome trend considering the objectives of the public libraries.

Community Information Services

(i) Community Information for Women: Information on whether these libraries are providing any community information services for women and if so on what aspects is shown in Table - 4.28.

It is interesting to note here that with some degree of variation in the aspects covered, all the seven public libraries are providing community information services to the women. The information is provided mainly on aspects such as family planning, women's health, child health, women's programmes, employment opportunities for women, adult education and distance education. Only few are covering other aspects like pulse polio, nutrition programmes, DWACRA, savings schemes and solar energy.

Table 4.28. Community Information for Women.

	RPL Visakha-patnam	*RPL Raja-mundry*	*RPL Guntur*	*RPL Tirupati*	*RPL Waran-gal*	*RPL Nizam-abad*	*SCL Hydera-bad*
(*a*) Whether providing community information to women?	Yes	Yes	Yes	Yes	Yes	Yes	Yes
(*b*) If yes, whether providng information on:							
Family planning	Yes	Yes	Yes	Yes	Yes	No	Yes
Women health	Yes	Yes	No	Yes	No	No	Yes
Child care	No	Yes	No	Yes	Yes	No	Yes
Pulse polio	Yes	No	No	Yes	No	Yes	Yes
Nutrition programmes	No	No	Yes	No	Yes	Yes	Yes
Women programmes	Yes	Yes	No	Yes	Yes	Yes	Yes
DWACRA	Yes	No	No	No	No	No	No
Employment opportunities	No	Yes	Yes	Yes	Yes	No	Yes
Adult education	Yes	Yes	Yes	Yes	Yes	No	Yes
Distance education	No	Yes	Yes	Yes	Yes	No	Yes
Savings schemes	No	No	No	Yes	No	No	No
Solar energy	No	No	No	No	No	No	No

(ii) Community Information on Agriculture: Information relating to the provision of community information on agriculture is presented in Table - 4.29.

Four out of the six RPLs at Rajahmundry, Guntur, Tirupati and Warangal and also the SCL at Hyderabad are providing community I information on agriculture. The aspects on which information is provided are mainly, agriculture, annadatha literature, farm literature, acqua culture, agro-products and prawn culture in that order.

Table 4.29. Community Information on Agriculture.

	RPL Visakha-patnam	*RPL Raja-mundry*	*RPL Guntur*	*RPL Tirupati*	*RPL Waran-gal*	*RPL Nizam-abad*	*SCL Hydera-bad*
(*a*) Whether providing information on agriculture?	No	Yes	Yes	Yes	Yes	No	Yes
(*b*) If yes, whether information provided on:							
Agriculture	—	Yes	Yes	Yes	Yes	—	Yes
Acqa culture	—	Yes	Yes	No	Yes	—	No
Prawn culture	—	Yes	Yes	No	No	—	No
Agro products	—	Yes	Yes	Yes	No	—	No
Farm literature	—	Yes	Yes	No	Yes	—	Yes
Farm technology	—	Yes	Yes	No	Yes	—	No
Annadatha liteature	—	Yes	Yes	Yes	Yes	—	Yes

(*iii*) Community Information on Medico-Legal aspects: Responses from the seven libraries regarding provision of community information on Medico-legal aspects and on which aspects information is provided are presented in Table - 4.30.

Table 4.30. Community Information on Medical and Legal Aspects.

	RPL Visakha-patnam	*RPL Raja-mundry*	*RPL Guntur*	*RPL Tirupati*	*RPL Waran-gal*	*RPL Nizam-abad*	*SCL Hydera-bad*
(*a*) Whether providing medical information?	No	Yes	Yes	Yes	Yes	Yes	No
If yes, on following aspects:							
Information about the Govt. and Private hospitals, Nursing homes and clinics	—	Yes	Yes	Yes	Yes	Yes	—
Information about the specialist doctors/surgeons	—	Yes	Yes	Yes	Yes	No	—
Information about the diagnostic labs, scanning centers, etc.	—	Yes	No	No	Yes	No	—

	RPL Visakha-patnam	RPL Raja-mundry	RPL Guntur	RPL Tirupati	RPL Waran-gal	RPL Nizam-abad	SCL Hydera-bad
(*b*) Whether providing legal information?	No	Yes	No	No	Yes	Yes	No
If yes, on following aspects:							
Information about the legal aid clinics (for the poor)	—	Yes	—	—	Yes	Yes	—
Information about consumer protection claims through consumer courts	—	Yes	—	—	Yes	No	—

Only five RPLs, excepting the RPL-Visakhapatnam and the SCL-Hyderabad have reported that they are providing community information on medical aspects.

Regarding the medical aspects, all the five RPLs mentioned that they are providing information about the government and private hospitals, nursing homes and clinics. While information about specialist Doctors and Surgeons is being provided by four of these five RPLs and only 2 are providing information about the diagnostic labs, scanning centers etc.

However, only three RPLs at Rajahmundry, Warangal and Nizamabad have reported that they are providing information on legal aspects. All these three RPLs are providing information mainly about the legal aid clinics useful for the poor and with the exception of RPL-Nizamabad, the remaining two are also providing information about consumer protection claims through consumer courts.

(iv) Form in which the Community Information is available: Information relating to the form in which the community information is available in these seven libraries is shown in Table - 4.31.

Table 4.31. Form in which the Community Information is Available.

Section	RPL Visakhapatnam	RPL Rajamundry	RPL Guntur	RPL Tirupati	RPL Warangal	RPL Nizamabad	SCL Hyderabad
1. Books	No	Yes	Yes	No	Yes	Yes	No
2. Booklets	No	Yes	No	No	Yes	Yes	Yes
3. Pamphlets	No	Yes	No	No	Yes	No	No
4. Govt. Publications	No	Yes	Yes	No	Yes	No	Yes
5. Govt. slogan posters	No	No	No	No	Yes	No	No
6. Pictorial posters	No	Yes	No	No	Yes	No	No
7. Through meetings	No	Yes	Yes	No	No	No	No
8. Govt. official programmes	No	Yes	Yes	No	Yes	No	Yes
9. Program sheets or posters	No	Yes	Yes	No	Yes	No	No
10. Hand bills	No	No	No	No	Yes	No	No

It can be noticed that the community information is available mainly in the form of books, booklets and pamphlets. Also through slogan posters and pictorial posters through government publication. This information is also reported to be disseminated through meetings and official government programmes.

Comparative picture of the status of the Regional Public Libraries in Andhra Pradesh

An attempt is made here to bring out a comparative picture regarding the status of these seven libraries considering some selected aspects like status of the building, sections of the library, staff position, library collection, collection by languages, registered borrowers, circulation and Audio-Visual equipment available. The details are shown in Table 4.31a and the presentation is self explanatory.

SECTION-II: User's Perception of the Functioning of the Public Libraries

User's perceptions of the functioning of the public libraries is discussed in this section. In all 1124 users or

Table 4.31a. Comparative Statement Showing the Status of the Regional Public Libraries in Andhra Pradesh.

Name of the Library	Sections	Status of the Building	Language Books available	Staff position		Book collection	Registered Borrowers	Circulation	A.V. Components
1. Government Regional Library, Visakhapatnam.	Periodical Section Reference Section Text Book Section Circulation Section	Rented Building 347.49 Sq. Meters	5 language books are available Telugu, English, Hindi, Urdu and Sanskrit	Sanctioned Retired In service	9 2 — 7	Books = 50,000 Periodicals = 53 Dailies = 12 Weeklies = 14 Fortnightlies = 5 Monthlies = 34	3,488 3,384 — 104	Books issued 117 Books consulted 137 per day.	Computer Radio, T.V., Tape recorder
2. Government Regional Library, Rajahmundry.	Text Book Section Reference Section Circulation Section Periodicals Section Technical Section Rare Book Collection Section	Own Building 3,100 sq. yards.	6 language books are available Telugu, English, Hindi, Urudu, Sanskrit and Tamil.	Sanctioned Retired In service	19 8 — 11 — —	Books = 70,375 Periodicals = 97 Dailies = 20 Weeklies = 26 Monthlies = 71	3,133 2,952 — 181	Books issued 160 per day Books consulted 158 per day	Radio, T.V., Tape recorder, computer.
3. Government Regional Library Guntur	Periodicals Section Text Book Section Reference Section Circulation Section Technical Section	Own Building 54,587 Sq. yards	5 language books are available Telugu, English, Hindi and Sanskrit.	Sanctioned Retired In service	31 11 — 20	Books = 1,27,672 Periodicals = 93 Dailies = 13 Weeklies = 15 Monthlies = 65 Quarterlies = 6 Annuals = 7	10,183 9,875 — 308 —	Books lent 9,875 Books consulted 2,61,050 per year	T.V., Radio, VCD OverHead Projector.

Name of the Library	Sections	Status of the Building	Language Books available	Staff position		Book collection	Registered Borrowers	Circulation	A.V. Components
4. Government Regional Library, Tirupati.	Reference Section Text Book Section Periodical Section Circulation Section	Rented Building 2,250 Sq. yards	4 language books are available Telugu, English, Hindi and Sanskrit.	Sanctioned Retired In service	14 6 8	Books = 55,793 Periodicals = 58 Dailies = 14 Weeklies = 15 Monthlies = 42 Annals = 1	4,609 3,590 — 1,019 =	Books issued = 40 Books consulted = 350 per day	Computer Radoio, T.V., Tape recorder
5. Government Regional Library, Warangal.	Reference Section Circulation Section Text Book Section Periodical Section	Own Building 1,516.28 Sq. yards	5 language books are available Telugu, English, Hindi, Urudu and Sanskrit.	Sanctioned Retired In service	13 6 7	Books = 52,919 Periodicals = 108 Dailies = 13 Weeklies = 28 Monthlies = 80	3,977 3,419 — 558 =	Books issued = 24 Books consulted = 74 per day	T.V., Radio, VCD, Xerox, Tape recorder, Projector.
6. Government Regional Library, Nizamabad.	Circulation section Periodical Section Reference Section Text Book Section	Own Building 1,404 Sq. Meters.	4 language books are available Urudu, Hindi, English and Telugu	Sanctioned Retired In service	6 2 — 4 =	Books = 48,835 Periodicals = 14 Dailies = 9 Weeklies = 10 Fortnightlies = 4	1,735 1,636 — 97 =	Issues demand = 45 per day Books consulted = 102 per day	Computer, Radio, T.V., Tape recorder, projector.

Name of the Library	Sections	Status of the Building	Language Books available	Staff position	Book collection	Registered Borrowers	Circulation	A.V. Components
7. State Central Library, Hyderabad	16 Sections, Technical Section Circulation Section Reference Section Periodic Section Children Section Text Book Section English Section Telugu Section Urdu Section Hindi, Marathi and Kannada Section Arabic and Persian Section Rare Book Section Binding Section Reprographic Section Social Education Wing Administrative Office	Own Building 1,52,492 Sq. ft.	9 language books available Telugu, Urudu, Hindu, Marati, Kannada, Arabi, Persian, Tamil and English	Sanctioned = 133 Retired = 41 — In service = 92 =	Books = 6,86,311 Periodicals = 304 Dailies = 29 Weeklies = 65 Fortnightlies = 30 Monthlies = 180	22,555 22,031 — 524 =	Books lent = 90 per day Books consulted = 3,300	T.V., Projector, Tape Recorder, Computer, Internet (computers) Scanners

readers were covered from the six Regional Public Libraries (RPL) and the State Central Library (SCL). The satisfaction of the users, in other words, to what extent these public libraries are able to meet the needs of their clients is of importance. In fact, the goals or objectives of this type of libraries are set to meet the information needs of the users. Unlike in academic libraries, the users group in this context is a heterogeneous one with a variety of needs. There is diversity in age, sex as well as status of the users. Consequently, the needs also vary from entertainment to information seeking for specific purposes. Hence, the views of the readers are of utmost importance in understanding the functioning of the public libraries.

Details of coverage of users

As mentioned earlier a total of 1124 users from all the seven libraries covered in the present study. The details of coverage of these respondents were shown in Table - 4.32 and Fig. 9.

Table 4.32. Coverage of Respondents from Different Libraries.

	Name of the library	*Respondents*	
		Number	*Percentage*
1.	RPL, Visakhapatnam	157	14.0
2.	RPL, Rajahmundry	157	14.0
3.	RPL, Guntur	161	14.3
4.	RPL, Tirupati	161	14.3
5.	RPL, Warangal	159	14.1
6.	RPL, Nizamabad	156	13.9
7.	SCL, Hyderabad	173	15.4
	Total	1124	100.0

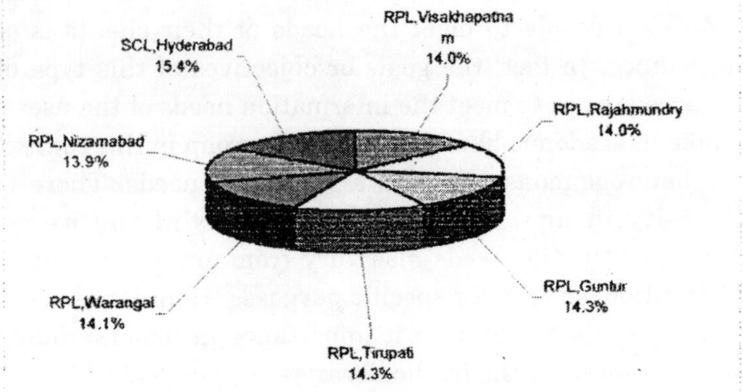

Fig. 9. Coverage of the Users from different libraries.

Composition of the users

Before making any observations from the responses, it is also important to know the composition of the respondent group by different background characters. Composition of the respondents covered in the present study by sex, age and status is shown in Table - 4.33 and Fig. 10.

Nearly 83 percent of the respondents are males and the remaining 17 percent are females. It is very interesting to note that about 60 percent of the users of these public libraries are in the age group of 31 - 34 years and 31 percent are aged below 31 years. Nearly 8 percent are in the age group of 35-64 years and the remaining one percent are aged 65 years or above.

Table 4.33. Composition of the Users Interviewed in the Study.

	Users covered	
	Number	*Percentage*
(*a*) Gender		
Male	930	82.7
Female	194	17.3
(*b*) Age group (in years)		
Below 31	348	31.0
31-34	679	60.4
35-64	86	7.7
65 and above	11	1.0
(*c*) Status		
Students	901	80.2
Employees	127	11.3
Retired Employees	40	3.6
Businessmen	56	5.0

Regarding the status of the respondents, it can be seen that a majority of the users (80 percent) are students. The remaining 20 percent consists of employees (11 percent), retired employees (4 percent) and businessmen (5 percent).

Duration of the use of the Regional Public Libraries

All the respondents interviewed were asked to mention for how long they have been coming to these libraries and their responses were presented library wise in Table - 4.34.

In total, about 34 percent of the users reported that they have been using the services of these libraries for 1 - 4 years while nearly 31 percent said that they were coming to these libraries only since few months. On the other hand, 13 percent were using these libraries for the last 5-10 years and only 9 percent were using them for more than 10 years. The

a) By Gender:

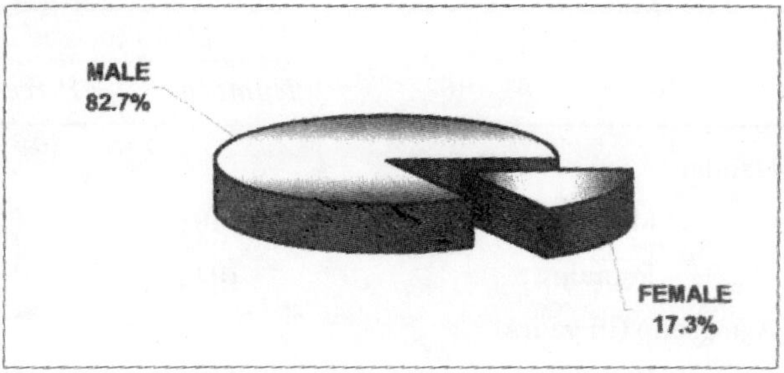

b) By Age group:

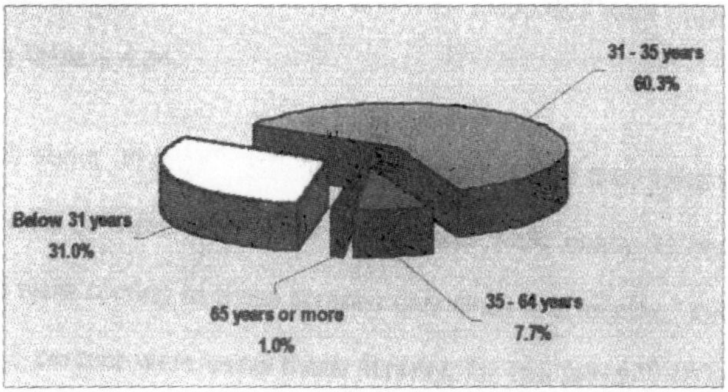

c) By Status group:

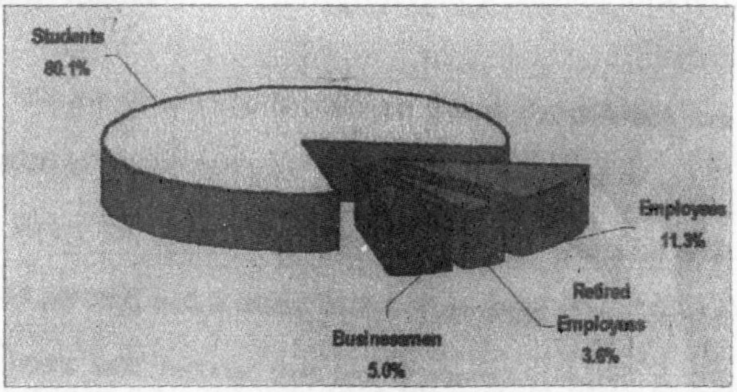

Fig. 10. Composition of the User Group.

Table 4.34. Duration of the Use of the Regional Public Library

Name of the Library	*Number*	*For how long have been coming to this library*									
		Over 10 years		*5-10 years*		*1-4 years*		*Few months*		*First Visit*	
		No.	*%*	*No.*	*%*	*No.*	*%*	*No.*	*%*	*No.*	*%*
1. RPL, Visakhapatnam	157	5	3.2	14	8.9	57	36.3	57	36.3	24	15.3
2. RPL, Rajahmundry	157	22	14.0	23	14.6	58	36.9	44	28.0	10	6.4
3. RPL, Guntur	161	20	12.4	20	12.4	55	34.2	57	35.4	9	5.6
4. RPL, Tirupati	161	8	5.0	17	10.6	38	23.6	56	34.8	42	26.1
5. RPL, Warangal	159	19	11.9	29	18.2	44	27.7	45	28.3	22	13.8
6. RPL, Nizamabad	156	3	1.9	23	14.7	63	40.4	38	24.4	29	18.6
7. SCL, Hyderabad	173	23	13.3	19	11.0	72	41.6	46	26.6	13	7.5
Total	1124	100	8.9	145	12.9	387	34.4	343	30.5	149	13.3

Chi-square value = 97.310 df = 24 Sig. 0.000

remaining 13 percent stated that it was their first visit to the public libraries.

More or less the same trend is observed among the different libraries with little variation in the percentages. The percentage of users who were coming to the library for more than 10 years is more in the case of RPL - Rajahmundry (14 percent) and is lowest in RPL - Nizamabad (2 percent). The percentage of users who reported their first visit to the library is more in RPL-Tirupati (26 percent) and low in RPLs - Rajahmundry and Guntur (6 percent each). However, most of the users are coming to the library for the last 1 - 10 years and this percentage is more in RPL - Nizamabad (55 percent) and low in RPL - Tirupati (34 percent). The percentage using the services of the library for less than 1 year is more in RPLs - Guntur and Tirupati (35 percent each) and is low in the SCL - Hyderabad (27 percent). In order to examine whether the proportion of users reporting different durations of use of these libraries differ significantly, the chi-square analysis is done and it is found that the proportions differ significantly among the seven public libraries.

Differentials in the duration of use of the library by sex, age and status of the users

Differentials in the duration of use of the public libraries by sex, age and status of the users along with the computed chi-square values is shown in Table - 4.35.

When the duration of the use of these libraries among the two sexes is considered, in both the sexes, the proportion reporting 1-4 years of use is more, followed by those reporting a few months of use, 5-10 years of use and more than 10 years of use. Those reporting first visit is more among the females (23 percent) compare to the males (11 percent). However, it is noticed that the proportion of males is more in all these duration categories compared to females with the exception of 1 - 4 years category.

Table 4.35. Differentials in the Use of Library by Sex, Age and Status of the Users.

	Number	*Duration of the use of the library*										Chi-square (df)	Significant
		Over 10 years		*5-10 years*		*1-4 years*		*Few months*		*First Visit*			
		No.	*%*	*No.*	*%*	*No.*	*%*	*No.*	*%*	*No.*	*%*		
Differentials by:													
(*a*) Sex:													
Male	930	92	9.9	129	13.9	313	33.7	292	31.4	104	11.2	29.726	
Female	194	8	4.1	16	8.2	74	38.1	51	26.3	45	23.2	df=4	0.000
(*b*) Age group (years):													
Upto 21	348	16	4.6	19	5.5	130	37.4	122	35.1	61	17.5		
21-34	679	48	7.1	104	15.3	234	34.5	209	30.8	84	12.4	160.630	
35-64	86	30	34.9	22	25.6	19	22.1	12	14.0	3	3.5	df=12	0.000
65+	11	6	54.5	—	—	4	36.4	—	—	1	9.1		
(*c*) Status:													
Students	901	45	5.0	89	9.9	322	35.7	308	34.2	137	15.2		
Employees	127	26	20.5	33	26.0	36	28.3	24	18.9	8	6.3	159.305	
Retired Employees	40	15	37.5	9	22.5	8	20.0	5	12.5	3	7.5	df=12	0.000
Businessmen	56	14	25.0	14	25.0	21	37.5	6	10.7	1	1.8		

Coming to the differentials in the duration of use of these libraries by age, it is noticed that more proportion of users aged 35 years or above are using the library for 5 years or more followed by those in the age group of 21-34 years and those who are aged 21 years or below. The proportion reporting 1-4 years of use is more in the 21 or below years age group (37 percent) followed by those who are aged 65 or above (36 percent), 21-34 years (35 percent) and 35-64 years (22 percent). The proportion reporting less than 1 year use is more in the younger age groups and obviously those reporting it as the first visit is also more among the younger age groups.

It is also noticed that the proportion visiting the libraries for more than 5 years is more among the retired employees (60 percent) followed by businessmen (50 percent), employees (47 percent) and students (15 percent). The proportion who are using the libraries for 1-4 years and less than 1 year is more among the students (70 percent) followed by businessmen (48 percent), employees (47 percent) and retired employees (33 percent). Those making a first visit are more among the students and retired employees compare to the other two groups.

The computed chi-square values indicate that there exist statistically significant differences in the duration of the use of the public libraries among the two sexes, between the four age and status groups considered in this study.

Frequency of using the Library

The frequency of use of the library by the readers is an important indicator because it indicates the information need on the part of the user and also indicates the usefulness of the library as source of information. Hence, all the users interviewed were asked to mention whether they frequently visit the library or not. Their responses are shown in Table 4.36 and Fig. 11.

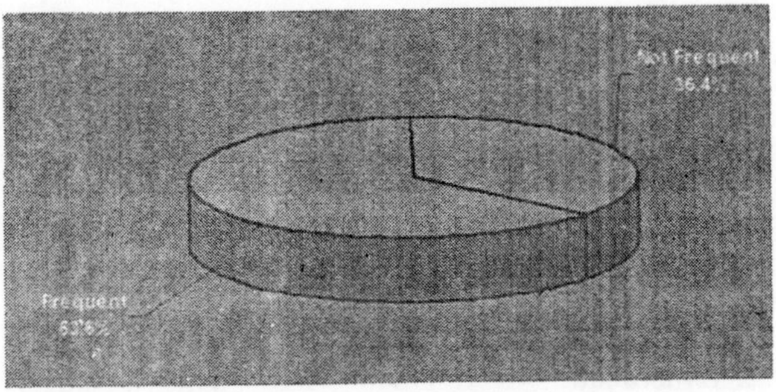

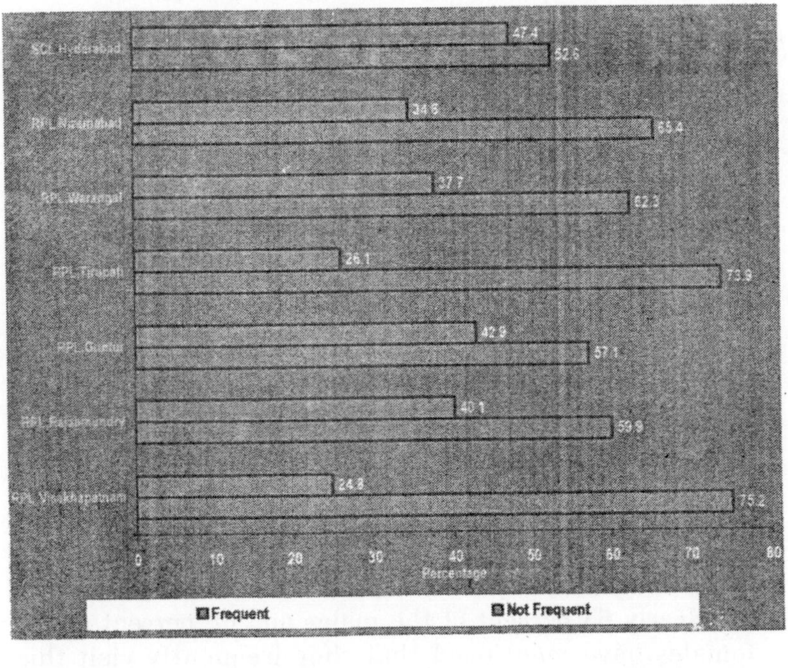

Fig. 11. Frequency of visit to the library by the Users.

Table 4.36. Frequency of Using the Library.

	Name of the Library	*Number*	*Frequency of use*			
			Frequent		*Non-frequent*	
			No.	*%*	*No.*	*%*
1.	RPL, Visakhapatnam	157	118	75.2	39	24.8
2.	RPL, Rajahmundry	157	94	59.9	63	40.1
3.	RPL, Guntur	161	92	57.1	69	42.9
4.	RPL, Tirupati	161	119	73.9	42	26.1
5.	RPL, Warangal	159	99	62.3	60	37.7
6.	RPL, Nizamabad	156	102	65.4	54	34.6
7.	SCL, Hyderabad	173	91	52.6	82	47.4
	Total	1124	715	63.6	409	36.4

Chi-square value = 29.682 df = 6 sig. 0.000

It is observed that nearly 64 percent of the users of these public libraries are frequent visitors while the remaining 36 percent are not. The proportion of users frequently visiting these libraries is found to more in RPL - Visakhapatnam (75 percent) followed by RPL-Tirupati (74 percent), RPL-Nizamabad (65 percent), RPL - Warangal (62 percent), RPL-Rajahmundry (60 percent), RPL - Guntur (57 percent)and this proportion is 53 percent in the SCL-Hyderabad. Differences in the proportion of frequent and non-frequent visitors are found to be statistically significant as indicated by the computed chi-square value.

Differentials in the frequency of using the library by sex, age and status of the users

Differentials by sex, age and status of users with regard to the frequency of visit to these libraries is shown in Table 4.37 along with the chi-square values.

Nearly 63 percent of the males and 68 percent of the females have mentioned that they frequently visit this library and the differences in these proportion are not statistically significant.

Table 4.37. Differentials in the Frequency of using the Library by Sex, Age and Status of the Users.

	Number	*Frequency of use*				*Chi-square (df)*	*Significant*
		Frequent		*Non-frequent*			
		No.	*%*	*No.*	*%*		
(*a*) Sex:							
Male	930	584	62.8	346	37.2	1.552	0.213
Female	14	131	67.5	63	32.5	df=1	
(*b*) Age group (years):							
Upto 21	348	219	62.9	129	37.1		
21-34	679	455	67.0	224	33.0	24.996	0.000
35-64	86	34	39.5	52	60.5	df=3	
65+	11	7	63.6	4	36.4		
(*c*) Status:							
Students	901	619	68.7	282	31.3		
Employees	127	57	44.9	70	55.1	55.423	0.000
Retired Employees	40	21	52.5	19	47.5	df=3	
Businessmen	56	18	32.1	38	67.9		

The proportion of frequent visitors is more in the 21-34 years age group (67 percent) followed by those who are aged 65 years and above (64 percent), who are aged 21 years or below (63 percent) and those in the age group of 35-64 years (40 percent). The relatively less percentage in the age group of 35-64 because it is the active working group who are engaged indifferent activities. Differences in the proportion of frequent visitors between the four age groups are found to be statistically significant.

In the same way, it is notice that the proportion of frequent visitors is among students (69 percent) followed by retired employees (53 percent), employees (45 percent) and businessmen (32 percent). This is more or less following the general exceptions and the chi-square value indicates significant differences in the proportion of the frequent and not-frequent visitors among the four groups of users interviewed in the present study.

Purpose of visit to the public libraries

It is also very essential to know on what purpose the visitors are coming to the public libraries. The responses of 1124 respondents to a question on this aspect are shown in Table - 4.38 and Fig. 12.

Three types of responses were mainly obtained with regard to the purpose of visit to the libraries. They are (i) for pleasure, (ii) on business and (iii) for some information. It is very heartening to note that 81 percent of the users are visiting the library to get some information. The proportion who are visiting to derive some pleasure is 12 percent and the remaining 7 percent have reported that their visit is related to some business.

Table 4.38. Purpose of Visit to the Regional Public Library

Name of the Library	*Number*	*Pupose of visit*					
		For pleasure		*On Business*		*For some information*	
		No.	*%*	*No.*	*%*	*No.*	*%*
1. RPL, Visakhapatnam	157	9	5.7	10	6.4	138	87.9
2. RPL, Rajahmundry	157	24	15.3	17	10.8	116	73.9
3. RPL, Guntur	161	19	11.8	7	4.3	135	83.9
4. RPL, Tirupati	161	11	6.8	5	3.1	145	90.1
5. RPL, Warangal	159	23	14.5	13	8.2	123	77.4
6. RPL, Nizamabad	156	19	12.2	16	10.3	121	77.6
7. SCL, Hyderabad	173	26	15.0	10	5.8	137	79.2
Total	1124	131	11.7	78	6.9	915	81.4

Chi-square value = 28.354 df = 12 sig. 0.005

The proportion of the users reporting that they are visiting these libraries for some information is more in RPL-Tirupati (90 percent) followed by RPL - Visakhapatnam (88 percent), RPL - Guntur (84 percent), RPL - Nizamabad (78

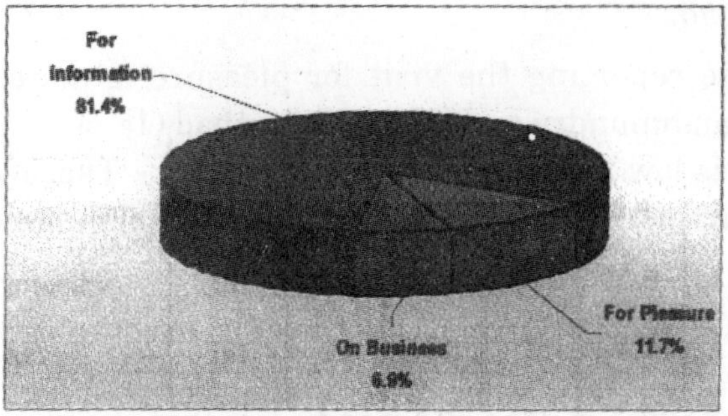

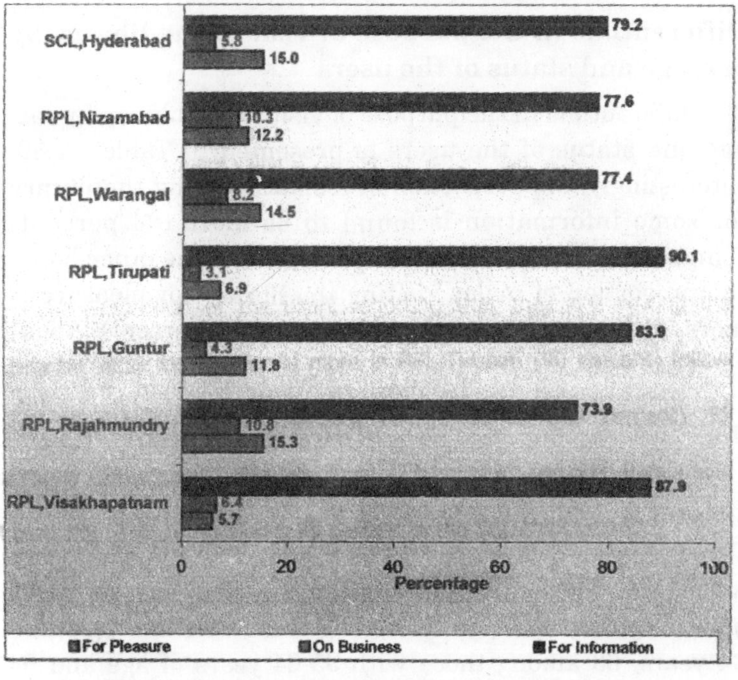

Fig. 12. Purpose of visit to the library by the Users.

percent), RPL-Warangal (77 percent) and RPL-Rajahmundry (74 percent). This proportion is 79 percent in the SCL-Hyderabad.

Those reporting the visit for pleasure is more in the RPL - Rajahmundry and SCL - Hyderabad (15 percent each) while it is low in RPL - Tirupati (7 percent). Those visiting the libraries on business is more in RPL - Rajahmundry (11 percent) and less in RPL - Tirupati (3 percent).

Again, in order to know whether the proportion of users reporting these three purposes differ significantly, the chi-square analysis is done and it indicates that the proportions differ significantly among the seven public libraries considered in the present study.

Differentials in the purpose of visit to the library by sex, age and status of the users

Differentials in the purpose of visit to the library by sex, age and status of the users is presented in Table - 4.39. Interestingly, the proportion of females visiting the library for some information is found to be more (84 percent) compared to that of males (81 percent). On the other hand, the proportion of males visiting the library for pleasure is more (13 percent) than that of females (5 percent). About 11 percent of the females and 6 percent of the males reported that they visit the library on some business. These differences are found to be statistically significant.

Majority of the users in all the four age groups reported that they are visiting the library for some information and this proportion is more in the younger age groups than among the older ones. This percentage is 85 among the users aged 21 years or below, 82 among those who are aged 21 - 34 years, 63 among those with 35-64 years of age and 64 among those who are aged 65 years or more. The proportion visiting the library for pleasure is more among the older age groups than among the younger ones. This percentage is 36 among those who are aged 65 years or more, followed by 26 among those with 35 - 64 years of age, 10 among those who are in the 21 - 34 years are group and 11 among those who are aged 21 years or below. The proportion of users visiting the library on business has increased from 4 percent among those who are 21 years or below to 12 percent among those who are in 35 - 64 years age group. Differences in the proportion of users who reported the three purposes are significant among the four age groups considered here.

Table 4.39. Differentials in the Purpose of Visit to the Library by Sex, Age and Status of the Users.

	Number	*Pupose of visit*						*Chi-square (df)*	*Signi-ficant*
		For pleasure		*On Business*		*For some information*			
		No.	*%*	*No.*	*%*	*No.*	*%*		
Differentials by:									
(*a*) Sex:									
Male	930	122	13.1	56	6.0	752	80.9	16.642	0.000
Female	14	9	4.6	22	11.3	163	84.0	df=2	
(*b*) Age group (years):									
Upto 21	348	39	11.2	14	4.0	295	84.8		
21-34	679	66	9.7	54	8.0	559	82.3	35.714	0.000
35-64	86	22	25.6	10	11.6	54	62.8	df=6	
65+	11	4	36.4	—	—	7	63.6		
(*c*) Status:									
Students	901	83	9.2	42	4.7	776	86.1		
Employees	127	23	18.1	18	14.2	86	67.7	75.639	0.000
Retired Employees	40	11	27.5	8	20.0	21	52.5	df=6	
Businessmen	56	14	25.0	10	17.9	32	57.1		

It can be seen that a higher proportion of the students (86 percent) are visiting the library for some information followed by the employees (68 percent), businessmen (57 percent) and retired employees (53 percent). This observation is in the expected direction and the reverse trend is true for those who reporting their visit for pleasure i.e. the proportion visiting the library for pleasure is more among retired employees (28 percent) followed by businessmen (25 percent), employees (18 percent) and students (9 percent). This trend is also more or less in the expected direction. However, the proportion reporting their visit to be on business is more among the retired employees (20 percent), followed by businessmen (18 percent), employees (14 percent) and students (5 percent). The computed chi-square value indicates that the differences in the proportion of users giving the three purposes for their visit are significant among the four groups of users considered here.

Time spent in the library during a visit

It is not only the frequency of visit but also the amount of time spent in library during a visit is very important for understanding whether the services are better utilized. Hence all the respondents were questioned accordingly and the responses are shown in Table - 4.40 and Fig. 13.

Table 4.40. Time Spent in the Library during the Visit

Name of the Library	*Number*	*Time spent*					
		Less than 1 hour		*1-2 hours*		*More than 2 hours*	
		No.	*%*	*No.*	*%*	*No.*	*%*
1. RPL, Visakhapatnam	157	31	19.7	69	43.9	57	36.3
2. RPL, Rajahmundry	157	30	19.1	82	52.2	45	28.7
3. RPL, Guntur	161	23	14.3	66	41.0	72	44.7
4. RPL, Tirupati	161	42	26.1	92	57.1	27	16.8
5. RPL, Warangal	159	21	13.2	92	57.9	46	28.9
6. RPL, Nizamabad	156	45	28.8	87	55.8	24	15.4
7. SCL, Hyderabad	173	12	6.9	49	28.3	112	64.7
Total	1124	204	18.1	537	47.8	383	34.1

Chi-square value = 142.037 df = 12 sig. 0.000

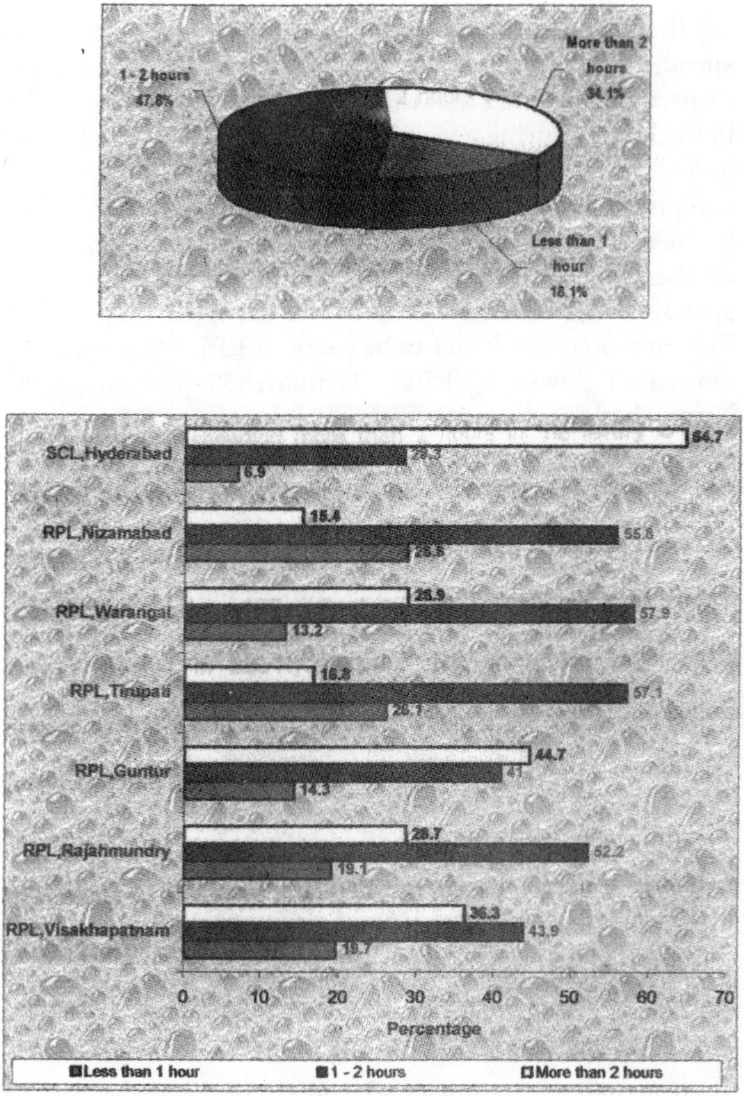

Fig. 13. Time spent in the library by the Users usually in a visit.

In all, nearly 48 percent of the users reported that they spend 1- 2 hours usually during their visit to the library and 34 percent have said that they spend more that 2 hours time in the library during a visit. The remaining 18 percent spend less than an hour in the library during a visit. With the exception of two RPLs, similar trend is observed with regard to the amount of time spent in the library during a visit. In all the seven libraries, majority of the users have reported spending of 1 - 2 hours only in the library during a visit. This proportion is found to be more in RPL - Warangal (58 percent) followed by RPL - Tirupati (57 percent), RPL-Nizamabad (56 percent), RPL - Rajahmundry (52 percent), RPL - Visakhapatnam (44 percent) and Guntur (41 percent). This percentage is only 28 in the SCL - Hyderabad while the percentage of users reporting more than 2 hours is nearly 65. The proportion reporting spending more than 2 hours in the library is more in RPL - Guntur (45 percent) and is low in RPL - Nizamabad (15 percent). Those spending less than 1 hour during a visit ranged from a high of 29 percent in RPL - Nizamabad to a low of 13 percent in RPL - Warangal while this proportion is only 7 percent in SCL - Hyderabad. The chi-square value indicates significant differences in the proportion of users regarding the amount of time spent among the seven libraries.

Differentials in the time spent in the library during a visit by sex, age and status of the users

Differentials in the time spent by the users by sex, age and status along with the computed chi-square values are shown in Table - 4.41.

It is noticed that about 47 percent of the males and 51 percent of the females are spending 1 - 2 hours time in the library during a visit. Interestingly, the proportion of users spending more than 2 hours time among males (37 percent) is nearly double than that among females (19 percent) and the reverse is true with the proportion reporting less than

1 hour time. Significant differences exist among the two sexes with regard to the amount of time spent during a visit, as indicated by the chi-square value.

Table 4.41. Differentials in the Time Spent in the Library by Sex, Age and Status of the Users.

	Number	*Time spent*						*Chi-square (df)*	*Significant*
		Less than 1 hour		*1-2 hours*		*More than 2 hours*			
		No.	*%*	*No.*	*%*	*No.*	*%*		
Differentials by:									
(*a*) Sex:									
Male	930	145	15.6	438	47.1	347	37.3	36.517	0.000
Female	14	59	30.4	99	51.0	36	18.6	df=2	
(*b*) Age group (years):									
Upto 21	348	75	21.6	184	52.9	89	25.6		
21-34	679	110	16.2	312	45.9	257	37.8	18.284	0.006
35-64	86	16	18.6	36	41.9	34	39.5	df=6	
65+	11	3	27.3	5	45.5	3	27.3		
(*c*) Status:									
Students	901	162	18.0	452	50.2	287	31.9		
Employees	127	25	19.7	48	37.8	54	42.5	15.718	0.015
Retired Employees	40	8	20.0	11	27.5	21	52.5	df=6	
Businessmen	56	9	16.1	26	46.4	21	37.5		

When the age group is considered, it can be noticed that most of the users in all the four groups have reported spending of 1 -2 hours during a visit. These percentages ranged from 42 in the age group of 35 - 64 years to 53 in the age group of 21 years or below. Those who are spending more than 2 hours time is more in the age group of 35 - 64 years (40 percent) followed by those in 21 - 34 years age group (38 percent), 65 years or above (27 percent) and 21 years or below (26 percent). The proportion of users spending less than 1 hour is low (16 percent) among 21 - 34 years age group and high (27 percent) among 65 years and above age group. The chi-square value indicates existence of significant differences among the four age groups of users with regard to the time spent during a visit.

It is observed that, by status of the users, 50 percent of the students, 46 percent of the businessmen, 39 percent of the employees and 28 percent of the retired employees are spending 1 - 2 hours time in the library during a visit while 53 percent of the retired employees, 43 percent of the employees, 38 percent of the businessmen and 32 percent of the students are spending more than 2 hours. The proportion of users reporting spending of less than 1 hour time in the library during a visit is 20 percent among retired employees and employers while it is 18 percent among students and 16 percent among businessmen. These differences by status were also found to be significant.

Purpose of visit to the Library

Responses of 1124 users who were interviewed in the present study regarding the usual purpose of their visit to the public libraries were presented in Table - 4.42 for all the seven public libraries.

In all, about 46 percent of the users have reported that they are visiting the library to look-up for some references of information while another 33 percent said that they are coming to use the reading room facility. About 4 percent said that they have come to borrow a fiction book and 7 percent borrowed a non-fictional book and 5 percent came to ask for some information. The remaining 5 percent have mentioned some other purposes.

The proportion of users who borrowed a fictional book ranged from 3 percent in RPL - Visakhapatnam to 5 percent in RPL - Nizamabad. In the same way the proportion of users who borrowed a non-fictional book ranged from 4 percent in RPL - Visakhapatnam to 13 percent in RPL -

Table 4.42. Purpose of Visit to the Library.

Name of the Library	Number	Purpose of the visit											
		Borrow a fictional book		Borrow a non-fictional book		Look-up for references / information		Ask staff for information		Use reading room		Other purpose	
		No.	%	No.	%	No.	%	No.	%	No.	%	No.	%
1. RPL, Visakhapatnam	157	5	2.5	6	3.8	93	59.2	3	1.9	44	28.0	7	4.5
2. RPL, Rajahmundry	157	5	3.2	20	12.7	69	43.9	11	7.0	45	28.7	7	4.5
3. RPL, Guntur	161	5	3.1	9	5.6	44	27.3	5	3.1	87	54.0	11	6.8
4. RPL, Tirupati	161	7	4.3	10	6.2	93	57.8	7	4.3	37	23.0	7	4.3
5. RPL, Warangal	159	7	4.4	13	8.2	64	40.3	10	6.3	55	34.6	10	6.3
6. RPL, Nizamabad	156	8	5.1	7	4.5	80	51.3	12	7.7	46	29.5	3	1.9
7. SCL, Hyderabad	173	12	6.9	16	9.2	77	44.5	3	1.7	60	34.7	5	2.9
Total	1124	48	4.3	81	7.2	520	46.3	51	4.5	374	33.3	50	4.4

Chi-square value = 91.480 df = 30 Sig. 0.000

Rajahmundry. These figures are 7 percent and 9 percent in the case of SCL-Hyderabad.

The proportion of users who came to look-up for some reference or information is high in RPL - Visakhapatnam (59 percent) and is low in RPL - Guntur (27 percent). This percentage is 45 in the case of SCL - Hyderabad. Those who came to ask for some information ranged from 2 percent in RPL - Visakhapatnam to 8 percent in RPL -Nizamabad. This percentage is 2 percent in SCL - Hyderabad.

Those who used the reading room facility is as high as 54 percent in RPL - Guntur and low in RPL - Tirupati (23 percent). Nearly 35 percent of the users in SCL - Hyderabad have come to use the reading room facility. The computed chi-square value indicate that there are significant differences in the proportion of users reporting different purposes of visit among the seven libraries covered in the study.

Differentials in the purpose of visit to the Library by sex, age and status of the users

In Table - 4.43, differentials in the purpose of visit to the library as reported by the users interviewed are presented by sex, age and status of the users.

Nearly 54 percent of the females and 45 percent of the males have come to look-up for some reference or information. There is not much variation in the proportion of users by sex among those who borrowed either a fictional book or non-fictional book. The proportion of those who came to ask for some information is more among females (7 percent) than among males (4 percent). The percentage of males (35) is more compared to females (23 percent) among those who came to use the reading room facility. These differences are found to be statistically significant.

When the age group of the users is considered, it is observed that the percentage who came to borrow a fictional

Table 4.43. Differentials in the Purpose of Visit to the Library by Sex, Age and Status of the Users.

	Number	What was done during the visit												Chi-square (df)	Significant
		Borrow a fictional book		Borrow a non-fictional book		Look-up for references/information		Ask staff for information		Use reading room		Other purpose			
		No.	%	No.	%	No.	%	No.	%	No.	%	No.	%		
Differentials by:															
(*a*) Sex:															
Male	930	40	4.3	65	7.0	416	44.7	37	4.0	329	35.4	43	4.6	14.337	
Female	194	8	4.1	16	8.2	104	53.6	14	7.2	45	23.2	7	3.6	df=5	0.014
(*b*) Age group (years):															
Upto 21	348	20	5.7	24	6.9	166	47.7	13	3.7	113	32.5	12	3.4		
21-34	679	21	3.1	44	6.5	324	47.7	27	4.0	229	33.7	34	5.0	35.966	
35-64	86	6	7.0	11	12.8	28	32.6	11	12.8	26	30.2	4	4.7	df=15	0.002
65+	11	1	9.1	2	18.2	2	18.2	—	—	6	54.5	—	—		
(*c*) Status:															
Students	901	36	4.0	4.0	5.1	451	50.1	32	3.6	294	32.6	42	4.7		
Employees	127	6	4.7	15	11.8	45	35.4	9	7.1	47	37.0	5	3.9	69.643	
Retired Employees	40	3	7.5	11	27.5	7	17.5	3	7.5	15	37.5	1	2.5	df=15	0.000
Businessmen	56	3	5.4	9	16.1	17	30.4	7	12.5	18	32.1	2	3.6		

or non-fictional book is more in the older age groups (35 years or above). Those who came to look-up for some reference or information is more in the younger age groups (below 35 years). The reading room facility is also reported more by the older age group. The difference in the proportion of users are found to be statistically significant for the purpose of visit reported among the four age groups considered in the analysis.

It is also noticed that more retired employees and businessmen have come to borrow either a fictional or non-fictional books compared to the students and employees. On the other hand, students and employees are mainly coming to look-up for some reference or information in larger proportions compared to the retired employees and businessmen. The percentage visiting the library to ask for information is more among businessmen (13 percent) and low among the students (4 percent). There is not much variation between the students and businessmen as well as between employees and retired employees with regard to using the reading room facility. However, these differences are found to be statistically significant as revealed by the computed chi-square value.

Users' opinion on the Library Collection

All the respondents were asked to give their opinion on the available library collection. Their responses were recorded in the form of ranking in terms of not good, fair, good and very good. These were shown in Table - 4.44 for all the seven libraries and diagrammatically in Fig. 14.

A little over half of the respondents (51 percent) have said that the collection is good in their respective libraries while 26 percent mentioned that the collection is very good and the remaining 23 percent felt that their libraries are having only a fair amount of collection.

The proportion of users who reported that the library collection is very good is more in RPL-Nizamabad (32

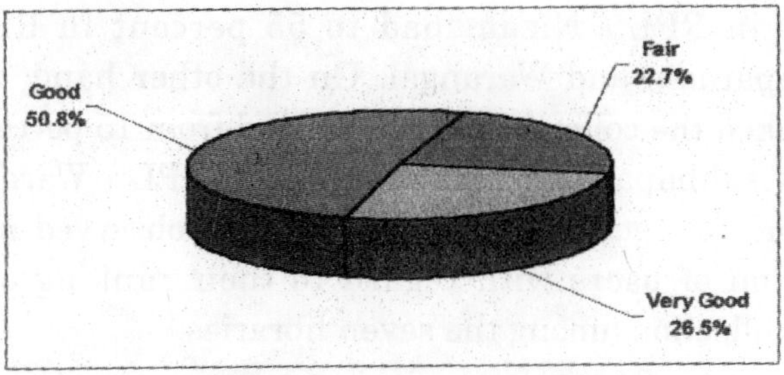

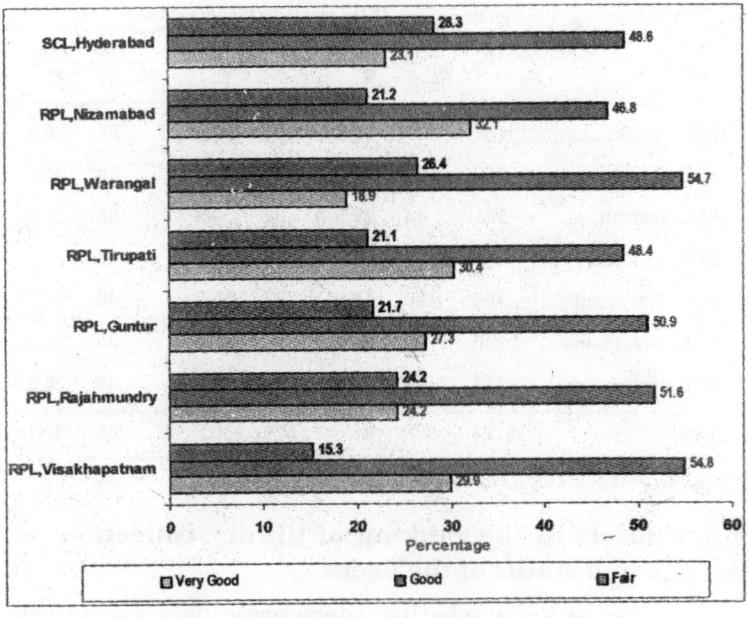

Fig. 14. Users views on existing Library Collection.

percent) followed by RPL-Tirupati and RPL - Visakhapatnam (30 percent each), RPL - Guntur (27 percent), RPL-Rajahmundry (24 percent) and RPL - Warangal (19 percent). Those who ranked the collection as good ranged from 47 percent in RPL - Nizamabad to 55 percent in RPLs - Visakhapatnam and Warangal. On the other hand, those who ranked the collection as fair ranged from 15 percent in RPL - Visakhapatnam to 26 percent in RPL - Warangal. However, no significant differences were observed in the proportion of users with regard to their ranking of the library collection among the seven libraries.

Table 4.44. Opinion on the Library Collection.

Name of the Library	*Number*	*Users' ranking of library collection*					
		Very good		*Good*		*Fair*	
		No.	*%*	*No.*	*%*	*No.*	*%*
1. RPL, Visakhapatnam	157	47	29.9	86	54.8	24	15.3
2. RPL, Rajahmundry	157	38	42.2	81	51.6	38	24.2
3. RPL, Guntur	161	44	27.3	82	50.9	35	21.7
4. RPL, Tirupati	161	49	30.4	78	48.4	34	21.1
5. RPL, Warangal	159	30	18.9	87	54.7	42	26.4
6. RPL, Nizamabad	156	50	32.1	73	46.8	33	21.2
7. SCL, Hyderabad	173	40	23.1	84	48.6	49	28.3
Total	1124	298	26.5	571	50.8	255	22.7

Chi-square value = 17.620 df = 12 sig. 0.128

Differentials in the ranking of library collection by sex, age and status of the users

In order to know whether there are differences in the opinion of the users by sex, age and status on the available library collection, chi-square test has been done and the chi-square values with the responses by sex, age and status of the users are presented in Table - 4.45.

Table 4.45. Differentials in the Ranking of Library Collection by Sex, and Status of the Users.

	Number	*Users' ranking of library collection*						*Chi-square (df)*	*Signi-ficant*
		Very good		*Good*		*Fair*			
		No.	*%*	*No.*	*%*	*No.*	*%*		
Differentials by:									
(*a*) Sex:									
Male	930	249	26.8	465	50.0	216	23.2	1.509	0.470
Female	14	49	25.3	106	54.6	39	20.1	df=2	
(*b*) Age group (years):									
Upto 21	348	97	27.9	189	54.3	62	17.8		
21-34	679	175	25.8	342	50.4	162	23.9	10.892	0.092
35-64	86	23	26.7	36	41.9	27	31.4	df=6	
65+	11	3	27.3	4	36.4	4	36.4		
(*c*) Status:									
Students	901	235	26.1	479	53.2	187	20.8		
Employees	127	30	23.6	59	46.5	38	29.9	18.307	0.006
Retired Employees	40	13	32.5	12	30.0	15	37.5	df=6	
Businessmen	56	20	35.7	21	37.5	15	26.8		

There appears not much difference between the two sexes in ranking the library collection. About 25 percent of females and 27 percent of the males ranked the collection as very good while 55 percent of females and 50 percent of males ranked is good. The remaining 20 percent of females and 23 percent of males mentioned the collection as fair. The differences in the proportion of the two sexes with regard to this ranking are not statistically significant.

Considering the age of the users, it is noticed that there is no variation in the proportion ranking the collection as very good between the four age groups considered. It ranged from 26 percent to 28 percent. Those who ranked the collection as good as more in the younger age groups (below

35 years) compared to the older age groups (above 34 years). The proportion of users reporting that the collection as fair is more in the age group 65 years or above (36 percent) and low in the age group 21 years or below (18 years). However, these differences in the proportion of users by age group with regard to the ranking of the collection are not statistically significant.

It is noticed that more proportion of users from businessmen (36 percent) and retired employees (33 percent) have ranked the collection as very good compared to that among students (26 percent) and employees (24 percent). Those who ranked the collection as good is more among students (53 percent) followed by employees (47 percent), businessmen (38 percent) and retired employees (30 percent). The proportion ranking the collection as fair ranged from 21 percent in students to 38 percent is retired employees. The chi-square value indicates significant differences in the proportion of users from the four categories considered here, with regard to the ranking of the library collection.

Users' view on co-operation and helpfulness of the Library Staff

All the respondents were asked to state whether they feel that the library staff are co-operative and helpful to them. Their responses are shown in Table-4.46 and Fig. 15.

It is quite welcoming to notice that a majority of the users in general (92 percent) have expressed that the library staff are co-operative and helpful. The proportion of users expressing this view is highest in the RPL - Guntur (98 percent) followed by RPL - Visakhapatnam (96 percent), RPL - Nizamabad (94 percent), RPL-Tirupati (90 percent), RPL - Warangal and RPL - Rajahmundry (89 percent each). This percentage is 88 in the SCL at Hyderabad. However, the chi-square value indicates that significant differences exist in the proportion of users' opinion on the co-operation and helpfulness of the staff among the seven libraries.

Table 4.46. Users' View on Staff Co-operation and Helfulness.

Name of the Library	Number	Whether staff are co-operative and helpful			
		Yes		*No*	
		No.	*%*	*No.*	*%*
1. RPL, Visakhapatnam	157	151	96.2	6	3.8
2. RPL, Rajahmundry	157	139	88.5	18	11.5
3. RPL, Guntur	161	157	97.5	4	2.5
4. RPL, Tirupati	161	145	90.1	16	9.9
5. RPL, Warangal	159	142	89.3	17	10.7
6. RPL, Nizamabad	156	146	93.6	10	6.4
7. SCL, Hyderabad	173	152	87.9	21	12.1
Total	1124	1032	91.8	92	8.2

Chi-square value = 19.427 df = 6 sig. 0.004

Differentials in the opinion on staff co-operation and helpfulness by sex, age and status of the users

Differentials by sex, age and status of the users regarding their opinion on co-operation and helpfulness of the library staff are presented in Table - 4.47. There is not much variation among the two sexes in the proportion of the users who felt that the library staff are co-operative and helpful. Nearly 92 percent of the males and 93 percent of the females expressed this view. These differences among the sexes are found to be not significant.

The proportion of users reporting that the staff are co-operative and useful is more in the younger age group i.e. those with 21 years or below (96 percent) followed by the age group of 21 - 34 years and 65 + years group (91 percent each) and relatively low in the age group of 35 - 64 years.

The chi-square value reveals significant differences in the proportion of users between the four age groups considered.

Table 4.47. Differentials in the Opinion on Staff Co-operation and Helpfulness by Sex, Age and Status of the Users.

	Number	*Whether staff are co-operative and helpful*				*Chi-square (df)*	*Signi-ficant*
		Yes		*No*			
		No.	*%*	*No.*	*%*		
Differentials by:							
(*a*) Sex:							
Male	930	851	91.5	79	8.5	0.687	0.407
Female	14	181	93.3	13	6.7	df=1	
(*b*) Age group (years):							
Upto 21	348	333	95.7	15	4.3	17.347	
21-34	679	618	91.0	61	9.0	df=3	0.001
35-64	86	71	82.6	15	17.4		
65+	11	10	90.9	1	9.1		
(*c*) Status:							
Students	901	848	94.1	53	5.9	32.542	
Employees	127	106	83.5	21	16.5	df=3	0.000
Retired Employees	40	33	82.5	7	17.5		
Businessmen	56	45	80.4	11	19.6		

By status, majority of the students have reported that the staff are cooperative and helpful (94 percent), followed by employees (84 percent), retired employees (83 percent) and businessmen (80 percent). The differences in the proportion of users from the four status groups are found to be statistically significant.

Users' opinion on establishing Computerized Information Network linking all the RPLs

Advancement in automation and Information Technology has facilitated for information sharing among institutions located at a distance in fairly quick time. It is in this background, the users were asked to mention whether they

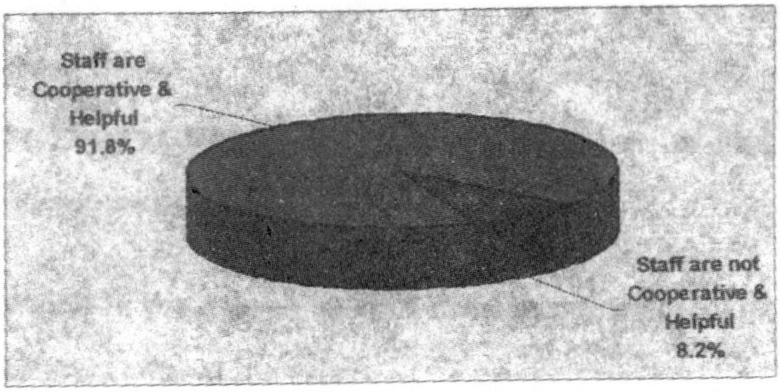

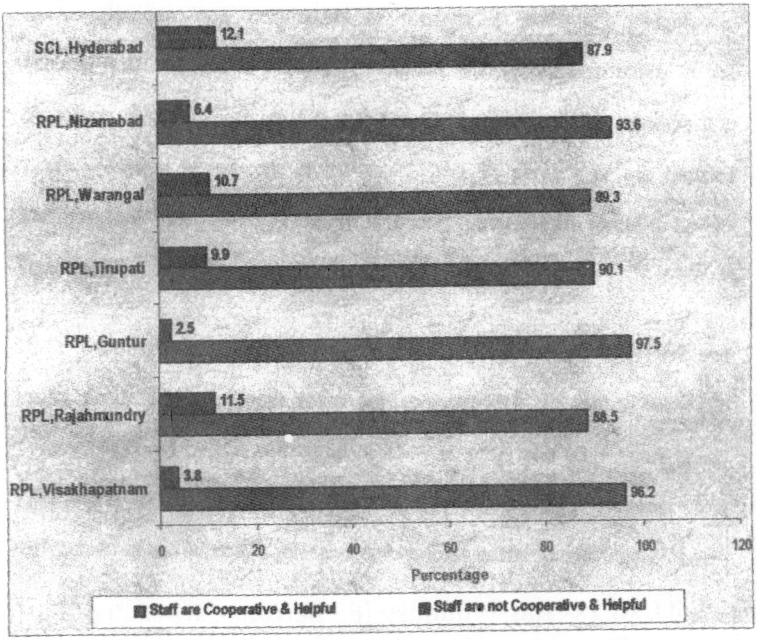

Fig. 15. Users' views on Staff Co-operation & Helpfulness.

feel that establishing computerized information network linking all the Regional Public Libraries in the state is required or it is not necessary. Their responses are shown in Table - 4.48 and Fig. 16.

Table 4.48. Users' Opinion on Establishing Computerized Information Network Linking All RPLs.

Name of the Library	*Number*	*Establishing computerized network linking all RPLs*			
		Required not useful		*Not necessary*	
		No.	*%*	*No.*	*%*
1. RPL, Visakhapatnam	157	142	90.4	15	9.6
2. RPL, Rajahmundry	157	134	85.4	23	14.6
3. RPL, Guntur	161	151	93.8	10	6.2
4. RPL, Tirupati	161	128	79.5	33	20.5
5. RPL, Warangal	159	141	88.7	18	11.3
6. RPL, Nizamabad	156	122	78.2	34	21.8
7. SCL, Hyderabad	173	151	87.3	22	12.7
Total	1124	969	86.2	155	13.8

Chi-square value = 25.729 df = 6 Sig. 0.000

In all, about 86 percent of the users of the RPLs have felt that establishing computerized information network linking all the RPLs in the state is very much required and useful. Among the different RPLs there is not much variation in the proportion of users reporting this view. This proportion is more in the RPL- Guntur (94 percent) followed by RPL - Visakhapatnam (90 percent), RPL - Warangal (89 percent), RPL - Rajahmundry (85 percent), RPL - Tirupati (80 percent) and RPL - Nizamabad (78 percent). This proportion is 87 percent from the SCL - Hyderabad. The computed chi-square value indicates that the differences in the proportion of users expressing this view are significant among the seven libraries considered here.

Differentials in the opinion of users on establishing computerized network linking all RPLs by sex, age and status

In Table - 4.49, the differentials in the opinion of the users on establishing computerized network linking all RPLs by sex, age and status are shown.

Among the two sexes, the proportion of users who reported that establishing computerized information network linking all RPLs in the state is required and useful is more among the males (87 percent) compared to the females (84 percent) and these differences in the proportions from the two sexes are not statistically significant.

Table 4.49. Differentials in the Opinion on Establishing Computerized Network Linking All RPLs by Sex, Age and Status of the Users.

	Number	*Establishing computerized networking linking all RPLs*				*Chi-square (df)*	*Significant*
		Required and useful		*Not necessary*			
		No.	*%*	*No.*	*%*		
Differentials by:							
(*a*) Sex:							
Male	930	807	86.8	123	13.2	1.443	0.230
Female	14	162	83.5	32	16.5	df=1	
(*b*) Age group (years):							
Upto 21	348	299	85.9	49	14.1	13.742	0.003
21-34	679	598	88.1	81	11.9	df=3	
35-64	86	64	74.4	22	25.6		
65+	11	8	72.7	3	27.3		
(*c*) Status:							
Students	901	794	88.1	107	11.9	27.126	0.000
Employees	127	107	-84.3	20	15.7	df=3	
Retired Employees	40	32	80.0	8	20.0		
Businessmen	56	36	64.3	20	35.7		

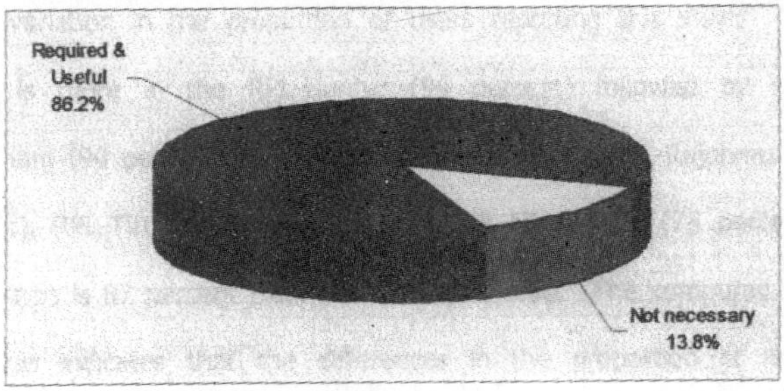

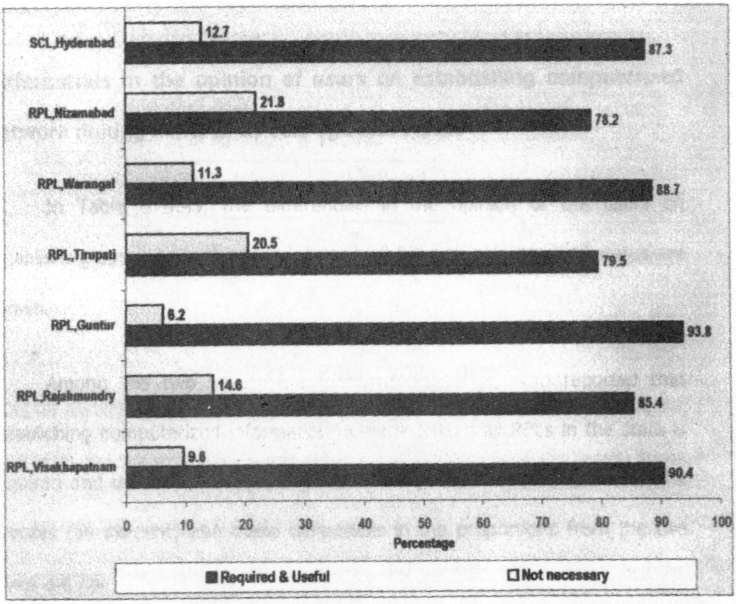

Fig. 16. Users' opinion on Establishing Computerized Information Network linking all the RPLs in the State.

The proportion of users feeling that it is required and useful to establish computerized networking of RPLs is more from the younger age groups compared to those from the older ones. Nearly 86 percent in the age group of 21 years or below, 88 percent in the age group of 21 - 34 years, 74 percent in the 35 - 64 years and 73 percent from 65 + years group have expressed this view. The chi-square value revealed significant differences in the proportion of users among the four age groups in the present study.

About 88 percent of the students, 84 percent of the employees, 80 percent of the retired employees and 64 percent of the businessmen have opined that establishing computerized information network linking all the RPLs in the state is very required and useful for information exchange. Differences in the proportion of users from the four status groups are found to be significant.

Users' view on establishing Data Banks

Views of the 1124 users on the need for establishing data banks in their Regional Public Libraries are shown in Table 4.50 and Fig. 17.

It is noticed that about 83 percent of the users are in favour of establishing data banks in RPLs as they reported it as required and ueful. Among the seven libraries also, there is not much variation in the proportion of users expressing this view. This proportion is slightly more in RPL - Guntur (86 percent) compared to RPLs - Visakhaptnam, Rajahmundry, Tirupati (83 percent each), RPL - Warangal (81 percent) and RPL - Nizamabad (80 percent). This proportion is 87 percent among the users from SCL - Hyderabad. The chi-square value revealed no significance difference in the proportion of users among the seven libraries with regard to their views on establishing data banks.

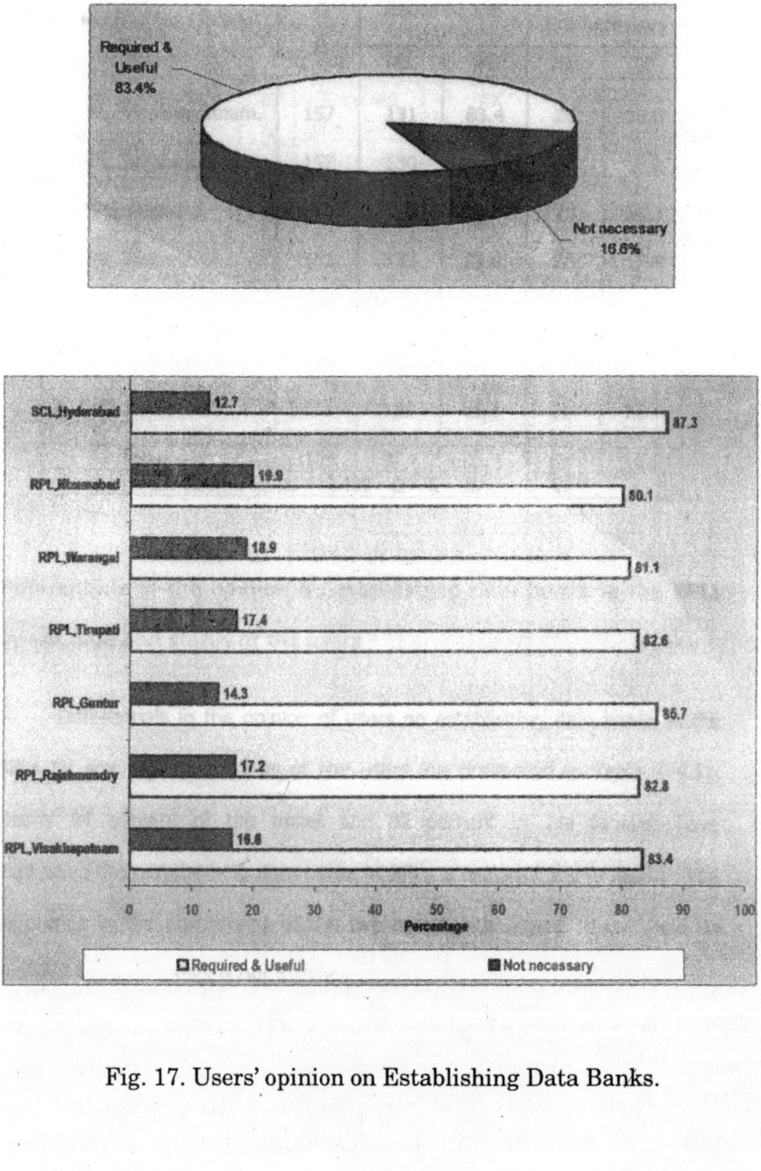

Fig. 17. Users' opinion on Establishing Data Banks.

Table 4.50. Users' View on Establishing Data Banks.

	Name of the Library	*Number*	*Establishing Data Banks*			
			Required not useful		*Not necessary*	
			No.	*%*	*No.*	*%*
1.	RPL, Visakhapatnam	157	131	83.4	26	16.6
2.	RPL, Rajahmundry	157	130	82.8	27	17.2
3.	RPL, Guntur	161	138	85.7	23	14.3
4.	RPL, Tirupati	161	133	82.6	28	17.4
5.	RPL, Warangal	159	129	81.1	30	18.9
6.	RPL, Nizamabad	156	125	80.1	31	19.9
7.	SCL, Hyderabad	173	151	87.3	22	12.7
	Total	1124	937	83.4	187	16.6

Chi-square value = 4.409 df = 6 Sig. 0.622

Differentials in the opinion on establishing data banks in the RPLs by sex, age and status of the users

Differentials in the opinion of users on establishing data banks in the RPLs by sex, age and status of the users are presented in Table - 4.51. Nearly 84 percent of the males and 82 percent of the females have expressed that establishing data banks in RPLs is required and is useful. The difference in the proportions of the two sexes with regard to the view on establishing data banks is not significant.

The proportion of users stating that establishing data banks is required and useful is nearly 81 percent in the age group of 21 years and below, 86 percent in 21 - 34 years age group, 74 percent in 35 - 64 years age group and 82 percent in the 65 + years age group. These differences in the proportion of users from the four age groups are statistically significant.

A majority of the students (86 percent), employees (77 percent), retired employees (78 percent) and businessmen

(68 percent) have expressed that the establishment of data banks in RPLs is required and useful. These differences are also statistically significant as revealed by the chi-square value.

Table 4.51. Differentials in the Opinion on Establishing Data Banks by Sex, Age and Status of the Users.

	Number	*Establishing Data Banks*				*Chi-square (df)*	*Signi-ficant*
		Required and useful		*Not necessary*			
		No.	*%*	*No.*	*%*		
Differentials by:							
(*a*) Sex:							
Male	930	778	83.7	152	16.3	0.333	0.564
Female	14	159	82.0	35	18.0	df=1	
(*b*) Age group (years):							
Upto 21	348	281	80.7	67	19.3	9.753	0.021
21-34	679	583	85.9	96	14.1	df=3	
35-64	86	64	74.4	22	25.6		
65+	11	9	81.8	2	18.2		
(*c*) Status:							
Students	901	770	85.5	131	14.5	17.075	0.001
Employees	127	98	77.2	29	22.8	df=3	
Retired Employees	40	31	77.5	9	22.5		
Businessmen	56	38	67.9	18	32.1		

Users' opinion on establishing links with District Central Library (DCL)

Opinions of the respondents on establishing links with the District Central Library (DCL) are shown in Table - 4.52 and Fig. 18.

Among the 1124 respondents, a majority (86 percent) are of the opinion that the RPLs should have links with the DCL.

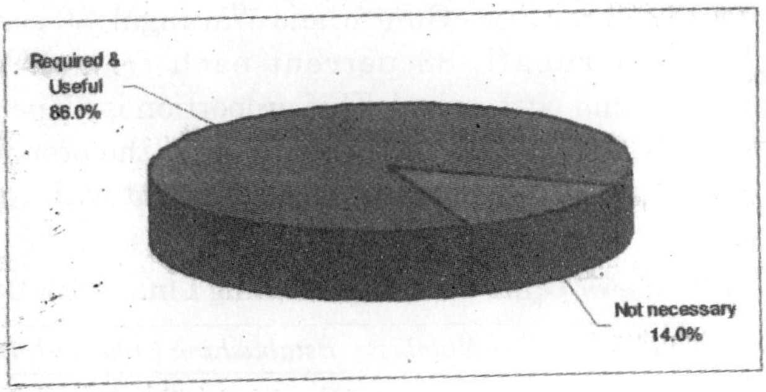

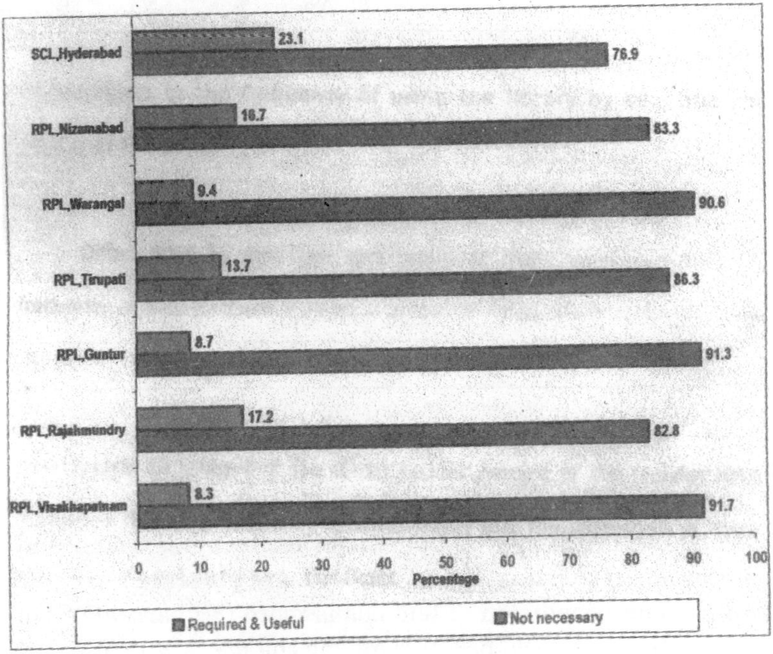

Fig. 18. Users' opinion on Establishing links with DCL.

The proportion of users reporting the need for establishing links with DCL is 92 percent in RPL - Visakhapatnam, 91 percent each from RPLs - Guntur and Warangal, 86 percent from RPL - Tirupati, 83 percent each from RPLs - Rajahmundry and Nizamabad. This proportion is 77 percent from the SCL - Hyderabad. The differences in the proportion of users from the seven libraries are significant with regard to their views on having links with DCL.

Table 4.52. Users' Opinion on Establishing Links with DCL.

Name of the Library	*Number*	*Establishing links with DCL*			
		Required not useful		*Not necessary*	
		No.	*%*	*No.*	*%*
1. RPL, Visakhapatnam	157	144	91.7	13	8.3
2. RPL, Rajahmundry	157	130	82.8	27	17.2
3. RPL, Guntur	161	147	91.3	14	8.7
4. RPL, Tirupati	161	139	86.3	22	13.7
5. RPL, Warangal	159	144	90.6	15	9.4
6. RPL, Nizamabad	156	130	83.3	26	16.7
7. SCL, Hyderabad	173	133	76.9	40	23.1
Total	1124	967	86.0	157	14.0

Chi-square value = 25.053 df = 6 Sig. 0.000

Differentials in the opinion of users on establishing links with DCL by sex, age and status

Differentials in the opinion of users by sex, age and status on establishing links with DCL are presented in Table 4.53. The proportion of females is more (89 percent) than that of the males (86 percent) among the users who feel that establishing links between RPLs and the DCL is required and useful. The chi-square reveals no significant differences in the proportion of users between the two sexes with regard to the views on establishing links with DCL.

Table 4.53. Differentials in the Opinion on Establishing Links with D.C.L. by Sex, Age and Status of the Users.

	Number	*Establishing Links with D.C.L.*				*Chi-square (df)*	*Signi-ficant*
		Required and useful		*Not necessary*			
		No.	*%*	*No.*	*%*		
Differentials by:							
(*a*) Sex:							
Male	930	795	85.5	135	14.5	1.347	0.246
Female	14	172	88.7	22	11.3	df=1	
(*b*) Age group (years):							
Upto 21	348	311	89.4	37	10.6	11.508	0.009
21-34	679	579	85.3	100	14.7	df=3	
35-64	86	66	76.7	20	23.3		
65+	11	11	100.0	—	—		
(*c*) Status:							
Students	901	799	88.7	102	11.3	27.314	0.000
Employees	127	98	77.2	29	22.8	df=3	
Retired Employees	40	29	72.5	11	27.5		
Businessmen	56	41	73.5	15	26.8		

All the respondents in the age group of 65 + years, 89 percent in the age group of 21 years or below, 85 percent in 21 - 34 years age group and 77 percent in the 35 - 64 years age group are in support of establishing links between RPLs and the DCL. The differences in these proportions of users are significant among the four considered age groups.

Nearly 89 percent of the students, 77 percent of the employees, 74 percent of the businessmen and 73 percent of the retired employees viewed establishing links between RPLs and DCL as required and useful. These differences in the proportion of users from the four status groups are statistically significant with regard to their views on establishing links with DCL as revealed by the chi-square value.

Opinion of the users on the facilities available in the Library

The respondents were asked to mention whether the facilities available in their libraries are up to the mark or there is any need to improve them. Their responses are shown in Table - 4.54.

Table 4.54. Opinion on the Facilities Available in the Library.

Name of the Library	*Number*	*Opinion on facilities available*			
		Upto the mark		*To be improved*	
		No.	*%*	*No.*	*%*
1. RPL, Visakhapatnam	157	78	49.7	79	50.3
2. RPL, Rajahmundry	157	116	73.9	41	26.1
3. RPL, Guntur	161	77	47.8	84	52.2
4. RPL, Tirupati	161	97	60.2	64	39.8
5. RPL, Warangal	159	84	52.8	75	47.2
6. RPL, Nizamabad	156	102	65.4	54	34.6
7. SCL, Hyderabad	173	87	50.3	86	43.0
Total	1124	641	57.0	483	43.0

Chi-square value = 36.702 df = 6 Sig. 0.000

The proportion of users who reported that the facilities are to be improved is more from RPL - Guntur (52 percent) followed by RPL - Visakhapatnam (50 percent), RPL - Warangal (47 percent), RPL - Tirupati (40 percent) RPL - Nizamabad (35 percent) and RPL - Rajahmundry (26 percent). This proportion is 50 percent in the SCL - Hyderabad. As indicated by the computed chi-square value, the differences in the proportion of users between the seven libraries are significant with regard to their views on the available facilities in their libraries.

Differentials in the opinion of users by sex, age and status on the facilities available at their libraries

In Table - 4.55, differentials in the opinion of the users on the available facilities at their libraries are shown by sex, age and status of the users. Nearly 62 percent of the females and 56 percent of the males are of the opinion that the facilities available at their libraries are up to the mark. Differences in the proportion of the two sexes with regard to their views on the adequacy of facilities are not statistically significant.

Table 4.55. Differentials in the Opinion on the Facilities Available in the Library by Sex, Age and Status of the Users.

	Number	*Opinion on available facilities*				*Chi-square (df)*	*Signi-ficant*
		Upto the mark		*To be improved*			
		No.	*%*	*No.*	*%*		
Differentials by:							
(*a*) Sex:							
Male	930	521	56.0	409	44.0	2.229	0.135
Female	14	120	61.9	74	38.1	df=1	
(*b*) Age group (years):							
Upto 21	348	200	57.5	148	42.5	5.097	0.165
21-34	679	377	55.5	302	44.5	df=3	
35-64	86	55	64.0	31	36.0		
65+	11	9	81.8	2	18.2		
(*c*) Status:							
Students	901	500	55.5	401	44.5	6.421	0.093
Employees	127	77	60.6	50	39.4	df=3	
Retired Employees	40	24	60.0	16	40.0		
Businessmen	56	40	71.4	16	28.6		

The proportion of users who are satisfied with the available facilities in their libraries is more in older groups compared to the younger ones. Nearly 82 percent in the age group of 65 + years, 64 percent in 35 - 64 years age group, 56 percent in 21-34 years age group and 58 percent in the age group of 21 years or below have reported that the available facilities are up to the mark at their libraries. These differences in the proportion of users from the four age groups with regard to the facilities is found to be not statistically significant.

About 71 percent of the businessmen, 61 percent of the employees, 60 percent of the retired employees and 56 percent of the students have mentioned that the facilities available at the libraries are up to the mark and the chi-square value reveals no significant differences in the four status groups of users with regard to their views on the available facilities in the library.

Opinion of the users on the furniture available in their Libraries

Opinion of the respondents with regard to the furniture available in their libraries is shown in Table - 4.56. It is noticed that only 37 percent of the users say that the available furniture is up to the mark and the remaining 63 percent feel that it should be improved. The proportion reporting that the furniture should be improved is more from the RPL - Guntur (76 percent) followed by RPL - Warangal (75 percent), RPL - Rajahmundry (71 percent), RPL - Nizamabad (55 percent), RPL - Visakhapatnam (52 percent) and RPL - Tirupati (43 percent). About 69 percent of the users from the SCL - Hyderabad feel that there is the need for improving the furniture. The chi-square value indicates that the differences in the proportion of users from the seven libraries are significant with regard to their opinion on the available furniture.

Table 4.56. Opinion on the Furniture Available in the Library.

Name of the Library	Number	Opinion on available furniture			
		Upto the mark		To be improved	
		No.	%	No.	%
1. RPL, Visakhapatnam	157	76	48.4	81	51.6
2. RPL, Rajahmundry	157	45	28.7	112	71.3
3. RPL, Guntur	161	38	23.6	123	76.4
4. RPL, Tirupati	161	92	57.1	69	42.9
5. RPL, Warangal	159	40	25.2	119	74.8
6. RPL, Nizamabad	156	71	45.5	85	54.5
7. SCL, Hyderabad	173	53	30.6	120	69.4
Total	1124	415	36.9	709	63.1

Chi-square value = 71.350 df = 6 Sig. 0.000

Differentials in the opinion on the furniture available by sex, age and status of the users

Differentials in the opinion of the users by sex, age and status on the furniture available in the libraries are presented in Table - 4.57. Nearly 67 percent of males and 46 percent of the females have reported that the furniture in the libraries is not up to the mark and need to be improved. The differences in the proportion of users expressing their view on the furniture are significant among the two sexes.

Considering the age of the users, it is noticed that as high as 83 percent from the age group of 35 - 64 years, 73 percent from 65 + years age group, 62 percent from 21-34 years age group and 60 percent from 21 years or below age group feel the need for improving the furniture in their libraries. Chi-square value reveals significant differences among the four age groups with regard to their opinion on available furniture.

Table 4.57. Differentials in the Opinion on the Furniture Available in the Library by Sex, Age and Status of the Users.

	Number	*Opinion on available furniture*				*Chi-square (df)*	*Significant*
		Upto the mark		*To be improved*			
		No.	*%*	*No.*	*%*		
Differentials by:							
(*a*) Sex:							
Male	930	310	33.3	620	66.7	29.791	0.000
Female	14	105	54.1	89	45.9	df=1	
(*b*) Age group (years):							
Upto 21	348	139	39.9	209	60.1		
21-34	679	258	38.0	421	62.0	16.153	0.001
35-64	86	15	17.4	71	82.6	df=3	
65+	11	3	27.3	8	72.7		
(*c*) Status:							
Students	901	363	40.3	538	59.7		
Employees	127	33	26.0	94	74.0	24.754	0.000
Retired Employees	40	11	27.5	29	72.5	df=3	
Businessmen	56	8	14.3	48	85.7		

The proportion of respondents who feel the need for improving the furniture is more among the businessmen (86 percent) followed by employees (74 percent), retired employees (73 percent) and students (60 percent). The differences in the proportion of users among the four status groups expressing their opinion on the furniture available are significant as revealed by the computed chi-square value.

Opinion of the users on the existing library services

The respondents were asked to mention whether the existing library services are up to the mark or whether there is need for improving the services. Their responses, along with chi-square value are shown in Table - 4.58.

It is also interesting to note that about 67 percent of the users feel the need for improving the library services while only 33 percent stated that they are up to the mark.

Table 4.58. Users' Opinion on the Existing Library Services.

	Name of the Library	*Number*	*Existing library services*			
			Upto the mark		*To be improved*	
			No.	*%*	*No.*	*%*
1.	RPL, Visakhapatnam	157	72	45.8	85	54.1
2.	RPL, Rajahmundry	157	50	31.8	107	68.2
3.	RPL, Guntur	161	49	30.4	112	69.6
4.	RPL, Tirupati	161	64	39.8	97	60.2
5.	RPL, Warangal	159	27	17.0	132	83.0
6.	RPL, Nizamabad	156	68	43.6	88	56.4
7.	SCL, Hyderabad	173	44	25.4	129	74.6
	Total	1124	374	33.3	750	66.7

Chi-square value = 46.250 df = 6 sig. 0.000

The proportion of respondents feeling the need for improvement in the library services is more in RPL - Warangal (83 percent), RPL - Guntur (70 percent), RPL - Rajahmundry (68 percent), RPL - Tirupati (60 percent), RPL - Nizamabad (56 percent) and RPL - Visakhapatnam (54 percent). This proportion is 75 percent among the SCL - Hyderabad. The chi-square revealed statistically significant differences in the proportion of users from the seven libraries with regard to their opinion on the existing library services.

Differentials in the opinion on existing library services by sex, age and status of the users

Differentials in the opinion on existing library services by sex, age and status of the users are presented in Table - 4.59.

Table 4.59. Differentials in the Opinion on the Existing Library Services by Sex, Age and Status of the Users.

	Number	*Existing Library services*				*Chi-square (df)*	*Signi-ficant*
		Upto the mark		*To be improved*			
		No.	*%*	*No.*	*%*		
Differentials by:							
(*a*) Sex:							
Male	930	287	30.9	643	69.1	14.140	0.000
Female	14	87	44.8	107	55.2	df=1	
(*b*) Age group (years):							
Upto 21	348	132	37.9	216	62.1		
21-34	679	226	33.3	453	66.7	15.715	0.001
35-64	86	14	16.3	72	83.7	df=3	
65+	11	2	18.2	9	81.8		
(*c*) Status:							
Students	901	325	36.1	576	63.9		
Employees	127	31	24.4	96	75.6	16.839	0.001
Retired Employees	40	7	17.5	33	82.5	df=3	
Businessmen	56	11	19.6	45	80.4		

The proportion of users who feel the need for improvement in the library services is more among males (69 percent) compared to the females (55 percent). This proportion has shown increase from younger (62 percent) to older age groups (82 percent). This view is expressed more by the retired employees (83 percent) followed by businessmen (80 percent), employees (76 percent) and students (64 percent). The differences in the proportion of users by sex, age and also the status are found to be statistically significant as revealed by the chi-square values.

Users' opinion on the existing equipment in the library

The responses of the users regarding whether the existing equipment in the library is up to the mark or to be improved are shown in Table - 4.60.

Here also, the degree of dissatisfaction is seen to be more as 69 percent of the respondents reported that the equipment in their libraries is not up to the mark and need to be improved. This proportion is observed to be more from the RPL - Warangal (80 percent) followed by the RPL - Guntur (76 percent), RPL - Rajahmundry (74 percent), RPL - Tirupati (64 percent), RPL - Visakhapatnam (57 percent) and RPL - Nizamabad (55 percent). Nearly 76 percent of the users from the SCL - Hyderabad have also expressed the need for improving the equipment in their library. The differences in the opinion of users with regard to the equipment in the seven libraries are found to be statistically significant as revealed by the chi-square value.

Table 4.60. Users' Opinion on the Existing Equipment in the Library.

Name of the Library	*Number*	*Existing library services*			
		Upto the mark		*To be improved*	
		No.	*%*	*No.*	*%*
1. RPL, Visakhapatnam	157	68	43.3	89	56.7
2. RPL, Rajahmundry	157	41	26.1	116	73.9
3. RPL, Guntur	161	38	23.6	123	76.4
4. RPL, Tirupati	161	58	36.0	103	64.0
5. RPL, Warangal	159	32	20.1	127	79.9
6. RPL, Nizamabad	156	69	44.9	86	55.1
7. SCL, Hyderabad	173	42	24.3	131	75.7
Total	1124	349	31.0	775	69.0

Chi-square value = 45.335 df = 6 Sig. 0.000

Differentials in the opinion of users by sex, age and status on the existing equipment in the library

In Table - 4.61, differentials in the opinion of users by sex, age and status with regard to the existing equipment in the library are presented.

Table 4.61. Differentials in the Opinion on the Existing Library Equipment in the by Sex, Age and Status of the Users.

	Number	*Existing equipment*				*Chi-square (df)*	*Significant*
		Upto the mark		*To be improved*			
		No.	*%*	*No.*	*%*		
Differentials by:							
(*a*) Sex:							
Male	930	258	27.7	672	72.3	27.539	0.000
Female	14	91	46.9	103	53.1	df = 1	
(*b*) Age group (years):							
Upto 21	348	116	33.3	232	66.7		
21-34	679	215	31.7	646	68.3	8.040	0.045
35-64	86	16	18.6	70	81.4	df = 3	
65+	11	2	18.2	9	81.8		
(*c*) Status:							
Students	901	311	34.5	590	65.5		
Employees	127	22	17.3	105	82.7	25.536	0.000
Retired Employees	40	7	17.5	33	82.5	df = 3	
Businessmen	56	9	16.1	47	83.9		

The proportion of users who feel the need for improving the available equipment in the libraries is more among the males (72 percent) compared to females (53 percent). The proportion of users who are not satisfied with the existing equipment has increased from 67 percent in younger age group (21 years or below) to 82 percent among the oldest age group (65+ years).

The percentage of users who are dissatisfied with the equipment available is low in students (66 percent) compared to the other three categories (83-84 percent). Chi-square values indicate significant differences in the proportion of users expressing their views on equipment in libraries by sex, age and status also.

Users' opinion on the available book resources in the library

Opinion of the respondents regarding the available book resources or library collection is shown in the Table - 4.62 for the seven libraries covered in the present study.

Table 4.62. Users' Opinion on the Available Book Resources in the Library.

Name of the Library	*Number*	*Book resouces available*			
		Upto the mark		*To be improved*	
		No.	*%*	*No.*	*%*
1. RPL, Visakhapatnam	157	35	22.3	122	77.7
2. RPL, Rajahmundry	157	28	17.8	129	82.2
3. RPL, Guntur	161	25	15.5	136	84.5
4. RPL, Tirupati	161	36	22.4	125	77.6
5. RPL, Warangal	159	29	18.2	130	81.8
6. RPL, Nizamabad	156	41	26.3	115	73.7
7. SCL, Hyderabad	173	22	12.7	151	87.3
Total	1124	216	19.2	908	80.8

Chi-square value = 13.409 df = 6 Sig. 0.037

It is noticed that only 19 percent of the uses are satisfied with the available book resources or library collection while the remaining 81 percent reported that it should be improved. The proportion of respondents who are not satisfied with the available resources is more in RPL - Guntur (85 percent) followed by RPLs - Rajahmundry and Warangal (82 percent each), RPLs - Visakhapatnam and Tirupati (78 percent each) and RPL - Nizamabad (74 percent). This proportion is 87 percent in the case of SCL at Hyderabad. The differences in the proportion of users with regard to their opinion on available book resources are significant among the seven libraries as indicated by the chi-square value.

Differentials in the opinion on the available book resources by sex, age and status of the users

Differentials in the opinion of users on the available book resources by sex, age and status are shown in Table - 4.63. The proportion of users who feel that the available book resources or library collection need to be improved is more among males (82 percent) compared to females (77 percent). This proportion is found to be 78 percent among those aged 21 years or below, 81 percent among those in 21-34 years age group, 87 percent among 35-64 percent age group and 82 percent in the 65+ years age group. When the status is considered, it is noticed that the proportion of users who are dissatisfied with the available book resources is 81 percent among students, 80 percent among employees and retired employees and 88 percent among businessmen. The computed chi-square values indicate significant differences in the proportion of users by sex, age and status with regard to their views on library collection or available book resources.

Table 4.63. Differentials in the Opinion on the Available Book Resources in the Library by Sex, Age and Status of the Usres.

	Number	*Book resouces avaible*				*Chi-square (df)*	*Signi-ficant*
		Upto the mark		*To be improved*			
		No.	*%*	*No.*	*%*		
Differentials by:							
(*a*) Sex:							
Male	930	171	18.4	759	81.6	2.391	0.122
Female	14	45	23.2	149	76.8	df = 1	
(*b*) Age group (years):							
Upto 21	348	76	21.8	272	78.2		
21-34	679	127	18.7	552	81.3	3.952	0.267
35-64	86	11	12.8	75	87.2	df = 3	
65+	11	2	18.2	9	81.8		
(c) Status:							
Students	901	175	19.4	726	80.6		
Employees	127	26	20.5	101	79.5	1.797	0.616
Retired Employees	40	8	20.0	32	80.0	df = 3	
Businessmen	56	7	12.5	49	87.5		

The proportion of users who reported that the available facilities, furniture, services, equipment and book resources are upto to mark in their respective libraries is diagrammatically presented in Fig. - 19.

Willingness of the users to pay user charges

All the respondents were asked whether they are willing to pay user charges for the services utilized. Their responses are presented in Table - 4.64 and Fig. 20.

Table 4.64. Willingness to pay the User Charges.

	Name of the Library	*Number*	*Whether willing to pay user charges*			
			Yes		*No*	
			No.	*%*	*No.*	*%*
1.	RPL, Visakhapatnam	157	59	37.6	98	62.4
2.	RPL, Rajahmundry	157	65	41.4	92	58.6
3.	RPL, Guntur	161	65	40.4	96	59.6
4.	RPL, Tirupati	161	58	36.0	103	64.0
5.	RPL, Warangal	159	58	36.5	101	63.5
6.	RPL, Nizamabad	156	62	39.7	94	60.3
7.	SCL, Hyderabad	173	60	34.7	113	65.3
	Total	1124	427	38.0	697	62.0

Chi-square value = 2.600 df = 6 Sig. 0.857

It is noticed that only 38 percent of the users are willing to pay the user charges for the services they receive from the library. This proportion of the users is found to be more among those from RPL - Rajahmundry (41 percent) followed by RPLs - Guntur and Nizamabad (40 percent), RPL - Visakhapatnam (38 percent), RPL - Warangal (37 percent) and RPL - Tirupati (36 percent). Nearly 35 percent of the users have reported their willingness to pay user charges in the SCL - Hyderabad. The chi-square value indicates no significant differences in the proportion of users with regard to the willingness to pay user charges in the seven libraries.

Differentials in willingness to pay user charges by sex, age and status of the users

Differentials in willingness to pay user charges by sex, age and status of the users is shown in Table - 4.65.

The proportion of users who reported their willingness to pay user charges is more among the females (43 percent) than the males (37 percent). When the age group is considered, about 37 percent in the age group of 21 years or below, 38 percent in 21 - 34 years age group, 37 percent in 35 - 64 years age group and 45 percent in 65 + years age group are willing to pay the user charges. In the same way, when the status is considered, 38 percent each from the students and employees, 55 percent from retired employees and 29 percent from businessmen reported willingness to pay the user charges for the services they receive from their libraries. However, the chi-square values indicate that the differentials in the willingness to pay user charges by sex, age and status of the users are not statistically significant.

Table 4.65. Differentials in theWillingness to Pay User Charges by Sex, Age and Status of the Users.

	Number	*Willingness to pay user charges*				*Chi-square (df)*	*Signi-ficant*
		Yes		*No*			
		No.	*%*	*No.*	*%*		
Differentials by:							
(*a*) Sex:							
Male	930	344	37.0	586	63.0	2.288	0.130
Female	14	83	42.8	111	57.2	df = 1	
(*b*) Age group (years):							
Upto 21	348	129	37.1	219	62.9		
21-34	679	261	38.4	418	61.6	0.466	0.926
35-64	86	32	37.2	54	62.8	df = 3	
65+	11	5	45.5	6	54.5		
(*c*) Status:							
Students	901	341	37.8	560	62.2		
Employees	127	48	37.8	79	62.2	7.032	0.071
Retired Employees	40	22	55.00	18	45.0	df = 3	
Businessmen	56	16	28.6	40	71.4		

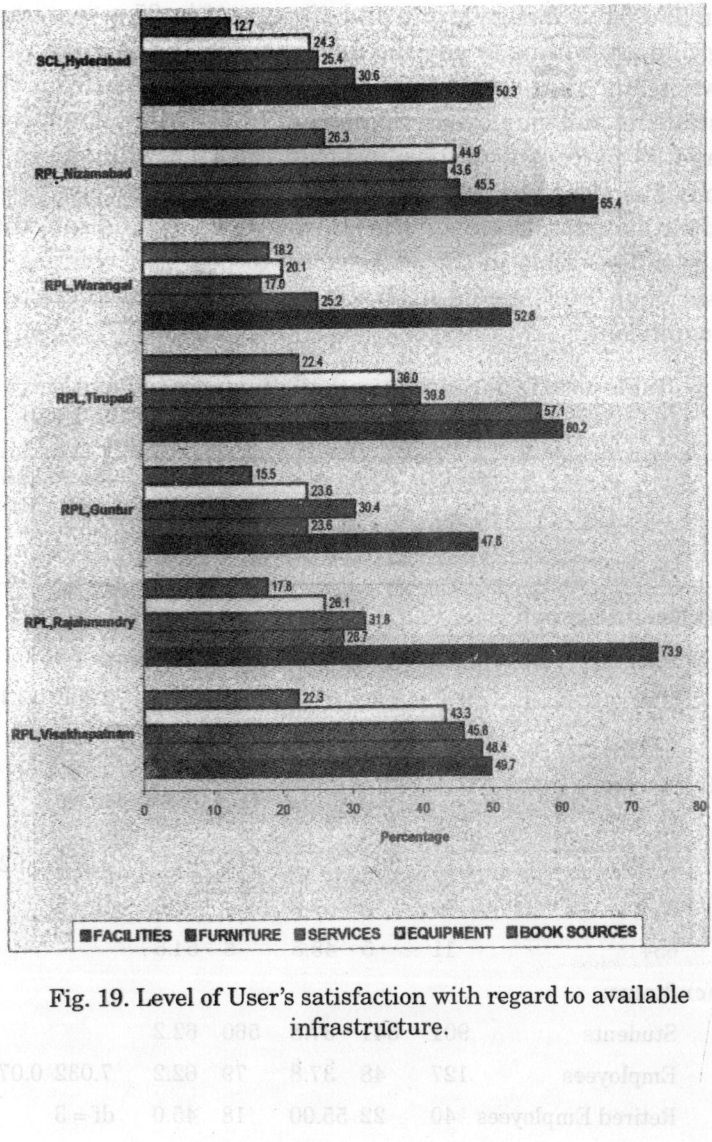

Fig. 19. Level of User's satisfaction with regard to available infrastructure.

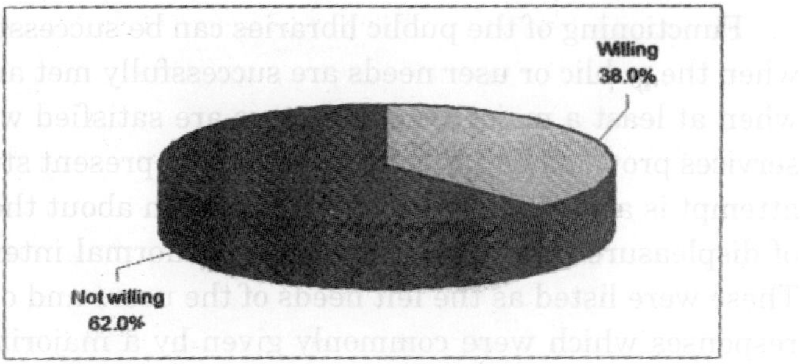

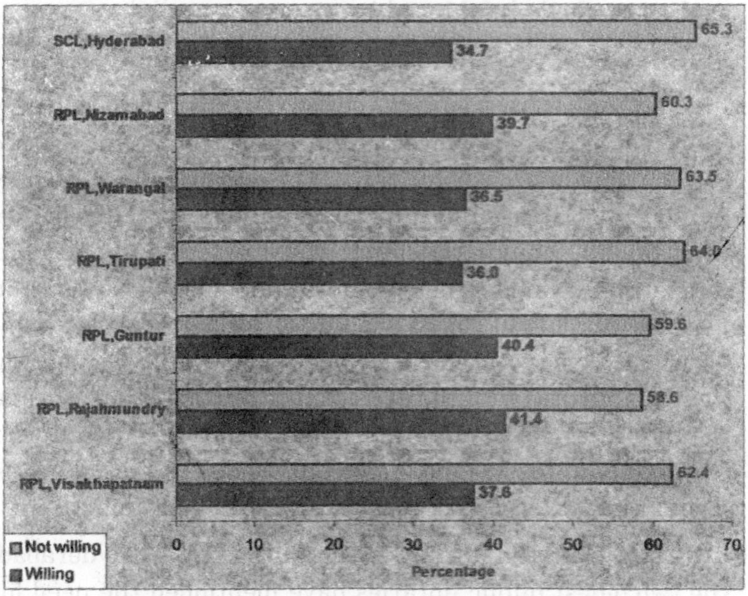

Fig. 20. Willingness to pay User charges.

Felt needs of the users

Functioning of the public libraries can be successful only when the public or user needs are successfully met and only when at least a majority of the users are satisfied with the services provided by these libraries. In the present study, an attempt is also made to gather information about the areas of displeasure from the users through informal interviews. These were listed as the felt needs of the users and only the responses which were commonly given by a majority were listed, hence not presented in the formal way through giving percentages. However, the needs are presented library wise as they can be helpful in taking-up any remedial measures.

Felt needs of the users regarding library collection

Felt needs or requirements regarding the library collection as stated by most of the users are shown in Table - 4.66. The major requirement regarding the library collection is the need for procuring all varieties of books i.e. text books, books on general knowledge, books for competitive exams, other technical and subject books. And also, the number of copies should be more or even sufficient for users. This requirement is mentioned by all the Regional Public Libraries (with the exception of RPL at Warangal) and the SCL at Hyderabad. The need for procuring more number of copies of at least some important books is stressed by the users from RPLs - Visakhapatnam and Rajahmundry.

Users from the RPL - Guntur and the SCL - Hyderabad, the two oldest public libraries have mentioned the need for immediate replacement of tornout or obsolete or lost books. The need for procuring latest editions or updated versions of books is stressed by the users from RPLs - Guntur and Visakhapatnam and also from the SCL - Hyderabad.

Another area needing concern is subscribing for all varieties of newspapers and all types of magazines in languages suited to the public from the surrounding areas. This is reported by RPLs - Visakhapatnam, Guntur and Nizamabad.

Table 4.66. *FELT* Needs of Users Regarding Libary Collection.

		Name of the library
1. All varieties of books (Text books, G.K. books, Books for competitive exams., Technical and subject books) need to be procured in sufficient numbers.	RPLs at	Visakhapatnam Rajahmundry Guntur Tirupati Nizamabad
	SCL at	Hyderabad
2. Number of copies of the important books should be increased.	RPLs at	Vikakhapatnam Rajahmundry
3. Torn-out/obsolete/lost books should be immediately replaced.	RPLs at SCL at	Guntur Hyderabad
4. New editions and updated books should be procured immediately and should be made available	RPLs at	Visakhapatnam Guntur
	SCL at	Hyderabad
5. All varieties of magazines and all news papers should be subscribed and should be made available.	RPL at	Visakhapatnam Guntur Nizamabad

Felt needs of the users regarding library services

Needs reported commonly by most of the users regarding the library services are shown in Table - 4.67.

Generally, the public libraries are scheduled to work for the convenience of the users from public. However, there appears some dissatisfaction with the hours of work is stressed by the RPLs - Rajahmundry, Visakhapatnam and Warangal. The same is also mentioned by relatively lesser proportion of users from the other libraries.

The need for automation of the RPLs for quicker access is mentioned by RPLs - Nizamabad, Guntur and Warangal. On the other hand, the need for providing internet facility is reported by RPLs - Visakhapatnam, Tirupati, Warangal and SCL - Hyderabad.

Table 4.67. *FELT* Needs of Users Regarding Libary Services.

	Type of service needed	*Name of the library where needed*	
1.	Need for extending the working hours of the library.	RPLs at	Rajahmundry Visakhapatnam Warangal
2.	Automation for quicker access	RPLs at	Nizamabad Guntur Warangal
3.	Internet facility	RPLs at	Visakhapatnam Tirupati Warangal
		SCL at	Hyderabad
4.	Timely binding of books, quick sorting and proper arrangement of books on racks	RPLs at	Nizamabad Rajahmundry Visakhapatnam Guntur
		SCL at	Hyderabad
5.	Should have separate reading rooms for newspapers and other subject books.	RPL at	Visakhapatnam Guntur
6.	Photocopying facility should be improved	RPLs at	Visakhapatnam Nizamabad
		SCL at	Hyderabad
7.	Loan period for books need to be increased	RPLs at	Tirupati Warangal
8.	New arrivals should be displayed	RPL at	Visakhapatnam
9.	Dusting activity should be taken up at regular intervals	SCL at	Hyderabad
10.	Staff need to work with more professional commitment and should be co-operative and helpful.	RPLs at	Rajahmundry Warangal
		SCL at	Hyderabad

Users from RPLs - Nizamabad, Rajahmundry, Visakhapatnam, Guntur and the SCL - Hyderabad have expressed displeasure with the condition of the books as well as arrangement of books on racks. They suggested that the books should be sent for binding as soon as they are damaged and action should be taken for quick sorting of consulted or used books and replacing them properly on racks. Users from

SCL-Hyderabad also suggested that dusting of books should be taken-up at frequent intervals.

The need for providing separate reading rooms for those who come to read news papers and for those who come to study subject or competitive examination books. This requirement was put forward by the users from RPLs - Visakhapatnam and Guntur. Users from RPLs - Visakhapatnam, Nizamabad and SCL - Hyderabad have asked for improving the photocopying facilities at their libraries.

It is also felt desirable that the new arrivals are displayed and is mostly reported by the users from RPL-Visakhapatnam. While the need for extending the loan period for books is mentioned by users from RPLs-Tirupati and Warangal.

Another important necessity reported by varying proportions of users is with regard to the library staff. They should be more committed to serve the clients in a better way, should be co-operative and helpful to the users as the user group is comprised of different age groups, different status groups and come with a variety of needs. Improvement in this aspect is needed by users from RPLs - Rajahmundry, Warangal and SCL - Hyderabad.

Felt needs of users regarding the facilities at the Libraries

Most commonly felt needs of the users with regard to the facilities at the libraries are listed in Table - 4.68.

The need for additional furniture especially the reading room chairs and tables is reported mostly by the users from RPLs - Tirupati, Visakhapatnam and Warangal. In the same way, necessity of improving the lighting and ventilation as well as providing fans, through stressed by users from RPLs -Visakhapatnam, Warangal and SCL - Hyderabad, also reported by relatively lesser proportion from other libraries.

Another important requirement reported by users with varying proportions in the provision of drinking water. This was stressed by those from RPLs - Rajahmundry, Tirupati, Warangal and also SCL - Hyderabad.

Table 4.68. *FELT* Needs of Users Regarding Facilities.

Facilities	*Name of the library where needed*	
1. More furniture required	RPLs at	Visakhapatnam Tirupati Warangal
2. Lighting and fans should be improved	RPLs at	Visakhapatnam Warangal
	SCL at	Hyderbad
3. Drinking water facility should be improved	RPLS at	Rajahmundry Tirupati Warangal
	SCL at	Hyderabad
4. Toilet and sanitation facilities need to be improved	RPLs at	Visakhapatnam Guntur Tirupati Warangal
	SCL at	Hyderabad
5. Seating capacity need to be improved	RPLs at	Visakhapatnam Guntur
	SCL at	Hyderabad
6. Space not sufficient and need to be increased	RPLs at	Visakhapatnam

It appears that the space available is not sufficient mainly at RPL - Visakhapatnam. The need for increasing the seating capacity is reported by users from RPLs - Visakhapatnam, Guntur and SCL - Hyderabad. This need is also mentioned by relatively few from other libraries.

Most importantly, the need for improving the sanitary conditions and toilet facilities is stressed by majority of the users from RPLs - Visakhapatnam, Guntur, Tirupati, Warangal and also the SCL - Hyderabad.

All these observations indicate that the Regional Public Libraries are having some constraints or impediments, as it appears that they are failing in providing basic amenities, sufficient reading material as well as in providing services.

SECTION-III: Views of the Librarians and Commissioner of Public Libraries on the Functioning of These Libraries

Librarians of the six Regional Public Libraries (RPLs) as well as the State Central Library (SCL) and also the Commissioner of Public Libraries were interviewed in order to know their views on the functioning of the public libraries in the state of Andhra Pradesh. The views of the Librarians and the Commissioner are separately presented in this section.

Views of the Librarians on the functioning of the RPLs

The seven Librarians were mainly asked to present their views on different aspects related to improving the functioning of the RPLs, their proposals and action so far taken and suggestion for improvement besides their previous association and experiences.

Past association and experiences of the Librarians with Public Library System

It is noticed that with the exception of the Librarians at RPLs - Warangal and Nizamabad who have been associated with public libraries for less than 5 years, the remaining four Librarians of the RPLs - Visakhapatnam, Rajahmundry, Guntur and Tirupati have been associated with the public libraries for 20-25 years while the Librarian of the SCL reported 30 years of association. These were associated in different capacities such as Assistant Librarian Grade-II, Grade-I and Librarian (Gazetted). The Librarians of the RPLs - Visakhapatnam, Warangal, Nizamabad and the SCL-

Hyderabad are members of the Indian Library Association (ILA), while the Librarians of the RPLs - Visakhapatnam and Guntur are having membership in Andhra Pradesh Public Libraries Association (APPLA).

The first impressions of these Librarians on assuming charge in Public Libraries is more or less uniform in the sense that they felt that the system has some good objectives and providing them a very good opportunity to serve readers of all types especially those who are poor and unemployed students. Most of them invariably felt that there is need to bring in lot of changes for extending better services to the public as these Libraries are special in the sense that they act as non-formal educational centres.

To a question as to what proposals they had for improving the functioning of these libraries and what steps have been taken - mainly the proposal for enhancing the budget allocations and need for improving the staff position by way of filling up the vacant positions and also the need for recruitment of additional staff were mentioned. In addition, proposals for introducing automation, providing internet facilities were also mentioned. Regarding the action taken, it was mentioned that in their capacity, they have sent the proposals for approval and sanction to their higher-ups. Automation has been initiated in RPLs - Guntur, Tirupati and SCL - Hyderabad and some other facilities are also being provided.

Librarians' views on some developmental aspects

All the seven Librarians supported the idea of establishing a computerized information network linking all the Regional Public Libraries and most of them are also in favour of establishing links with the District Central Library. Majority of them are also in support of establishing some databanks.

All these Librarians felt the need for introducing text books for Intermediate Courses while six of the seven

Librarians (with the exception of RPL - Visakhapatnam) also felt that text books for degree level, distance education/ entrance tests and general knowledge text books for competitive examinations are also need to be introduced why most of them suggested for inclusion of X - Class text books also under the Educational Information Activities. This is felt required in the context of changes in the educational system.

All these seven Librarians interviewed have expressed their willingness to utilize the services of the voluntary workers in Regional Public Libraries. This is felt essential in the light of the shortage of manpower as well as non-filling of the sanctioned posts, which are kept vacant for years.

These Librarians have also showed some agreement in reporting the need for improving the new lines of information services and the need for improving the resources for the public libraries. Four of them also opined that there is a need to introduce some special or new services in view of the changing public information needs.

Librarians' views on support from Library Associations and Committees

Six out of the seven Librarians (except the Librarian, RPL-Visakhapatnam) reported that the Library Associations are promoting the interests of the Public Libraries through library services. Five Librarians (excepting Librarians of RPL-Visakhapatnam and SCL-Hyderabad) have stated that the Library Associations are promoting the interests of Public Libraries through educational services and this promotion through bibliographical services is mentioned by three Librarians from RPLs - Guntur, Warangal and SCL-Hyderabad. While five Librarians (excepting the Librarians of RPL-Rajahmundry and Warangal) have mentioned this kind of promotion through publicity work by the Library Associations.

To another question on whether they have taken the help and cooperation of the Library Associations, only four Librarians out of the seven from RPLs - Rajahmundry, Warangal, Nizamabad and the SCL - Hyderabad have said that they have taken the help and co-operation of the Library Associations and persons interested in the public library development.

Three Librarians - from RPLs-Visakhapatnam, Tirupati and SCL - Hyderabad have expressed the view that the State Library Committee is of no help for them and all the seven Librarians have stated that they feel the need to have the public support for library development in the state and their efforts in getting the public support are yielding good results to some extent. They have also mentioned that they face some obstacles in implementing their programs mostly related to finance and manpower, and they are some how managing the situation and overcoming the obstacles. Some financial requirements are met through donations from donors while other problems related to the personnel are tackled with patience in motivating the available staff to go ahead with the programs.

Librarians' suggestions for public library development in State

The following are the main suggestions given by the Librarians for public library development in the state.

* One public library should be established for every 5,000 population.
* Collection of cess.
* Allocation of more funds for developing the collection as well as to improve the quality of services.
* Linking of all the libraries in the state for promoting better co-operation and loan facilities etc.
* Automation of the libraries and providing internet facility to the users and public.

* Establishing links with the District Central Library.
* Improving the staff position through filling up vacancies and also by making new recruitments.
* Providing funds to improve infra-structural facilities for the readers.

Views of the Commissioner of Public Libraries on the functioning of Public Libraries in the State

An IAS Officer in the cadre of secretary in the A.P. State Government was posted as the Commissioner of Public Libraries at the time of conducting this interview. Prior to this the office was treaded by a Director, who coordinates and controls the public library system in the state. Very recently, it is understood that again a Director was posted in place of the Commissioner.

By the time of taking this interview, the Commissioner had only one month association with the public libraries of the state. He opined that there is a need for strengthening the public libraries as per the Echora Committee recommendations. Initially he had plans to improve the infrastructural facilities in the existing public libraries of the state by seeing to it that at least there are basic amenities in all these libraries. And also he expressed that he had plans for networking of District Central Libraries and the Regional Public Libraries in the state.

He also mentioned that there is a state level committee which gives suggestions and monitors the Regional/Public library system in the state and he stressed that such committees are necessary to look into the functioning of the public library system. He also opined that periodical meetings of the state Regional Public Library Committees are helpful in improving the public library system in the state.

It is also mentioned that organizing meetings of the State Library Committee with the Regional Public Library Committees at regular intervals, help in identifying the local needs of the Regional Public Libraries through the Regional Public Library Committees and to chalk out remedial action plans through the State Library Committee's endorsement. The support of the State Library Committee is very essential in developing these libraries.

Speaking about his goals for development of the public library system, he state that he had plans to develop the Regional Public Libraries into Research and Reference Libraries linking them with the Zilla Grandhalaya Samstha Libraries (DCLs). He also had some plans for strengthening the public libraries which are existing now and also to open more number of village libraries. He agreed that there are some obstacles in achieving these objectives mainly related to allocation of funds and filling-up of vacant posts as well as creating new employment opportunities. He suggested acceptance of donations from public and pursuing the Non-Resident Indians (NRIs) of the respective areas to help in developing the libraries as the measures that can be taken to overcome some of the problems or obstacles related to finances.

He is aware of the Raja Ram Mohan Roy Library Foundation's policy on Public Libraries and also the National Policy on Public Libraries. As it is only one month since he has taken-up the responsibilities, he has concentrated his efforts on the implementation of the previous plans on a priority basis. He suggested the following aspects for improving the Public Library System in the state:

* Implementation of the Public Libraries Act.
* Enforcement of laws regarding cess collection.
* Appointing qualified professional staff in these libraries.
* Linking the regional libraries with the DCLs.
* Linking the public library system with school education and adult education.
* Establishing Regional Directorates for better monitoring of the functioning of the Regional Public Libraries.

5
Summary, Conclusions and Suggestions

The reading of books for education, for information, for social status, for emotional relief, for spiritual satisfaction, and for pleasure became a universal phenomenon. Library is an organized collection of books and other materials used for study, research and recreation.

A library should be developed not with a view to achieve prestige by having large number of books but to make it as a useful institution that spreads education among the people. The main reason for the development of Public libraries could be the expanded avenues for education, research and evolution of democratic ideas of the states responsibility towards common citizens.

A public library is a tax-supported institution serving a city, town, country or other local area. A public library functions as an intellectual powerhouse, aspiring to meet the intellectual, educational, recreational, informal and cultural requirements of the masses. A public library should act as a multi-purpose information - education - culture agency.

A public library is one that serves the entire population of a community. Everyone in the community, regardless of nationality, race, colour, creed, age, sex, status, educational attainments, language or any such considerations has a claim to its services as a matter of right. It is generally established and maintained out of public funds under the mandate of legislation. Public library service is generally free of charge, but some libraries charge a nominal fee. They are usually referred to as subscription libraries. This contention finds support in the modern definition of a public library as approved by the UNESCO and IFLA, which is "Public

Libraries are those libraries which serve the population of a community or region free of charge or for a nominal fee". The UNESCO manifesto has envisaged four functions for the public library, viz., (i) promoting education, (ii) fostering culture, (iii) disseminating information, and (iv) providing recreation. In addition, it highlights the need for public library service to children and to the handicapped sections of the society.

According to APPL Act 1960 the Andhra State Library situated at Hyderabad was declared as the State Central Library. After the formation of Andhra Pradesh, the State Central Library at Visakhapatnam was converted as the State Regional Library. That is how the first Regional Library was established at Visakhapatnam. In 1958, the Visakhapatnam State Regional Library was shifted to Guntur and this was only State Regional Library functioning in the State till the end of 1963. At present, there are seven regional libraries, in the state out of these seven regional libraries, the State Central Library at Hyderabad is also covered in the present study as this is also a Government Regional Library.

In actual practice, the Regional Libraries have failed miserably in the implementation of their objectives. As per the Government's expectations each Regional Library has to expand its library services atleast to five districts. There may be District Central Library of the Zilla Grandhalaya Samstha functioning in each District headquarters and the branch libraries in the rural areas. As these Regional Libraries were established at the district headquarters to supplement the services of the District Central Library.

The regional libraries should show 'high standards of service' to stand as a model to guide the district central libraries. In reality, these regional libraries were unable to show any leadership to the District central libraries. Neither these regional libraries are unable to collect and preserve the manuscripts to develop local history collections, nor providing any facilities to the research scholars and historians. Even the basic reference collections in these libraries are of poor quality.

The libraries directly managed by the Government in Andhra Pradesh happen to be the State Central Library, Hyderabad and five Regional Libraries at Tirupathi, Guntur, Visakhapatnam, Warangal and Nizamabad including mobile library at Eluru. These libraries appear to have failed in delivering the goods, by not playing their legitimate role, in the absence of clarity in the set goals and objectives. All these libraries are simply duplicating the services of the Samastha Libraries at the District level.

Although, the process of automation and providing technical training to the professionals has been initiated, the situation is not uniform in the Regional Libraries in the State of Andhra Pradesh as these Libraries were set up in different periods of time.

Study Design

Hence, in the above backdrop, it is felt that there is a need for studying the functioning of these Public Libraries and related social issues and their influence on the society. Accordingly, the present study was proposed and it is decided to cover all these libraries in order to understand the functioning of these Regional Public Libraries and the study is designed to be taken-up with the following objectives :

(*i*) To study the facilities and services available in these Regional Public Libraries at present.

(*ii*) To understand the opinion of the librarians as well as users regarding the functioning of these libraries.

(*iii*) To identify the felt needs of the users in utilizing the services of these libraries.

(*iv*) To collect the opinion of the librarians and users on the areas in which interventions for development are required, and

To obtain suggestions from these respondents for making recommendations for strengthening public library system in the state.

Keeping in mind the objectives, the study is planned and three areas are identified for obtaining the needed information.

(*i*) Institutions - i.e., the Regional Public Libraries.

(*ii*) Library Professionals - Librarians and the higher authorities i.e., the Commissioner, Public Libraries, Andhra Pradesh.

(*iii*) Users - users or readers of these libraries.

The user or reader community in case of the Regional Public Libraries is heterogeneous comprising of students, employees, businessmen, retired people, women and children. All these people visit the libraries according to their convenient timings and selecting a strictly random sampling is a difficult task. Hence, in the present study, each library was visited for 6 - 7 days for covering the user sample. Each day one hour in the morning and one hour in the evening these users were covered and each day, the interviews were done at different timings. The interviews were done in the form of exit interviews - i.e. during the fixed one-hour, some of the users who are leaving the library were selected for interviews irrespective of their status. Each day 20 - 25 interviews were conducted during the selected two hours time in the two sessions and it is decided to collect information from users in excess of 150 from each of the seven selected libraries.

Direct personal interviews and obtaining information through structured questionnaires are the two methods employed for data collection in the present study. Structured questionnaires have been used for obtaining information regarding the functioning of the library and also for obtaining user information. For getting the views and suggestions from the librarians and higher-ups, direct personal interview (using a check list of aspects on which questions are to be asked) is employed. Two types of questionnaires were constructed and pre-tested. Finalized questionnaires were used for obtaining the needed information and the information elicited from the structured questionnaires were analysed using the SPSS package (Version 8.0) on personal computers.

Simple statistical methods have been used in the study keeping in mind the purpose of the study. Mostly comparisons were made using the percentages and chi-square values were computed for notifying the significance of differences among the groups.

Observations of the Study

Information gathered from the three types of respondents was analysed and discussed under the following sections.

SECTION - I: FUNCTIONING OF THE REGIONAL PUBLIC LIBRARIES

Four of the seven librarians are having graduate degrees while the remaining three are post-graduates. On the other hand four of them are having MLISc. and the remaining three are having BLISc. degrees as professional qualifications. Although, these librarians are having professional qualification, most of them expressed that they need special courses and training programmes on application of computer in libraries in order to cope up with the latest development.

Details of space available

Except two Regional Public Libraries (RPLs) at Visakhapatnam and Tirupati, the rest of the libraries are housed in their own buildings. The librarian expressed the need for independent building to cater various information services. Nearly 50 percent of the librariès are located at the places convenient to users. It is advisable to shift the libraries that are located in places not convenient to users to suitable places, to facilitate the user group, as well as to attract the users in large numbers to these libraries.

Almost all the libraries reported that they have reasonable space to house the library materials, but many of them expressed that the available space would not be sufficient for future expansion. Many of the libraries are not able to keep the book collection in a proper way, as the space is not sufficient. To go along with the fifth law of library science 'library is a growing organism' the buildings of these libraries need to be expanded both horizontally and vertically at least once in 10 years.

Accommodation for different sections in the Library

All the seven libraries covered in the study have reported that they are having separate accommodation for different sections. All these have reported separate accommodation for Librarian's room, stack room, reference section and technical section. All the libraries, with the exception of RPL at Tirupati reported availability of accommodation for computer section. It is an appreciating feature that all the libraries have various selections in their libraries to attend and offer various services to users. The librarians are of the opinion that space for computer section be provided on a priority basis.

Normal Schedule of Work

All the six RPLs and the SCL have reported that they work for 6 days in a week and normally have 20 holidays in a year excluding the weekly holidays. Four out of the six RPLs, those at Visakhapatnam, Rajahmundry , Tirupati and Nizamabad are working for 6 hours a day in two shifts i.e. 8 am to 11 a.m. and 4 p.m. to 7 p.m. The remaining two RPLs at Guntur and Warangal and also the SCL at Hyderabad are functioning for 12 hours a day on all working days between 8 am and 8 p.m. Except the SCL, all the RPL have reported, that the working hours for 6 hours in two shifts. It is suggested that the library working hours be increased to 8 - 10 hours per day by sanctioning other facilities like staff, infrastructures etc. If the library is kept opened for long hours, there is scope for offering services to more users.

Furniture available and future requirements

All these seven libraries covered in the present study are having sufficient number of reading tables and chairs and book racks as well as office furniture and also reported that all the libraries are having electricity and fans in their reading rooms. The major requirement mentioned by all the six RPLs is the Internet facility. The SCL has reported that they need some additional tables and chairs for the reading room, book racks, audio-visual equipment, some electronic equipment and also some more computer systems for use in their library. Necessary equipment and needed furniture should be provided to these libraries periodically. Otherwise it becomes difficult to manage the books and periodicals without having necessary bookracks.

Staff position

In all the six RPLs, there is one Librarian (Gazetted) and a minimum of one Assistant Librarian (Grade-I). Regarding the semi-professionals, 3 card writers are there in RPL-Rajahmundry, 2 in Nizamabad, 1 each in Tirupati and Warangal and none in Visakhapatnam and Guntur. Except in RPL - Nizamamad, Record Assistants are functioning in all the remaining five RPLs. The staff position at the SCL, Hyderabad is totally different from that of the RPLs. Altogether there are 72 staff members working in the SCL.

Income and Expenditure for the year 2002-2003

The major source of income for these libraries is reported to be the annual grant released by the state government and the amount accumulated through user subscriptions. While the major component under expenditure is mentioned to be the payment of staff salaries and other allowances.

All the library staff expressed that there is a need for more staff to open the library for longer hours and offer better information services.

Ways of Library Collection

All the six RPLs and the SCL, with the exception of RPLs at Tirupati and Nizamabad, are having a set selection policy for the development of print materials while there is no such policy for the development of non-print materials. Regarding the methods of procuring the documents as well as other library materials, all the RPLs and SCL have mentioned that they do mostly purchase from the available grants or get them by way of gifts from other agencies or individuals.

Type of Material Available

All the six RPLs and SCL have reported the availability of book materials, periodicals and newspapers in their libraries. All of them have reported the availability of cartographic material. Seminar papers are not reported by any of the six RPLs.

Average Book Collection during the past 5 years

Average collection of books during the last five years ranged from a low of 39,519 in RPL - Visakhapatnam to a high of 1,15,011 in RPL - Guntur. This figure is 4,17,424 at the SCL. This book collection is RPLs mainly include books in Telugu, English, Hindi, Urdu and Sanskrit. Where as books in Marathi, Kannada and Tamil languages are also reported in addition by the SCL.

Average collection of Periodicals during the past 5 years

The average collection of periodicals among the six RPLs ranged from a low of 33 in Nizamabad to a high of 111 in Rajahmundry. This average collection is 205 in the SCL. When the periodicals by language are considered periodicals in Telugu are more in RPLs at Visakhapatnam, Rajahmundry and Nizamabad.

Availability and Maintenance of non-book material

Five out of the six RPLs, with the exception of RPL at Tirupati and also the SCL have reported the availability of all the three types of cartographic material viz., maps, globes and atlases in their libraries. RPLs at Tirupati, Warangal and SCL have reported the availability of all the three types of graphic material - charts, film clips and slides.

Manuscripts, audio-video recordings and microfilms are reported to be available at RPL - Rajahmundry. The facilities available to house cartographic materials, manuscripts etc., are not sufficient. Therefore, it is suggested that these libraries should develop the storage facilities on a priority basis for the non-book materials and special materials etc. Cartographic material is one of the important library collections. It is observed that most of the libraries are not giving any kind of preference to acquire them, may be due to the space and funds problem. Since the cartographic material depicts crucial information, a plan should be prepared to acquire them in these libraries.

Display of charts/models/posters and preservation of News Papers

All the six RPLs and the SCL are displaying charts, models, posters and other exhibits that carry government and public interests. These display items are in general, carry messages regarding health awareness, family welfare, national book week and book exhibitions.

Extent of Library Automation

Three out of the six RPLs (Visakhapatnam, Tirupati and Nizamabad) and also the SCL, were not so far automated. The remaining three RPLs are partially automated. This shows the need for automation in the public libraries, which is very essential in the days of technological revolution. All these libraries should be automated on priority basis otherwise it would be no use to acquire any kind of electronic media and difficult to get the facilities available in Information Technology.

Maintenance of Registers and frequency of stock verification

Accession register is maintained by all the RPLs and the SCL while maintenance of staff list cards is reported by RPL-Guntur and the SCL. All these libraries have stated that the stock verification is carried out only periodically but not on annual basis. It is not fair to make the librarians responsible for the loss of books. The guidelines followed in the case of the degree colleges may be extended to these libraries in this regard.

Book access, classification and cataloguing

All the RPLs and the SCL have reported that they are following the open access system and the RPL - Rajahmundry mentioned that access is closed for reference section in their library. All these seven libraries have also mentioned that the library collection is classified and they are following the DDC scheme for the purpose of classification. It is a good sign that all the libraries are maintaining accession registers, an authority record. Most of the librarians expressed that due to paucity of staff, it would not be possible for them to maintain shelf list.

A catalogue is reported to be maintained in all the six RPLs and the SCL. Regarding the type of catalogue used, there is some variation between these libraries.

Membership

All these libraries have reported that they follow some special conditions in giving book-borrowing facility to their members. However, they all mentioned that the registered members will have the borrowing facility while in RPL-Rajahmundry and SCL - Hyderabad, all the permanent members are also having this book borrowing facility. None of these seven libraries have reported loan facility to the non-members.

Book - borrowing Procedures

Only three out of the six RPLs - Rajahmundry, Tirupati and Warangal and also the SCL have informed that they are providing services to the non-resident borrowers who include adults (persons who have completed their studies), students (persons in school or college i.e. from 9th class to Graduation or above) and children (any child below 9th grade in school).

Reading material other than print material is not lent in any of these seven public libraries. In general, books are given for a period of two weeks and periodicals and reference books are not lent in any of these libraries.

Library Committee

Only three RPLs at Visakhapatnam, Rajahmundry and Warangal and the SCL at Hyderabad have reported that they have a library committee. In the SCL, the library committee is constituted by the state government under the provisions of A.P. Public Libraries Act 1980. Other committees like book selection committee, library development committee, weeding out of books committee and readers forum are constituted at the local level involving the relevant persons from different fields. All the seven libraries have reported that they are having a book selection committee comprising of 5 - 7 members through the government nomination.

Inter- Library Loan facility

Regarding the inter-library loan facility, it is reported that the RPL - Rajahmundry is having inter-library loan facility with four libraries while the RPL at Warangal is having this facility with libraries all over the state. However, the SCL has mentioned that they are having inter-library loan facility with only two other libraries. It is suggested that the inter-library loan facility should be established as it helps in meeting the varied information requirements of the users.

Proposals for extending co-operation among the RPLs

Only two RPLs - Tirupati and Warangal and also the SCL at Hyderabad are having some proposals for establishing co-operation among all the Regional Public Libraries at the state level. None of these seven public libraries are contributing to the national bibliography. Co-operation among these libraries are very essential and necessary efforts should be made to coordinate all these libraries for maximum utilization of resources and to develop the Union Catalogues of the State Regional Libraries. The Union Catalogues will help and develop the Bibliography of the Andhra Pradesh State.

Material available for Extension and other Activities

Computers and television are available with all the RPLs and the SCL. Availability of audio-visual material is reported by only four RPLs at Rajahmundry, Tirupati, Warangal and Nizamabad. The availability of Internet, VCD, Record Player, Xerox services etc., are far from satisfaction in any of these libraries, though getting information and transfer of information through Internet is least expensive. Therefore the Internet facility should be made available on priority basis in all the libraries.

Publicity, Extension and Other Activities

All these seven public libraries are celebrating the National Library week. All these libraries are organizing activities such as book exhibitions, arranging popular lecturers and public meetings, felicitations to renowned persons, conducting sports during festivals and festive occasions and organizing some special activities for women.

The mobile library service is not reported in any of these libraries. Hence, it is suggested that mobile library services need to be established in order to reach people at their door-steps especially in villages, where libraries are not established.

Community Information Services

(i) Community Information for Women: With some degree of variation in the aspects covered, all the seven public libraries are providing community information services to the women. The information is provided mainly on aspects such as family planning, women's health, child health, women's programmes, employment opportunities for women, adult education and distance education. These services are very crucial for social, political and economic development of women. These services should be strengthened faster to attract all women to use the services offered.

(ii) Community Information on Agriculture: Four out of the six RPLs at Rajahmundry, Guntur, Tirupati and Warangal and also the SCL at Hyderabad are providing community information on agriculture. The information relating to various aspects of agriculture is useful for farmers to strengthen them economically. These services should be planned according to the local requirements of farmers.

(iii) Community Information on Medico-Legal aspects: All the RPLs mentioned that they are providing information about the government and private hospitals, nursing homes and clinics availability around their city. Only three RPLs at Rajahmundry, Warangal and Nizamabad have reported that they are providing information on legal aspects. The medical and legal information is crucial for people living in rural and urban areas. The knowledge of hospitals in public and private sector is necessary for people and also legal knowledge at least to protect their interest. It is desirable to have this kind of services in all regional libraries in true sense.

(iv) Forms of Community Information available: The community information is available mainly in the form of books, booklets and pamphlets. Also through slogan posters and pictorial posters through government publication. This information is also reported to be disseminated through

meetings and official government programmes. It is reported that all libraries are not offering the community information services. It is high time for these libraries to make available all kinds of community information for the benefit of users.

SECTION - II: FUNCTIONING OF THE PUBLIC LIBRARIES AND USER'S PERCEPTION

Composition of the users

The composition of the users interviewed reveals that nearly 83 percent of them are males and the remaining 17 percent are females. Interestingly about 60 percent of these users are in the age group of 31 - 34 years and 31 percent are aged below 31 years. Special efforts be put-forth to encourage women to use the library resource for improvement of their personality.

Duration of the use of the Regional Public Libraries

About 34 percent of the users reported that they have been using the services of these libraries for 1 - 4 years while nearly 31 percent said that they were coming to these libraries only since few months. The percentage of users who were coming to the library for more than 10 years is more in the case of RPL - Rajahmundry (14 percent) and is lowest in RPL - Nizamabad (2 percent).

In both the sexes, the proportion reporting 1-4 years of use is more, followed by those reporting a few months of use, 5-10 years of use and more than 10 years of use. Those reporting first visit is more among the females (23 percent) compared to the males (11 percent). Considering use of these libraries by age, it is noticed that more proportion of users aged 35 years or above are using the library for 5 years or more followed by those in the age group of 21-34 years and those who are aged 21 years or below. The proportion using the library for more than five years is more among the retired employees (60 percent) followed by businessmen (50 percent), employees (47 percent) and students (15 percent). Thus, there are significant differences in the duration of the use of the public libraries among the two sexes, between the four age and status groups considered in this study.

Frequency of using the Library

Nearly 64 percent of the users of these public libraries are frequent visitors while the remaining 36 percent are infrequent and occasional.

Nearly 63 percent of the males and 68 percent of the females have mentioned that they frequently visit this library. This proportion is more in the age group of 21-34 years (67 percent) followed by those who are aged 65 years and above (64 percent), who are aged 21 years or below (63 percent) and those in the age group of 35-64 years (40 percent). By status, students are the frequent visitors (69 percent) followed by retired employees (53 percent), employees (45 percent) and businessmen (32 percent). Differences in the proportion of users with regard to the frequency of visit are significant by age and status of the users while they are not significant by sex of the users.

Purpose of visit to the public libraries

Three types of responses were mainly obtained with regard to the purpose of visit to the libraries. They are: (i) for pleasure, (ii) on business and (iii) for some information. It is very heartening to note that 81 percent of the users are visiting the library to get some information.

The females visiting the library for some information is found to be more (84 percent) compared to that of males (81 percent). Majority of the users in all the four age groups are visiting the library mainly for some information and this proportion is more in the younger age groups than among the older ones. The students (86 percent) are visiting the library for some information followed by the employees (68 percent), businessmen (57 percent) and retired employees (53 percent). These differences in the purpose of visit by sex, age and status of the users are found to be statistically significant.

Time spent in the library during a visit

Nearly 48 percent of the users reported that they spend 1-2 hours usually during their visit to the library and 34 percent spend more than 2 hours time in the library during a visit. Most of the users expressed the need for improving the furniture, proper ventilation; artificial and natural air and light, important facilities like, drinking water and toilets, etc. This would not only attract more readers but also encourage them to sit for longer hours.

About 47 percent of the males and 51 percent of the females are spending 1-2 hours time in the library during a visit. The users in all the four groups have reported spending of 1-2 hours during a visit. These percentages ranged from 42 in the age group of 35-64 years to 53 in the age group of 21 years or below. By status of the users, 50 percent of the students, 46 percent of the businessmen, 39 percent of the employees and 28 percent of the retired employees are spending 1-2 hours time in the library during a visit. Differentials in the time spent in library during a visit by sex, age and status of the users are found to be statistically significant.

Purpose of visit to the Library

On the day of this interview, about 46 percent of the users came to the library to look-up for some references of information while another 33 percent for using the reading room facility. About 4 percent came to borrow a fiction book and 7 percent borrowed a non-fictional book and 5 percent came to ask for some information. The remaining 5 percent have mentioned some other purposes.

Nearly 54 percent of the females and 45 percent of the males have come to look-up for some reference or information. It is observed that the percentage who came to borrow a fiction or non-fiction book is more in the older age groups (35 years or above). The retired employees and businessmen have come to borrow either a fictional or non-fictional book compared to the students and employees. On the other hand, students and employees have mainly come to look-up for some reference or information in larger proportions compared to the retired employees and businessmen. Again differentials by sex, age and status of the users are found to be significant.

Users' opinion on the Library Collection

A little over half of the respondents (51 percent) have said that the collection is good in their respective libraries. The proportion of users who reported that the library collection is very good and more in RPL-Nizamabad (32 percent) followed by RPL-Tirupati and RPL-Visakhapatnam (30 percent each), RPL-Guntur (27 percent), RPL-Rajahmundry (24 percent) and RPL-Warangal (19 percent).

About 25 percent of females and 27 percent of the males ranked the collection as very good while 55 percent of females and 50 percent of males ranked it good. Considering the age of the users, it is noticed that there is no variation in the proportion ranking the collection as very good between the four age groups considered. Users from businessmen (36 percent) and retired employees (33 percent) have ranked the collection as very good compared to that among students (26 percent) and employees (24 percent). However, significant differences are observed only by status of the users in this aspect.

Users' view on co-operation and helpfulness of the Library Staff

A majority of the users (92 percent), in general have expressed that the library staff are co-operative and helpful. There is not much variation in the two sexes with regard to this expression and this proportion is more in the younger age group i.e. those with 21 years or below (96 percent) followed by the age group of 21 - 34 years and 65 + years group (91 percent each) and relatively low in the age group of 35 - 64 years. Majority of the students have reported that the staff are co-operative and helpful (94 percent), followed by employees (84 percent), retired employees (83 percent) and businessmen (80 percent). Differentials by age and status of users are found to be statistically significant.

Users' opinion on establishing Computerized Information Network linking all the RPLs

In all, about 86 percent of the users of the RPLs have felt that establishing computerized information network, linking all the RPLs in the state is very much required and useful.

This proportion is more among the males (87 percent) compared to the females (84 percent) and is more from the younger age groups compared to the older ones. A majority of the students (88 percent), employees (84 percent) and retired employees (80 percent) have also supported this view. However, differentials by age and status the users are only found to be significant.

Users' view on establishing Data Banks

About 83 percent of the users are in favour of establishing data banks in RPLs as they reported it as required and useful. Among the seven libraries also, there is not much variation in the proportion of users expressing this view.

Nearly 84 percent of the males and 82 percent of the females have expressed that establishing data banks in RPLs is required and is useful. This proportion is nearly 81 percent in the age group of 21 years and below, 86 percent in 21 - 34 years age group, 74 percent in 35 - 64 years age group and 82 percent in the 65 + years age group. A majority of the students (86 percent), employees (77 percent), retired employees (78 percent) and businessmen (68 percent) have supported this, the differentials by age and status with regard to this view being statistically significant.

Users' opinion on establishing links with District Central Library (DCL)

Out of the 1124 respondents, a majority (86 percent) are of the opinion that the RPLs should have links with the District Central Libraries (DCLs).

The proportion of females is more (89 percent) than that of the males (86 percent) regarding the opinion that establishing links between RPLs and the DCL is required and useful. All the respondents in the age group of 65 + years, 89 percent in the age group of 21 years or below, 85 percent in 21 - 34 years age group and 77 percent in the 35 - 64 years age group are in support of this view. Nearly 89 percent of the students, 77 percent of the employees, 74 percent of the businessmen and 73 percent of the retired employees viewed the same as required and useful. Here also, the differentials by age and status of the users were found to be significant.

Opinion of the users on the facilities available in the Library

More than half of the respondents (57 percent) feel that the facilities available at their libraries are up to the mark while the remaining 43 percent said that the facilities are to be improved. Nearly 62 percent of the females and 56 percent of the males are of the opinion that the facilities available at their libraries are up to the mark. The proportion of users who are satisfied with the available facilities in their libraries is more in older age groups compared to the younger ones. About 71 percent of the businessmen, 61 percent of the employees, 60 percent of the retired employees and 56 percent of the students have mentioned that the facilities available at the libraries are up to the mark. Differentials by sex, age and status with regard to their view are not significant.

Opinion of the users on the furniture available in their Libraries

Only 37 percent of the users reported that the available furniture is up to the mark and the remaining 63 percent felt that there is need for improvement.

Nearly 67 percent of males and 46 percent of the females were not satisfied with the available furniture in the libraries. Considering the age of users, 83 percent from the age group of 35 - 64 years, 73 percent from 65 + years age group, 62 percent from 21 - 34 years age group and 60 percent from 21 years or below age group have reported the need for improving the furniture in their libraries. The proportion of respondents who feel this need is more among the businessmen (86 percent) followed by employees (74 percent), retired employees (73 percent) and students (60 percent). These differentials are statistically significant. It is evident that most of the users of all these libraries have expressed the available furniture is not sufficient to use the material to full extent. Therefore, there is a need to improve the level of furniture to the satisfaction of users, which in turn improves the use of library materials.

Opinion of the users on the existing library services

Regarding the existing library services about 67 percent of the users feel the need for improving the library services while only 33 percent stated that they are up to the mark.

The proportion of users who feel the need for improvement in the library services is more among males (69 percent) compared to the females (55 percent). This proportion has shown increase from younger (62 percent) to older age groups (82 percent). This view is expressed more by the retired employees (83 percent) followed by businessmen (80 percent), employees (76 percent) and students (64 percent). Differentials by sex, age and status of the users in this regard are significant. Since many of the respondents are not satisfied with the existing library services like compilers of bibliography, internet research, employment opportunities, pervious examination question papers to students, etc., should be made available.

Users' opinion on the existing equipment in the library

About 69 percent of the respondents reported that the equipment in their libraries is not up to the mark and need to be improved.

This proportion is more among the males (72 percent) compared to females (53 percent). And it is more in the older age groups than in the younger ones, while low among the students compared to other categories of users. Differentials by sex, age and status with regard to this opinion are found to be statistically significant.

Users' opinion on the available book resources in the library

It is noticed that only 19 percent of the uses are satisfied with the available book resources or library collection while the remaining 81 percent reported that it should be improved.

The proportion of users who feel that the available book resources or library collection need to be improved is more among males (82 percent) compared to females (77 percent). This proportion is found to be 78 percent among those aged 21 years or below, 81 percent among those in 21 - 34 years age group, 87 percent among 35 - 64 percent age group and 82 percent in the 65 + years age group. When the status is considered, it is noticed that the proportion of users who are dissatisfied with the available book resources is 81 percent among students, 80 percent among employees and retired employees and 88 percent among businessmen, the differentials being significant. So necessary steps need to be taken for improving the quality and standards of book resources and there is a need to take into account local needs of users and their requirements while selecting books.

Willingness of the users to pay user charges

Only 38 percent of the users are willing to pay the user charges for the services they receive from the library.

This proportion is more among the females (43 percent) than the males (37 percent). When the age group is considered, about 37 percent in the age group of 21 years or below, 38 percent in 21 - 34 years age group, 37 percent in 35 - 64 years age group and 45 percent in 65 + years age group are willing to pay the user charges. In the same way, when the status is considered, 38 percent each from the students and employees, 55 percent from retired employees and 29 percent from businessmen reported willingness to pay the user charges for the services they receive from their libraries. Hence, there is no wrong in collecting user changes for the sustenance of the libraries and not for earning profits. This is useful as the grants are not adequate for these libraries.

Felt needs of the users

The major requirement regarding the library collection is the need for procuring all varieties of books i.e., text books, reference books, books on general knowledge, books for competitive exams, other technical and subject books. And also, the number of copies should be more or should be sufficient for users.

Felt needs of the users regarding library services

Some dissatisfaction is reported with the hours of work by the users from RPLs-Rajahmundry, Visakhapatnam and Warangal. The need for automation of the RPLs for quicker access is mentioned by users from RPLs-Nizamabad, Guntur and Warangal. Users from RPLs-Nizamabad, Rajahmundry, Visakhapatnam, Guntur and the SCL-Hyderabad have expressed displeasure with the condition of the books as well as the shelf arrangement of books on racks.

The users from RPLs-Visakhapatnam and Guntur reported that the need for providing separate reading rooms for those who come to read news papers and those who come to study subject or competitive examination books. The staff should be more committed to serve the clients in a better way, should be co-operative and helpful to the users as the user group is comprised of different age groups, different status groups and come with a variety of needs.

Felt needs of users regarding the facilities at the Libraries

The need for additional furniture especially the reading room chairs and tables is reported mostly by the users from RPLs - Tirupati, Visakhapatnam and Warangal. The space available is said to be not sufficient mainly at RPL-Visakhapatnam. The need for improving the sanitary conditions and toilet facilities is stressed by majority of the users from RPLs-Visakhapatnam, Guntur, Tirupati, Warangal and also the SCL-Hyderabad. All these observations indicate that the Regional Public Libraries are having some constraints or impediments, as it appears that they are failing in providing basic amenities, sufficient reading material as well as in providing services. So, reasonable attention should be paid to improve the existing facilities and implement new facilities.

SECTION - III: VIEWS OF THE LIBRARIANS AND COMMISSIONER OF PUBLIC LIBRARIES ON THE FUNCTIONING OF THESE LIBRARIES

The first impressions of these Librarians on assuming charge in Public Libraries is more or less uniform in the sense that they felt that the system has some good objectives and providing them a very good opportunity to serve readers of all types especially those who are poor and mostly unemployed students. Proposals for introducing automation, providing Internet facilities were also mentioned. Regarding the action taken, it was mentioned that in their capacity, they have sent the proposals for these facilities for approval and sanction to their higher-ups. Automation has been initiated in RPLs-Guntur, Tirupati and SCL - Hyderabad and some other facilities are also being provided.

Librarians' views on some developmental aspects

All the seven Librarians supported the idea of establishing a computerized information network linking all the Regional Public Libraries and most of them are also in favour of establishing links with the District Central Library. The need for introducing text books for Intermediate Courses while six of the seven Librarians (with the exception of RPL-Visakhapatnam) also felt that text books for degree level, distance education/entrance tests and general knowledge text books for competitive examinations.

These Librarians have also showed some agreement in reporting the need for improving the new lines of information services and the need for improving the resources for the public libraries.

Librarians' views on support from Library Associations and Committees

Most of the librarians (except the Librarian, RPL-Visakhapatnam) reported that the Library Associations are promoting the interests of the Public Libraries through library services. Majority of the librarians said that they have taken the help and co-operation of the Library Associations and persons interested in the public library development.

All the seven Librarians have stated that they feel the need to have the public support for library development in the state and their efforts in getting the public support are yielding good results to some extent.

Librarians' suggestions for public library development in State

For public library development interests, one library for every 50,000 population, requirements in collection of cess, offer services, cooperation among these libraries, automation in libraries, etc., were suggested by these librarians.

The Commissioner of Public Libraries felt that there is a need for strengthening the public libraries as per the Ecbote Committee recommendations. He also suggested for improvement of the infrastructural facilities in the existing public libraries of the state and networking of District Central Libraries and the Regional Public Libraries in the state.

Organizing meetings of the State Library Committee with the Regional Public Library Committees at regular intervals help in identifying the local needs of the Regional Public Libraries through the Regional Public Library Committees and to chalk out remedial action plans through the State Library Committee's endorsement. For developing the Regional Public Libraries into Research and Reference Libraries linking them with the Zilla Grandhalaya Samstha Libraries (DCLs) is a necessity. He also suggested strengthening the public libraries which are existing now and also to open more number of village libraries.

For improvement of public library system in Andhra Pradesh, the implementation of public library act, collection of cess, appointment of qualified staff in libraries, networking of libraries, linking the public libraries with school and adult education progammes are requested.

In conclusion, it can be said that the functioning of the Regional Public Libraries in the state of Andhra Pradesh is not quite satisfactory, regarding several lacunae that need to be reminded. Observations of the present study clearly indicate that these libraries have failed in providing even basic amenities and infrastructural facilities and also in providing services to the satisfactions of their clients. Hence, there is an urgent need on the part of the authorities to analyse the existing system, find out the constraints or impediments in meeting the goals of these libraries. First, they should pay attention for improving the existing facilities as well as services in these libraries and then should take-up improvements and new interventions as quickly as possible because the traditional library environment is rapidly changing to electronic environment.

Basing on a careful analysis of the observations made from the present study the following suggestions are made for improving the functioning of the Regional Public Libraries.

Suggestions

(A) Suggestions for improving infrastructural facilities

* All these libraries should be accommodated in own buildings with sufficient space for organizing all activities and also keeping in mind the future needs in the process of development. These should be located at places more accessable and convenient to users.
* Infrastructure like reading room chairs, tables, book racks should be provided sufficiently. Necessary items should be supplied at regular intervals in order to organize the accumulated collection.
* More attention should be provided for improving basic amenities like - proper lighting, ventilation, good drinking water, better toilet facilities and care should be taken on cleanliness and sanitation.

Vacant posts should be filled and also providing additional staff at places where needed can be considered.

(B) Suggestions for improving Library Services

* Efforts for automation and providing Internet facility should be taken up on priority basis.
* The staff should be given special training especially in the use of computers and periodical refresher training activities should be planned.

* Arrangements should be made for display of the new arrivals and also are should be taken to replace the books used on racks as well as on quick rack arrangement.
* Books which are important and are in bad condition should be immediately binded and made available.
* All varieties of books should be procured and the number of important books should be more and should be sufficient for users. Always, latest editions should be made available. Book selection committees should be committed to develop the collection according to the local needs.
* .Steps should be taken to acquire and provide all sorts of newspapers and magazines to the users as per the local needs and also cartographic material.
* Period of loan for books borrowed need to be increased.
* Other services like photo copying etc. should be improved.
* The Library should be kept open for longer hours as per the needs of the users. If not, at least some sections as requested by majority of the users should be kept open for longer hours.
* Separate reading rooms should be provided for those reading only the newspapers and for those who study for different examinations.
* Steps are needed to attract more women users byway of providing suitable services.
* Staff should work with more commitment and service motto. They should be cooperative and helpful to users.

(C) Suggestions for improving the Functioning of Regional Public Libraries

* Computerized information network linking all the RPLs in the state is essential.

* RPLs should be linked with DCLs and efforts are needed to establish data banks at the respective RPLs.
* There is also need for improving the inter-library loan services.
* Need for improving the community information services.
* Staff position in terms of number and skills should be improved.
* There is also a need for increasing the number of village libraries.
* Mobile service units should be implemented to increase the readership at village level.
* There is a need for text books for students for Intermediate and Degree level. These should be introduced along with books needed for distance education, entrance examinations and competitive examinations.
* These library services should be linked to school and adult education programmes also.
* Sufficient financial support in meeting the goals of these libraries should be extended. Other means like collecting cess, and user charges may also be considered for sustaining the activities of these libraries.
* Cooperation from the library associations and people who are interested should be taken for development of public libraries.
* Meetings of the State Library Committee with RPL committees should be organised at regular intervals in order to identify the local needs and to initiate action in the needed lines.

Bibliography

1. Adak, T.: Development of public libraries in Andaman and Nicobar Islands. Granthana, 4(1 and 2), 1994, p. 117-9.
2. Adimorah, Eno: An analysis of progress made by Public Libraries as social institutions in Nigeria, UNESCO Journal of Information Science, Librarianship and Archives Administration, 5(3), 1983.
3. Aggarwal, D.S.: Public Library and the new literate in India - A survey of developments. Library Herald, 12(1), 1970.
4. Agnoli, A.: L'emergence des bibliotheques pour la jeunesse. The emergence of chihldren's libraries. Bibliotheque(s), (1), 2002, p. 49-51.
5. Agrawal, S.P.: National and Public Libraries in India. International Library Review, 17(3), July 1985, p. 293-312.
6. Agrawal, S.P.; Walia, Meena; Lal, Manohar: Development of public libraries in India: review and projections. International Library Movement, 8(2), 1986, p. 82-99.
7. American Library Association and Public Library Association Standards Committee. Minimum Standards for Public Library Systems, 1966, ALA, 1967.
8. American Library Association, Coordinating Committee on Revision of Public Library Standards. Public Library Service, a guide to Evaluate with minimum standards, Chicago, ALA, 1956.
9. Andhra Pradesh Library Act (Amendment), 1989. Hyderabad, Govt. of A.P., 1989.
10. Andhra Pradesh: Review Committee for the working of the A.P. Public Libraries Act, 1960 and to suggest amendments to the Act. Report of the Review committee, Hyderabad, Deptt. of Public Libraries, 1978.
11. Anthony, L.J.: A National Information Policy for the United Kingdom, Aslib Proceedings, 33(3), 1981.

12. Ashburner, E.H.: Modern Public Libraries, New Delhi. Reliance Publishing House, 1986.

13. Asheim, Lester: Research on the reading of adults. Library Trends, 1(4), 1953.

14. Augustine, C.A. & G. Devarajan, ed.: Public Library System in India, New Delhi. SS Publications, 1990.

15. Babu, T.A.: Automation of public libraries. Herald of Library Science, 38(1), 1999, p. 47-52.

16. Bagari, N.D.: Manifold activities of Public Libraries. March of Karnataka, 18(5), 1980.

17. Baker, Sharon, L. and Ruey, Ellen Dew: Information and referral services-attitudes and Libraries - as survey of North Carolina Public Libraries, 28(2), 1985.

18. Baliarsingh, R.K.; Mahapatra, M.: Public's reading interest in the collection development of public libraries. Proceedings of the 19th All India Conference of IASLIC, Calcutta, India, 1993, p. 99-102.

19. Bandhopadhyay, A.R.: The Delivery of Books Act, 1954: Suggestions for fresh book. ILA Bulletin, 34(3), Oct.-Dec., 2000, p. 69-70.

20. Barnis, Harry Elmer: Social Institutions - in an Era of world upheaval. New York, Prentice-Hall, 1947.

21. Barreau, D.: Information systems and collection development in public libraries. Library . Collections, Acquisitions, and Technical Services, 25(3), 2001, p. 263-279.

22. Barugh, John: Community Information and the Public Library. Journal of public library, Journal of Librarianship, 16(2), 1984.

23. Bashiruddin, S.: Role of public libraries. Library Herald, 3(4), 1961.

24. Beer, E.; Flemming, A.; Glaubrecht, S.; Gratz, M.; Hamann, H.; Kaspar, A.; Natusch, M.; Schneider, G.; Schumann, A.; Ullrich, U.; Wagner, E.: The development of public libraries in the new German federal states. Bibliothek Forschung und Paxis, 19(3), 1995, p. 295-321.

25. Berelson, Bernard: The library's public - A report of the public library inquiry. New York, Columbia University press, 1949.
26. Bergeijk, D. Van : Overcoming the language barrier in information transfer, Unesco Journal of Information Science, Librarianship and Archives Administration, 3(3), 1981.
27. Bernier, G.: The information resources of the public libraries of tomorrow. Documentation et Bibliotheques, 46(4), 2000, p. 173-8.
28. Berrigan, Frances, J.: Community communications - the role of community media in development, Paria, UNESCO, 1981.
29. Bhargava, G.D.: Public Libraries in India - A Review. Indian Librarian, 18(3), Dec. 1963, p.144-150.
30. Bhattacharjee, R.: Role of Raja Rammohun Roy Library Foundation in the promotion of public library movement in India. Herald of Library Science, 38(1-2), 1999, p. 14-20.
31. Biswas, S. : Can the Internet and digital libraries compensate for the lack of pubic libraries in India ? New Zealand Libraries, 49(8), 2003, p. 280-2.
32. Blake, Fey, M. and Irby, Jane: The selling of the Public Library. Drexel Library Quarterly, 12(1-2), 1976.
33. Bloss, Meredith: Responding to manifest needs. Library Journal, 89(16), 1964.
34. Boadi, B.Y.: SCECSAL: a lesson in regional library co-operation. Libri, 48(2), 1998, p. 116-23.
35. Bolles, C: Federal and state support for public library development. Idaho Librarian, 48(3), 1996, p. 61-64.
36. Bone Larry Earl: Introduction. Library Trends, 24(3), 1976.
37. Books for the Millions at their Doorsteps: Information Manual, 5th Ed., RRRLF, B.B.Co., Calcutta, 1997.
38. Borm, J.V.: Regional Library cooperation in Belgium. European Research Libraries Cooperation, 5(4), 1995, p. 373-82.

39. Boscheinen, C.: The role of personnel development in public libraries: results of a survey. Buch und Bibliothek, 51(10/11), 1999, p. 632-636.

40. Bowen Judith : Makaing information work for local people. London, British Library, 1989.

41. Braverman, Miriam (Ed.) : Information and referral services in the public library. Drexel Library Quarterly, 12(1-2), 1976.

42. Brezova, Lydia: A visit to the Department of Bibliographic and Information Services of the Regional Library in Trencin. Citatel, 35(10), 1986, p. 376-377.

43. Browne, Mairead: The territorial stakeout - Librarians, social workers and community information. Australian Library Journal, 25(16), 1976.

44. Bundy, Marry Lee and Wasserman Paul: Professionalism reconsidered. College and Research Libraries, 29(1), 1968.

45. Buragohain, A.: Public Library scenario in India - Problem and Prospects, Herald of Library Science, 38(1-2), 1999, p. 5-14.

46. Burrows, Brian, E.: The Public Library as a leisure resource in post-industrial society, Library Association Record, 84(9), 1982.

47. Campbell, H.C.: Developing public library system services. Paris: UNESCO, 1983.

48. Campbell, H.C.: Developing Public Library Systems and Services - A guide to the organization of National and Regional Public Library Systems as a part of overall National Information Service Planning. Paris, UNESCO, 1983.

49. Carnovsky, Leon and Martin, Lowell (Eds.): The Library in the community. Chicago University Press, 1949.

50. Census of India 1991: Provisional Population Totals - Rural and Urban distribution, New Delhi. Registrar General and Census Commissioner, India Ministry of Home Affairs.

51. Chakrabarti, N.C. : Library movement in Indian and Introductory essay. Delhi, Hindustan, 1962.

52. Chakravarty, N.C.: Report of the Advisory Committee for Libraries, 1959 and the future of Public Library Service in India. IASLIC Bulletin, 9(2), June 1964, p. 83-94.
53. Chandler, George: Libraries in the modern world, Oxford, Pergamon, 1965.
54. Chavez, G.T.: Workforce training and development in selected public libraries throughout the State of Oregon: patterns and implications. Rural Libraries, 21(1), 2001, p. 25-49.
55. Cherry, Susan Spaeth: Public Library branches in schools - the Kansas city experience. American Libraries, 13(1), 1982.
56. Childers, Thomas: The Neighbourhood information Centre Project. Library Quarterly, 46(3), 1976.
57. Childers, Thomas: The Trends in Public Library I and R services. Library Journal, 104(17), 1979.
58. Coleman, Pat: Community information policy and provision. Aslib Proceedings, 38(9), 1986.
59. Community Information and the library. Assistant Librarian, 74(6), 1981.
60. Conant, Ralph, W.(Ed.) : Public library and the city. Cambridge, The M.I.T. Press, 1965.
61. Coughlin, Robert, E.: Taibe, Fran Coise, and Stevens Benjamin. Urban analysis for branch library system planning, Westport, Connecticut, Greenwood Publishing Company, 1972.
62. Croneberger, Robert and Luck, Carolyn: Analyzing community human information needs - A case study. Library Trends, 24(3), 1976.
63. Curley, Arthur : Information from the people to the people. American Libraries, 10(6), 1979.
64. Daines, G.: New Ambitions for public libraries in the United Kingdom. Bulletin Des Bibliotheques de France, 46(1), 2001, p. 121-3.
65. Daniel, H.: Public Libraries for everyone. New York, Double day and company, 1961.

66. Dante, G.P. : Gestion, gestion de information, gestion del conocimiento, gestion del futuro [Management, management of information, management of knowledge, management of the future], Ciencias de la Information, 30(3), 1999, p. 43-52.

67. Das Gupta, R.K.: New education policy and libraries. Herald of Library Science, 25(1), 1986.

68. Das, H.: ICT and Libraries: a chance for an open goal. BibliotheekBlad, 3(23), 1999, p. 6-8.

69. Das, I.V.: Public Library movement in Kerala, Herald of Library Science, 38(1-2), 1999, p. 83-9.

70. Davies, D.W. : Public Libraries as culture and social centres. Metuchen, N.J. : Scare Crow Press, 1974.

71. Debeij, J.: A golden future for libraries in the knowledge society. BibliotheekBlad, 1(9), 1997, p. 12-13.

72. DeCandido, G.A.: Ten graces for new librarians. Trends in law Library Management and Technology, 10(5), 1999, p. 1-2.

73. Delcourt, T.: Internet et intranet a la bibliotheque municipale a vocation regionale de Troyes. "Internet and intranet at the Troyes municipal library with regional remit. Bulletin d'Informations de I'Association des Bibliothecaires Francais, 184-185 (3rd and 4th Quarter), 1999, p. 217-218.

74. Deshpande, K.S. ; Hungund, B.B.: Raja Rammohun Roy Library Foundation and its role in galvanizing the public library movement in India. SRELS Journal of Information Management, 38(3), 2001, p. 179-200.

75. Despande, K.S.: Staff pattern for a Public Library System. ILA Bulletin, 9(2), April-June 1973, p. 61-66.

76. District Central Library, Visakhapatnam. Accession Register.

77. District Central Library, Visakhapatnam. Daily Visitors Record.

78. District Central Library, Visakhapatnam. Register of Deposit-holders.

79. Dolinska, E.: A visit to the regional library in Zvolen. Citatel, 35(6), 1986. p. 234-235.

80. Dowlin, Kenneth, E.: the Technological setting of the public library. Library Quarterly, 48(4), 1978.

81. Dunstan, D.W.: The Functions of Public Libraries in the 1970s. Australian Library Journal, 20(7), 1971.

82. Editorial: Indian Library Association Bulletin, 24(1), 1988.

83. Eichhorn, S.: Enquiry service on new ground: CD-RM in public libraries. Bibliothek Forschung und Prasis, 20(1), 1996, p. 50-94.

84. Ekbote, Gopalarao: Public Library System. Hydeabad, Ekbote Brother, 1987.

85. Ekbote, Gopalrao: Public Libraries System, Hyderabad. Ekbote Brother, 1987.

86. Ennis, Phillip, H.: Social change - some cautionary notes. Library Trends, 20(2), 1971.

87. Epstein, R.: Openbare biblioteke en skole [Public libraries and schools]. Cape Librarian, 42(3), 1998, p. 14-15.

88. Esdalle, Arudalle: National Libraries of the World, London, Library Association, 1957.

89. Estabrock, Leigh: Emerging tends in community library services. Library Trends, 28(2), 1979.

90. Ewart, Geraldine Sydney: Endeavouring to reach the information poor. Drexel Library Quarterly, 12(1-2), 1976.

91. Finnegan, Gerry: Public library and community development. Library services to the disadvantaged edited by William Martin. Hamden, Conn., Linnet Books and London, Clive Bingley, 1975, p. 32-46.

92. Frey, A.L. and Spigel, S.: Education adult users in public library. Library Journal, 104(8).

93. Fruin, D.: Women's needs and community information. Tendril, 3(2), 1981.

94. Gardner, Frank, M.: The Public Library - An Evaluation Report. Paris: UNESCO, 1957.

95. Garish, Sarel : Community information Service. Cape Librarian, 31(3), 1987.

96. Ghurye, G.S.: Caste and race in India. Bombay, Popular Prakashan, 1969.

97. Gilmore, Ken : Developed and developing countries on evolutionary process? In William Martin (Ed.). Library service to the Disadvantaged. London, Clive Bingley.

98. Goedel-Hoche, G.: Zusammenarbeit, eine Aufgabe for Schule and offentliche Bibliothek. "Cooperation, a task for school and public library". Schulbibliothek Aktuell, (2), 1994, p. 133-5.

99. Gour, P.N. : Public library services in India and national adult education programme - a plea for their integration. Indian Library Association Bulletin, 16(1-2), 1980.

100. Gour, P.N.: Public library services in India and National Adult Education Programme: a plea for their integration. Indian Library Association Bulletin, 16(1-2), 1980, p. 3-9.

101. Government of Andhra Pradesh: Review Committee for the working of the A.P. Public Libraries Act 1960 and to suggest amendments to the Act. Report of the Review Committee. Hyderabad, Deptt. of Public Libraries, 1978.

102. Govind, Vijai: Financing public libraries. Lucknow Librarian, 20(1), 1988, p. 1-6.

103. Great Britain, Ministry of Education: Working partly on standards of Public Library Service in England and Wales. Standards of Public Library Service in England and Wales - Report. London, HMSO, 1962.

104. Great Britain, Reconstruction (Ministry of—). Adult Education Committee, 1919, Final Report (HMSO).

105. Gregory, Ruth, W.: The search for information about community needs. Library Trends, 17(1), 1968.

106. Groombridge, Brain: The Londoner and his library. London: Research Institute for Consumer Affairs, 1964.

107. Guerin, C; De l'importance de la mediatheque en milieu hospitaller [About the importance of the media centre in the hospital milieu]. Bulletin d'lnformations del'Association des Bibiothecaires Francais, 181(4th quarte), 1998, p. 63-65.

108. Guha, B. and Rajan, T.N.: Towards a national information policy for India. IASLIC Bulletin, 24(4), 1979.

109. Guruswamy Naidu, N.: Information for developing countries. Paper presented at FID Congress, Havana, 1990.

110. Hamby, P. and Najowitz, I: The Public Libraries Act of 1850: utilitarian pragmatism and idealist humanitarianism in action. Public and Access Services Quarterly, 2(4), 1998, p. 73-88.

111. Hanks, Gardner and Schnidt, James : An alternative model of a profession for libraries. College and Research Libraries, 36(3), 1975.

112. Harmse, R.: The public library as alternative source of income for local authorities. Mousaion, 7(2), 1989, p. 2-33.

113. Harris, Roma, M.: The information needs of battered women. R.Q., 28(1), 1988.

114. Harrison, K.C.: The Library and the Community, 2nd ed. London, Andre Deutsch, 1966.

115. Harvey, Graham: Public library impact-breaking down the barriers. Assistant Librarian, 66(7), 1973.

116. Hayes, R.M: Information Science in Librarianship, Libri, 19(3), 1969.

117. Healy, Sue: Community profiles. Tendril, 15(3), 1983.

118. Healy, Sue: Public Libraries and community information - a study of attitudes. Tendril, 6(2), 1984.

119. Heitzman, J.; Asundi, A.Y.: Evaluation of public libraries in India. Information Development, 16(3), 2000, p.142-53.

120. Hennessy, J.A.: Choices for library services - comments on the socio-economic dimension. Journal of Librarianship, 11(2), 1979.

121. Henry, Alice, C: The importance of resource files in information and referral delivery. Information and Referral, 9(1), 1987.

122. Hiese, P.: Regional library work in Denmark. Scandinavian Public Quarterly, 24(3), 1991, p. 4-5.

123. Hu, I-Chin: Information and referral services should be offered in the public library. Journal of Educational Media and Library Sciences, 21(3), 1984.

124. Humphrevs, K.W.: Standards for libraries in Great Britain. Library Tends, 21(2), Oct., 1972, p. 312-329.

125. Inamdar, N.B.: Development of public libraries in Andhra Pradesh. Granthana, 3(2), 1992, p. 115-31.

126. India, Ministry of Education: Advisory Committee for Libraries. Report for the Advisory Committee for Libraries, New Delhi, Manager of Publications, 1970.

127. India: Census of India (1991) Series-2, Andhra Pradesh Paper-I (supplement) Provisional Population Totals. Coimbatore-Government of India Press, 1992.

128. Irving, A.: Libraries central role in informing the community. Library Association Record, 80(1), 1978.

129. Issac, K.A. and Devarajan, G. (Eds.) : Libraries in distance education. New Delhi Ess Ess, 1989.

130. Issac, K.A.: Libraries and Librarianship. Madras, S.Viswanathan Pvt. Ltd., 1987.

131. Ito, Satoru: Trial construction of Kitami regional libraries' network [in Japanese]. Toshokan Zasshi/Library Journal, 83(5), 1989, p. 253-255.

132. Itou, S.; Kato, H.; Kawata, T.; Sato, T.; Muraoka, K.; Murabayashi, M.; Yamamoto, A.; Wakisaka, S.: These wrong thoughts arrest the development of public library. Toshokan-Kai (The Library World), 51(2), 1999, p.110-119.

133. Jackman, Peter: Public Libraries information and the community. Assistant Librarian, 66(2), 1973.

134. Jambhekar, N.: National policy on public libraries in India. Third World Libraries, 5(2), 1995, p. 8-21.

135. Jefferson, G.: Libraries and Society. London, Jame's Clark, 1969.

136. Jefferson, George: Public Library Administration: An Examination Guidebook. Bombay. Asia Publishing House, 1965.

137. Jessup, Frank, W.: Libraries and adult education. Unesco Bulletin for Libraries, XXVII (6), 1973.

138. Johnstone, Marea, A.: Public library users - some characteristics and perceptions. Australian Library Journal, 22(9), 1973.

139. Jones, C: How to prove public libraries are really necessary - an interview with Clara Jones, Australian Library Journal, 25(16), 1976.

140. Jong, J.D.: Verscharling of versterking? Collectievorming in de OB ter discussie. Reducing or improving services? A review of collection development in public libraries. Open, 28(5), 1996, p. 123-125.

141. Justa, H.R.: Development of public libraries in Himachal Pradesh. Granthana, 4(1 and 2), 1994, p. 57-60.

142. Kalia, D.R.: A Review of Public library development in Asia. Lucknow Librarian, 13(3), 1981.

143. Kalia, D.R.: A Review of the Public Library Development in India. laslic Bulletin, 18(2 & 3), June & Sept., 1973, p. 162-167.

144. Kaminska, Halina : Udostepnianie pity w bibliotekach publicznych za granica. Record facilities in public libraries abroad. Poradnik Bibliotekaza, 30(11-12), 1978, p. 244-247.

145. Kanakachary, M.; More, S.: Computerisation of public libraries in India: manpower development through in-service training. Lucknow Librarian, 24(4), 1992, p. 133-7.

146. Kapoor, A.L.: A.P. Public Libraries Act, 1960. Library Herald, 5(2), July 1962, p. 81-96.

147. Kapoor, A.L. A.P. Public Libraries Act, 1960. Library Herald 5(2) July 1962, p. 81-96.

148. Karun, B. : Slovene Public Libraries. New Library World, 100 (1146), 1999, p. 20-3.

149. Kaula, P.N. : Higher Education and Libraries. Herald of Library Science, 25(1&2), 1986.

150. Kaula, P.N.: A study of public library development and services for rural upliftment. Herald of Library Science, 39(3-4), 2000, p. 184-190.

151. Kaula, P.N.: Facets and Phases of Indian Library Development. In: Sen, N.D. ed. Development of Libraries in New India, New Delhi. New Book Society of India, 1965, p. 158-167.

152. _____: Library Service and Andhra Pradesh. Herald of Library Science, 19(1), 1980, p. 62-72.

153. ____: Some hints on the development of college and public libraries. Herald of Library Science, 34(1-2), 1995, p. 92-7.

154. ______: Some observations on networking of public libraries. Herald of Library Science, 38(1-2), 1996, p. 62-8.

155. Kempson, Elaine: Information for self-reliance and self-determination - the role of community information services. IFLA Journal, 12(3), 1986.

156. Khan, H.A.: Public library development: policies, problems and performance. Timeless Fellowship, (10), 1975-76, p. 20-33.

157. Khan, M.A. Majeed: Andhra Pradesh Public Libraries Act 1960 (As modified upto April, 1989) with Amendments of Commentaries. Hyderabad, Andhra Pradesh Public Libraries Association, 1990.

158. Khan, M.A.M.: Some observations on public library service in Andhra Pradesh, Herald of Library Science, 38(1-2), 1999, p. 106-8.

159. Khanna, J.K.: Library and Society, Kurukshetra, Research Publication, 1987.

160. Khanna, J.K.: Library and Society. Kurukshtra, Research Publications, 1987, p. 121-130.

161. Khanna, S.N.: Mobile library service with a special reference to Delhi Public Library. Resource Sharing and Information Networks, 9(2), 1994, p. 119-26.

162. Kisimu, F.N.: Collection development in the public library system in Kenya: constraints, solutions and the way forward. IFLA Journal, 28(2), 2002, p. 66-68.

163. Kraft, J., Geist, C., Frohss, W., Leutemann, C, Walther, B.: Bibliotheksforderung im Land Brandenburg, Die Forderung Offentlicher Bibliotheken in Thuringen. Das sachsische Kulturraumgesetz and die Bibliotheks-forderung. Library development in the state of Brandenburg. The development of public libraries in Thuringia. Saxony's culture laws and library development. Buch and Bibliothek, 51(4), 1999, p. 224-229.

164. Krishna Kumar: Library manual, New Delhi. Vani Educational Books, 1985.

165. Krishna Murthy, C.S.: Role of Library Association in Standardizing the Library Practice, Library Herald, 11(4), Jan. 1970, p. 254-260.

166. Kumar, R.P.; Nagpal, S.P.: Public libraries: a pivot to adult education. International Library Movement, 2(1 and 2), 1980, p. 45-48.

167. Kumbar, M.; Biradar, B.S.: Use of mass media and public library by the rural community: a study. Annals of Library Science and Documentation, 44(3), 1998, p. 86-92.

168. Landry-Hyde, D.: Outreach at a public, academic, regional libray - Texas AandM University at Corpus Christi. Reference Librarian, (67/68), 1999, p. 289-98.

169. Larsen, Harald : The role of the public libraries in public information. Scandinavian Public Library Quarterly, 12(2), 1979.

170. Layman, Helen Huguenor: Library programs and services to the disadvantaged - Intoduction. Library Trends, 20(2), 1971.

171. Lee, Donald, W.: One way in the alternative information scene. Aslib Proceeding, 35(9), 1983.

172. Lee, W-n.: A library is a lifetime learning place [in Chinese]. Bulletin of the Library Association of China, (53), 1994, p. 35-41.

173. Leskien, H.: Regional libraries on the way to specialization. Zeitschrift for Bibliothekswesen und Bibliographic, 46(4), 1999, p. 297-309.

174. Lianzama, C: Status report of public library development in Mizoram. Granthana, 4(1), 1994, p. 75-8.

175. Librarian Association of Australian Information Policy, 1976 the need to know. Australian Library Journal, 25(7), 1976.

176. Lick, T. East and Shearouse, Jr. Henry, G.: Organisation of a Branch system. Library Trends, 14(4), 1966.

177. Linley, R.: Use of focus groups in a public library research project. Assignation, 16(2), 1999, p. 11-13.

178. Lipsman, Claire, K.: The disadvantaged and library effectiveness. Chicago, American Library Association, 1972.

179. Loeb, Janet, Orin, Carol and Hedtke, Lorraine : Community planning as part of a multi-service I and R agency. Information and Referral. 6(1&2), 1984.

180. Lorenz, John, G.: The Role of libraries in economic and social development. UNESCO Bulletin for libraries, 16(5), 1962.

181. Lund, Ruth: Community involvement. Cape Librarian, 39(1), 1987.

182. Lynch, Mary, Jo : Educational, cultural and recreational services of the public library for adults. Library Quarterly, 48(4), 1978.

183. MacCallan, Norma, J.: Delivery systems and programs. Library Trends, XXVII(4), 1980.

184. Mackenzie, Christine: Library services to people with disabilities at Dandenong Valley Regional Library Service. Australasian Public Libraries and Information Services, 3(2), 1990, p. 84-88.

185. Majeed Khan, M.A.: A.P. Public Libraries Act, 1960 - as modified upto April, 1989 (with amendments and communications). Published by A.P. Public Library Association, 1990.

186. Manghani, P.: Community development and the public library service: an innovative training course in the London Borough of Merton. Assignation, 16(4), 1999, p. 18-21.

187. Mangla, P.B.: Library legislation in India. In R.K.Rout (Ed.) Library legislation India: problems and prospects. New Delhi. Reliance Publication House, 1986.

188. Mangla, P.B.: Role of the public library in developing countries with particular reference to literacy. Journal of Library and Information Science (India), 9(1), 1984. p. 1-15.

189. Marshall, Margaret, R.: Librarian and literature for teenagers, London, Andre Deutsch, 1966.

190. Martin Susan, Library Net Works, 1981-82. New York, Knowledge Industry Publications, 1981.

191. Martin, Allie Beth: Studying community - an overview. Library Trends, 24(3), 1976.

192. Martin, L.A.: Public Library - middle-age crisis or old age (Tenth of the R.R. Bowker memorial Lectures, New Series). New York, Bowker, 1982.

193. Martin, Lowell, A.: User studies and library planning. Library Trends, 24(3), 1976.

194. Martin, Lowell: Standards for Public Libraries. Library Trends, 21(2), Oct. 1972, p.164-177.

195. Masling, Charles: The Public library and community information - The Houston Program. Information and Referral, 4(2), 1982.

196. McAllister, N.; Cury, A.: Canada's country and regional library systems: a national survey. Feliciter, 43(2), 1997, p. 30-3.

197. McColvin, L.R.: Public Library extension. Paris, UNESCO, 1950.

198. McGarry, K.J.: Changing context of information - An introductory analysis. London, Clive Bingley, 1981.

199. Medowar, C: Public right to know. Aslib Proceedings, 28(2), 1976.

200. Menou, Michel, J.: National information policy in the less developed countries - an educational perspective. International Library review, 23(1), 1991.

201. Miller, Euan: Community information - the library's role. Tendril, 2(1), 1980.

202. Minai, H.: What is necessary for public library development? Issues and trends for 5 years hence. Toshokan Zasshi (The Library Journal), 93(10), 1999, p. 866-869.

203. Minai, Hideki : Public libraries and bibliographies of literary works. Annals of Japan Society of Library Science, 30(1), 1984, p. 13-32.

204. Miranda, Antonio: Aspects of the development of public libraries systems and networks in Brazil. Revista de Biblioteconomia de Brasilia, 7(2), 1979, p. 230-235.

205. Mohan Rajan, P.A.: The Relevance of second and third laws of library science on the role of public libraries in

community information and distance education. Indian Library Association Bulletin, 33(1&2), 1987.

206. Monroe, Margaret, E. and Heim, Kathleen, M.: Emerging patterns of community service. Library Trends, 28(2), 1979.

207. Mookerjee, S.K.: Development of Libraries and Library Science in India, Calcutta. World Press, 1969.

208. Morse Philip, M.: Measures of library effectiveness. Library Quarterly, 42(1), 1971.

209. Mukherjee, S.K.: Development of Library and Library Service in India, Calcutta, Wald Press, 1969.

210. Murison, W.J.: The public library - Its origins purpose and significance. London, Harrap, 1971.

211. Murphy, Paula: Visual literacy, libraries and community development. Collection building, 3(1), 1981.

212. Murrison, W.J.: The Public Library, its origins, purpose and significance, 2nd ed., London, George, G.: Hamap & Co., 1971.

213. Murrison, W.J.: The Public Library; its origins, purpose and significance, 2nd ed. London. George, G. Harrap & Co., 1971.

214. Musib, S.K.: Community analysis and the library collection building: a survey report. IASLIC Bulletin, 34(3), 1989, p. 121-127.

215. Naidu, G.H.S.; Narasimhulu, A.; Rao, V.S.; Ramesh, L.S.R.C.V. : User services in modern public libraries towards improving readership. Herald of Library Science, 38(1-2), 1999, p. 70-5.

216. Narasimham, P.V.A.: A.P. Public Libraries Act, 1960 with a latest amendments and commentaries, Hyderabad. A.P. Public Library Association, 1980.

217. Narayana Rao and Ramachandra Rao, T.: Rise and Growth of the Public Library Movement in India. Eluru, lyyanki Library awards Committee, 1981.

218. Neigel, C.: A blue-print for action: a needs assessment for the South Fraser Health Regional Library. Bibliotheca Medica Canadiana, 21(4), 2000, p. 51-6.

219. Nyeng, P.: When Randers Regional Libraries inaugurated their new hit of a media bus. Bibliotekspressen, (8), 2000, p. 248-9.

220. O'Hara, W. : Literacy service at the Echuca Regional Library. Link-up, 1996, p. 17-18.

221. Okko, M.: Education of public library personnel in Finland. Scandinavian Public Library Quarterly, 13(4), 1980.

222. Onadiran, G.T.; Onadiran, R.W. : Public library development: an assessment of present trends in Nigeria. Annals of Library Science and Documentation, 28(1-4), 1981, p. 119-123.

223. Osborne, L.: Driving the bush track to the superhighway: the Maroochy Mobile Library experience. Electronic Library, 16(5), 1998, p. 301-4.

224. Ostendorf, J.E. : Internet policies for Public Libraries, Georgia Librarian, 34(4), 1997, p. 4-7.

225. Ostrom, Kriss Taya: Public Libraries and community I and R agencies: Partners in the same business, R.Q., 15(1), 1975.

226. Owino Henry: The need for community information service. Journal of Ugandan Libraries, 6(1), 1984.

227. Panda, B.D.: Handbook of Public Library System, New Delhi. Anmol Publications, 1993.

228. Panda, B.D.: Public Library networking programme: some action plan for the State of Orissa. Informatin management in academic and research libraries. Proceedings of the 5th National Convention for Automation of Libraries in Education and Research (CALIBER-98), Bhubaneswar, India, ISBN: 81-900825-1-5, 1998, p. 319-321.

229. Parker, S.; Banweli, L., and K. Ray: The LOGOPLUS Project - A Seamless transition?, Library Management, 20(5 & 6), 1999, p. 273-82.

230. Penland, Patrick, R.: Community Information Science management certificate. Public Libraries, 24(4), 1985.

231. Phillips, H.M.: Literacy and development. Paris, UNESCO, 1970.

232. Phinney, Eleanor: Trends and needs - the present condition and future improvement of group services. Library Trends, 17(1), 1968.

233. Proctor and Simmons, S.: Public Library closures: the management of hard decisions. Library Management, 21(1 & 2), 2000, p. 25-34.

234. Prucess, J.: Tampines Regional Library, Singapore. Asian Libraries, 4(3), 1995, p. 8-12.

235. Public Library development in India. Herald of library science, 16(2-3), 1977.

236. Rabinson, H. Alan; Korn, Florence and Winters, Shirley, N.: The Library and the disadvantaged reader. Library Trends, 20(2), 1971.

237. Rajan, T.N.: The role of libraries in a Changing Society, Indian Library Association Bulletin, 16(1-2), 1980.

238. Raju, A.A.N.: Government's books acquisition policy: its impact on collection development in the public library system in Andhra Pradesh. Proceedings of the 19th All India Conference.of IASLIC, Calcutta, India, 1993, p. 43-8.

239. Raju, A.A.N.: Public Library Devefopment in Andhra Pradesh. ILA Bulletin, 23(3), Oct.-Dec. 1987, p. 127-139.

240. Raju, A.A.N.: Public Library development in Andhra Pradesh. Indian Library Association Bulletin, 9(1), 1987.

241. Raju, A.A.N.: Regional Libraries in Andhra Pradesh. Indian Library Association Bulletin, 8(1-2), 1972.

242. Raju, A.A.N.: Regional Libraries in Andhra Pradesh. ILA Bulletin, 9(1), Jan.-March 1973, p. 7-12.

243. Raju, K.A.: Information technology and public libraries in 21st century. Herald of Library Science, 38(1-2), 1999, p. 52-62.

244. Ramachandra Rao, P. : Significance of the Library Movement in Andhra Pradesh, 1900-1948. Library Herald, 20(2-4), July 1981 - March 1982, p. 151-154.

245. Ramachandra Rao, P.: Significance of the Library Movement in Andhra Pradesh, 1900-1948. Library Herald, 20(2-4), July 1981 - March 1982, p. 151-154.

246. Ramaiah, L.S.: Public libraries and public finances in India. A critical perspective. Herald of Library Science, 32(3-4), 1993, p. 171-80.

247. Ramanaya, I.V.: Role of the Public Library in Adult Literacy Work. Herald of Library Science, 16(2), 1977, p. 204-208.

248. Ramanayya, I.V.: Role of the Public Library in Adult Literacy Work. Herald of Library Science, 16(2), 1977, p. 204-208.

249. Ranganathan, S.R., ed.: Free Book service for all - An International Survey, Bombay. Asia Publishing House, 1968.

250. Ranganathan, S.R., ed.: National Grid of Public Library System based on Legislation. Call for the Silver Jubilee Year, laslic Bulletin, 17(3), Sept., 1972, p.139-150.

251. Ranganathan, S.R., ed.: Public Library Systems, Bombay. Asia Publishing House, 1972.

252. Rao, P. Bhaskar: Information Networks and Resource Sharing, New Delhi. Reliance Publishing House, 1986.

253. Rao, S.R.: Public Library System. Asia Publishing House, Bombay, 1972.

254. Rayward, W. Boyd: Introduction. The Public Library - a perspective and some questions. Library Quarterly, 48(4), 1978.

255. Regional Public Library System. Library Trends, 13(3), Jan. 1965.

256. Reid, Barrett: Community information and library. Australian Library Journal, 26(2), 1977.

257. Revesz, B.: Politicas de information , bibliotecas publicas y desarrollo local y reginal. Information policies, public libraries, and local and regional development. Revista Interamericana de Bibliotecologia, 24(2), 2001, p. 45-63.

258. Richardson, W.D.; Ried, K.B.; Vaughan, J. and Watson, C.S.: It's all a matter of what you know - submission by the Library Association of Australia to the committee of inquiry into public libraries. Australian Library Journal, 24(9-10), 1975.

259. Ridgway, Helen, A.: Country and Regional Libraries in the United States. Library Trends, 1(4), April, 1953, p. 491-502.

260. Roberts, W.: The FORCE Foundation : A new international organisation in the field of visual handicap. Bulletin d'lnformations de l'Association des Bibliothecaires Francais, 181, (4th Quarter), 1998, p. 54-56.

261. Robinson, W.C. : Price of materials and collection development in large public libraries. Library Acquisitions: Practice and Theory, 19(3), 1995, p. 299-312/

262. Rohlf, Robert, H.: Standards for Public Libraries. Library Trends, 31(1), Summer 1982, p. 65-76.

263. Rohlf, Robert, H.: Standards of public libraries. Library Trends, 31(1), 1982.

264. Romer, Gerhard : The Study Group on Regional Libraries. Autumn Conference in Oldenburg. Bibliotheksdienst, 23(1), 1989, p. 29-30.

265. Rout, R.K.: Library legislation in India. New Delhi, Reliance Publishing House, 1986.

266. Ruby, Joseph, L.: A methodology for information and referral need assessment. Information and Referral, 1(1), 1979.

267. Ryder, Julie, (Ed.): Library services to house bound people. London, Library Association, 1987.

268. Sager, Donald, J.: Answering the call for Health Information. American Libraries. 9(8), 1978.

269. Sager, Donald, J.: Managing the Public Library, New York. Knowledge Industry Publications, Inc., 1984.

270. Sahai, Shrinath: Library and the community. New Delhi, Today and Tomorrow's printers and publications, 1973.

271. Salmon, R.: Growth and vitality for the library. Rural Libraries, 19(1), 1999, p. 7-29.

272. Sarada, K.: A Plea for Centralised Library services - plan for Andhra Pradesh, Indian Library Association Bulletin, 14(4), 1978.

273. Sarada, K.: Rural Library Services in India. New Delhi, Ess Ess Publications, 1986.

274. Sardana, J.L.: Indian Standards in Library and Information Science - A Review. ILA Bulletin, 19(1-3), April-Dec. 1983, p. 53-60.

275. Schaefer, M.T.: Changes in CD-ROM industry benefit libraries, Information Retrieval and Library Automation, 34(1), 1998, p. 1-3.

276. Scholarly Press Books for Public Libraries. Public Library Quarterly, 3, 1982.

277. Schulman, S.: Big changes in Library system selection criteria: now, its "end users rule!" when selecting automation products, Information Today, 15(9), 1998, p. 56, 58.

278. Sciacca, J.: Economic development and the public libraries: perspectives on the impact of an LSCA funded research project. Illinois Libraries, 80(2), 1998, p. 80-83.

279. Sen, N.B. ed.: Development of Libraries in New India, New Delhi, New Books Society of India.

280. Sewa Singh : Public library development in Northern India - A critique. Lucknow Librarian, 12(3), 1980.

281. Sharma, Pandey, S.K.: Public Libraries in India, New Delhi, Ess Ess, 1985.

282. Shera, J.H. : The Foundation of Education for Librarianship. New York, Becker and Hayes, 1972.

283. Silver Jubilee Souvenir, 1982, Guntur: State Regional Library, 1982.

284. Simsova, Sylva : The Public Library and the acculturation of migrants - a personal view of the British experience. Journal of Librarianship, 11(4), 1979.

285. Sinclair, Dorothy: Administration of the small public library, Chicago. ALA, 1985.

286. Singh, P.A.: Public library development in Manipur. Granthana, 4(1&2), 1994, p. 69-74.

287. Slanker, Barbara, O.: Research needed for a public library's community information centre. R.Q., 15(1), 1975.

288. Somasekhara Rao, K.: Junior College Libraries - Perspectives, trends and Challenges (Ph.D. Thesis), 1992.

289. Stanton, J.: Measuring value for money in public library collection development. Australasian Public Libraries and Information Services, 14(2), 2001, p. 58-61.

290. Stephens, A.K. : Public library collection development in the information age. Acquisitions Librarian, (20), 1998, p. 1-202.

291. Stevenson, Gordon: Popular culture and the public library. In Melvin J.Voigt, (Ed.). Advances in Librarianship, New York Academic Press, 7, 1977.

292. Stevenson, Gordon: The Public Library in a communications setting. Library Quarterly, 48(4), 1978.

293. Subramani, T.K. : Public relations in Libraries. IASLIC Bulletin, 31(3), 1986.

294. Suggestions for the development of public libraries in Andhra Pradesh. Herald of Library Science, 14(1), 1975.

295. Swiegelaar, Johan: A community information service- some comments. Cape Librarian, 32(7), 1988.

296. Tait, H.M.: Current developments in public libraries - New Zealand. LAA NZLA conference proceedings, 1981, p. 548-553.

297. Tauber, Maurice, F. and Stephens, Irlene, R: Library Surveys. New York, Columbia University Press, 1967.

298. Tayal, A.S.: Standards and Specificatins. Library Herald, 4(1), April 1961, p. 26-30.

299. Thillainyagarri, V.: The first true public library. Herald of Library Science, 20(3-4), 1981.

300. Thomas, V.K.: Public library financing: analysis of RRRLF schemes of assistance. Herald of Library Science, 38(1-2), 1999, p. 27-39.

301. Tocatlian, Jacques: Information for development - the role of UNESCO's General Information Programme. UNESCO Journal of Information Science, Librarianship and Archives Administration, 3(3), 1981.

302. Trehan, G.L.: Library Services for developing Society. Indian Library Association Bulletin, 16(1&2), 1980.

303. Triloknath,: Libraries in the Life of the Nation. Indian Librarian, 21(4), March 1867, p. 179-182.

304. Ude, C.C. : Mobile library services in Nigeria. Bibliotheek Samenleving, 11(1), 1983, p. 12-17.

305. Umlauf, K. : Principle: content - Function - demands - development -implementation, Buch and Bibliothek, 51(2), 1999, p. 98-105.

306. UNESCO Public Libraries Manifesto, 1994, NISSAT New Letter, 13, 14, Oct.-Dec., 1994.

307. UNESCO Public Libraries Manifesto, 1994. NISSAT News Letter, 13-14, Oct.-Dec., 1994.

308. UNESCO Public Library Manifesto, ILA Bulletin, 9(1), Jan.-March 1973, p. 30-32.

309. UNESCO Public Library Manifesto. ILA Bulletin, 9(1), Jan.-March 1973, p. 30-32.

310. UNESCO Public Library Manifesto: Library Association Record. 75(1), 1973.

311. Vashishth, C.P.: Advancement of Librarianship in India. Journal of Library and Information Science, 17(1), 1992.

312. Veatch, Julian Lamar : Library architecture and environment design: the application of selected environmental design factors to the planning of public library facilities. Ann Arbor, Michigan, University Microfilms International, 1979, p. 298.

313. Veeranjaneyulu, K.; Rao, T.S.: Role of public library in development of culture and civilization: an overview. Herald of Library Science, 38(1-2), 1999, p. 39-42.

314. Venkata Ramanayya, lyyanaki: Role of the public library in adult literacy work. Herald of library science, 16(2-3), 1977.

315. Venkatappaiah, V. : Some observations on the public library system in Kerala State, Herald of Library Science, 38(1-2), 1999, p. 89-95.

316. Venkatappaiah, Velaga: A New Book at the Public Library System in Andhra Pradesh. A.P. Public Libraries (comprehensive) Act, 1978, Paper presented at the A.P. Libraries Conference, 9-11 March, 1979 at Hyderabad.

317. Venkatappaiah, Velaga: Model Public Libraries Act, New Delhi. Indian Library Association, 1991.

318. Venkatappaiah, Velaga: Public Library System in Andhra Pradesh, Waltair, Andhra University, 1982.

319. Venugopal, M.V.: Regional Libraries in Andhra Pradesh. ILA Bullegin, 9(3 & 4), July-Dec. 1973, p. 105-108.

320. Vermeulen, C.H. : What about the non-users of the public library ? South African Journal for Librarianship and Information Science, 49(1), 1981, p. 10-14.

321. Vijayakumar, P.: Ekbote Committee on the A.P. Public Libraries Act 1960: A Study of the Recommendations. Herald of Library Science, 18(3), July 1979, p. 292-299.

322. Vishwa Mohan, V.: Community information sources; A framework for handling and services. Indian Library Association Bulletin, 24(2), 1988.

323. Viswanathan, C.G.: Public Library Organisation with special reference to India. Rev. 4th ed., New Delhi, Ess-Ess Publications, 1990.

324. Waizer, N.; Gruidl, J.J.: Rural Public libraries and community economic development. Illinois Libraries, 79(4), 1993, p. 178-181.

325. Waknis, T.D.: Changing concept of library service with reference to public libraries. Indian Library Association Bulletin, 12(3-4), 1976.

326. Wang, M-l: Collection Development of Public Libraries in Taiwan. Bulletin of the Library Association of China, (65), 2000, p. 29-43.

327. Warncke, Ruth: Library objectives and community needs. Library Trends, 17(1), 1968.

328. Warren, Althea : The needs of Readers. Library Trends, 3(2), 1954.

329. Wavada, Jim : Access - a community information service. Reference Services Review. 15(3), 1987.

330. Wells, A.R.: Information service to laymen. South African Journal for Librarianship, and Information Science, 49(1), 1981.

331. Wheeler, Joseph, L.: Practical Administration of Public Libraries. New York, Harper & Row, 1962.

332. Wigell-Ryynanen, B.: Library facilities in Finland. Scandinavian Public Library Quarterly, 33(2), 2000, p. 21.

333. Williamzon, Kirsty: Information seeking by users of a citizen advice Bureau. Australian Library Journal, 35(4), 1986.

334. Wilson, Patrick: Public knowledge and private ignorance - toward a library and information policy. West Port, Green Wood Press, 1977.

335. Winston, M.D., Neely, T.Y.: Leadership development and public libraries, Public Library Quarterly, 19(3), 2001, p. 15-32.

336. Withers, F.N.: Standards for Library Service: An International Survey, Paris, Unesco, 1974.

337. Witwer, M.: Intelibray loan in Regional library service systems. Colorado Libraries, 22(3), 1996. p. 42-3.

338. Yang, C; Chen, C; Lin, L. : Development of a general public library digitization system. Bulletin of the Library Association of China, (69), 2002, p. 24-31.

339. Yilmaz, B.: Halk Kutuphaneleri uzerine guncel bir karsilastirma. [A recent comparison on public libraries]. Turk Kutuphaneciligi/Turkish Librarianship, 13(1), 1999, p. 28-39.

340. Zilla Grandhalaya Samastha, Visakhapatnam. Administration report for the year 1991-92 (unpublished).

341. Zweizig, Douglas, L.: With our eye on the user needed research for information and referral in the public library. Drexel Library Quarterly, 12(1-2), 1976.

gentrification in the following areas: building and acquisitions; collection building; services to the public; automation and organization.

Wagner, M. (1989) traces the development of interlibrary loan in the Colorado, USA, regional [illegible] service system. The system routes requests from local library to system headquarters to the Denver Public Library, which acts as the Colorado Resource Center. Interlibrary loan peaked in the early 90s, but declined after [illegible] increased demand led to slow turn around [illegible] had not been resolved. Use of technology [illegible] with development of the Access Colorado Library Information Network, [illegible] training support and technology [illegible].

[illegible] M.T. (1998) [illegible] undergoing rapid change. Industry [illegible] product life cycle, [illegible] continued popularity of [illegible] and Asian predominance in the manufacture of [illegible] drives. Highlights the benefit of CD [illegible] libraries and assesses the implications of industry developments for library CD use. Covers network environments, Web CD-ROM servers, CD recordable and CD Rewritable, [illegible] longevity, preserving CD-ROM quality and the recently released standards for writable optical discs.

Shulman, S. (1998) traces the changes in selection [illegible] of new replacement library automation systems as they have been influenced by the rapidly developing technology. How libraries [illegible] availability [illegible] reasons for this and [illegible] selection criteria.

Salmon, R. (199[illegible]) [illegible] for successful small rural libraries. Suggests [illegible] a [illegible] cooperative [illegible] of

Index